GERMANY PROFILED

GERMANY
PROFILED

Essential facts on society, business and politics in Germany

Edited by Barry Turner

ST. MARTIN'S PRESS
NEW YORK

GERMANY PROFILED

St Martin's Press, Scholarly and Reference Division,
175 Fifth Avenue, New York, N.Y. 10010

First published in the United States of America in 1999

Printed in the United Kingdom

ISBN: 0–312–22726–4

Library of Congress Cataloging-in-Publication Data
Germany profiled / essential facts on society, business, and politics
in Germany / edited by Barry Turner.
        p. cm. — (SYB factbook series)
    Includes bibliographical references and index.
    ISBN 0–312–22726–4 (pbk.)
        1. Germany—Social life and customs. 2. National
    characteristics, German. 3. Political culture—Germany.
    4. Germany—Intellectual life. 5. Etiquette—Germany.
    I. Turner, Barry. II. Series.

    DD290.26 G47 1999
    943—dc21   99–050165

Contents

Territory and Population *2*
Länder (area and population) *3*
Principal Towns (population) *4*

Key Historical Events *5*
A United Germany *22*

Chronology *23*
The Romans and Celtic Tribes *23*
The Frankish Empire *23*
The First Reich *23*
Holy Roman Empire *24*
Hapsburg Dynasty *24*
The Reformation *25*
Rise of Prussia *25*
Fall of the Holy Roman Empire *26*
Towards German Unification *26*
The Bismarck Era *26*
The Second Reich *27*
The First World War *27*
The Weimar Republic *27*
The Third Reich *28*
The Second World War *28*
Post-War Germany and the Cold War *29*
The Federal Republic *29*

Cultural Briefing *30*
Architecture and Design *30*
 Romanesque *30*
 Gothic *30*
 Renaissance *31*
 Baroque and Rococo *31*
 Neo-Classicism *32*
 Modern and Contemporary Movements *32*
 The Third Reich *33*
Painting and Sculpture *33*
 9th–15th century *33*
 10th century *34*
 Gothic *34*
 Renaissance *34*

Baroque and Rococo 35
Neo-Classicism 35
Romanticism 36
Realism and Naturalism 36
Impressionism 36
Expressionism 37
Die Brücke 37
Der Blaue Reiter 37
Neue Sachlichkeit 37
Early 1950s 38
1960s 38
1970s to the Present 38
Neue Wilde 38
Music 39
Middle Ages 39
Renaissance 39
Baroque 39
The Viennese School 40
The Romantics 40
Modern Germany 42
Literature and Theatre 43
Middle Ages 43
The Baroque 44
The Age of Enlightenment (Aufklärung) 44
Sturm und Drang 45
Neo-Classicism 45
The Romantic Movement 45
Naturalism and Realism 46
Existentialist Movement 47
National Socialism 47
Post-War Period 47
Cinema 48
Silent Films 48
Sound Films of the 1930s 48
Post-War Films 49
Major Cities 50
Berlin 50
Introduction 50

Transport *51*
Airports *52*
Trains *52*
Roads *52*
Buses *52*
Local Transport *53*
Ferries *53*
Taxis *53*
Car Hire *53*
Bicycle Hire *53*
Travellers Information *54*
Tourist Offices *54*
Financial and Currency *54*
Post Office *54*
Consulates *54*
Emergency *55*
Medical Emergency *55*
Pharmarcies *55*
Internet Access *55*
Hotel Reservations *55*
Leading Museums and Galleries *55*
Tiergarten-Kulturforum *55*
Kunstbibliothek/Kupferstichkabinett *56*
Kunstgewerbemuseum (Museum of Applied Arts) *56*
Neue Nationalgalerie *56*
Musikinstrumenten-Museum *56*
Museumsinsel (Museum Island) *57*
Pergamon Museum *57*
Alte Nationalgalerie *57*
Bodemuseum *57*
Altes Museum (Old Museum) *58*
Dahlem-Museen (Dahlem Museums) *58*
Landmarks *58*
The Reichstag *58*
Brandenburger Tor (Brandenburg Gate) *58*
Schloss Charlottenburg *59*
Apartments of Frederick I and Sophie-Charlotte (Historische Räume) *59*
Knobelsdorff Wing (Neuer Flügel) *59*

Gallery of Romanticism (Nationalgalerie) 59

Royal Apartments 59

Schlosspark 60

Potsdamer Platz 60

Alexander Platz 60

Performing Arts *61*

Philharmonie 61

Opera 61

Further Reading *62*

Hamburg *62*

Introduction *62*

Transport *63*

Airport 63

Trains 63

Roads 63

Buses *64*

Local Transport 64

Ferries 64

Taxis 64

Car Hire 64

Bicycle Hire 64

Boat Hire *65*

Travellers Information *65*

Tourist Office 65

Financial and Currency *65*

Post Offices *65*

Consulates *66*

Emergency *66*

Medical Emergency *66*

Pharmacies *66*

Internet Access *66*

Hotel Reservations *66*

Leading Museums and Galleries *67*

Hamburger Kunsthalle (Fine Arts Museum) 67

Galerie der Gegenwart 67

Museum für Kunst und Gewerbe (Museum of Decorative Arts) 67

Landmarks *67*

Aussenalster 67

Hamburg Hafen (Port of Hamburg) 68

Harbour cruises 68

Hadag 68

Grosse Michaelskirche 68

Fernsehturm (Television Tower) 69

Munich (München) 69

Introduction 69

Transport 71

Airport 71

Trains 71

Roads 71

Buses 71

Local Transport 71

Taxis 72

Car Hire 72

Bicycle Hire 72

Travellers Information 72

Tourist Offices 72

Financial and Currency 72

Post Office 73

Consulates 73

Emergency 73

Medical Emergency 73

Pharmacies 73

Internet Access 74

Hotel Reservations 74

Leading Museums and Galleries 74

Residenz 74

Residenz Museum 74

Porcelain Chambers 74

Schatzkammer (Treasury) 74

Altes Residenztheater (Old Residence Theatre) 75

Schloss Nymphenburg 75

Marstallmuseum 75

Nymphenburger Porzellan Sammlung Bäuml 75

Museum Mensch und Natur 75

Botanical Garden 75

Alte Pinakothek 76

Neue Pinakothek 76

Deutsches Museum 76

BMW Museum 76

Landmarks 77

Marienplatz and the Old Town 77

Cologne (Köln) 77

Introduction 77

Transport 79

Airport 79

Trains 79

Roads 79

Buses 79

Local Transport 79

Boat 80

Taxis 80

Travellers Information 80

Tourist Offices 80

Financial and Currency 80

Post Office 81

Consulates 81

Emergency 81

Medical Emergency 81

Internet Access 81

Hotel Reservations 81

Leading Museums and Galleries 81

Römische-Germanisches Museum 81

Heinrich-Böll-Platz 82

Wallraf-Richartz Museum 82

Museum Ludwig 82

Agfa-Foto-Historama 83

Beatles Museum 83

Landmarks 83

The Kölner Dom (Cathedral) 83

The Old Town 84

Rathaus (Town Hall) 84

Romanesque Churches 84

Gross St. Martin 85

St. Maria im Kapitol 85

St. Gereon 85

Frankfurt am Main 85

Introduction 85

Transport 87
Airport 87
Trains 87
Roads 87
Buses 87
Local Transport 87
Taxis 88
Car Hire 88
Bicycle Hire 88
Travellers Information 88
Tourist Offices 88
Financial and Currency 89
Post Office 89
Consulates 89
Emergency 89
Medical Emergency 89
Internet Access 90
Hotel Reservations 90
Leading Museums and Galleries 90
Museumsufer 90
Städelsches Kunstinstitut und Städtische Galerie 90
Museum für Kunsthandwerk (Museum of Applied Arts) 91
Deutsches Filmmuseum (German Museum of Cinema) 91
Museum für Post und Kommunikation (Museum of Post and
    Communication) 92
Deutsches Architektur-Museum (German Architecture Museum) 92
Landmarks 92
Römerberg (Old Town) 92
Dom (Bartholomäuskirche) 92
Kaisersaal (Imperial Hall) 93
Paulskirche (St. Paul's Church) 93
Goethe Haus (Birthplace of Goethe) 93
Zoo 93
Bonn   94
Introduction 94
Transport 94
Airport 94
Local Transport 95
Roads 95

Buses 95

Taxis 95

Car Hire 95

Bicycle Hire 95

Travellers Information 96

Tourist Offices 96

Financial and Currency 96

Post Office 96

Consulates 96

Emergency 96

Medical Emergency 96

Pharmacies 97

Hotel Reservations 97

Leading Museums and Galleries 97

Beethoven Geburtshaus (Birthplace of Beethoven) 97

Münster Basilika (Collegiate Church) 97

Haus der Geschichte der Bundesrepublik Deutschland 97

Kunstmuseum Bonn (Bonn Museum of Art) 98

Deutsche Museum Bonn 98

Landmarks 98

Poppelsdorfer Schloss 98

Düsseldorf 98

Introduction 98

Transport 99

Airport 99

Trains 100

Local Transport 100

Travellers Information 100

Tourist Offices 100

Financial and Currency 100

Post Office 101

Consulates 101

Emergency 101

Medical Emergency 101

Hotel Reservations 101

Leading Museums and Galleries 102

Kunstsammlung Nordrhein-Westfalen 102

Hochschule für bildende Künste 102

Kunstmuseum 102

Schloss Jägerhof *102*
Goethe Museum *102*
Theatres *102*
Düsseldorf Schauspielhaus *102*
Oper am Rhein *102*
Leipzig *103*
  Introduction *103*
  Transport *104*
  Airport *104*
  Trains *104*
  Local Transport *104*
  Taxis *104*
  Travellers Information *105*
  Tourist Offices *105*
  Financial and Currency *105*
  Post Offices *105*
  Consulates *105*
  Emergency *105*
  Medical Emergency *106*
  Hotel Reservations *106*
  Leading Museums and Galleries *106*
  Ägyptisches (Egyptian) Museum *106*
  Grassi Museum Complex *106*
  Musikinstrumenten-Museum *106*
  Museum für Völkerkunde (Museum of Ethnology) *106*
  Museum für Kunsthandwerk (Museum of Arts and Crafts) *106*
  Landmarks *107*
  Battle of Leipzig/Battle of the Nations Monument *107*
  Opernhaus *107*
  Neues Gewandhaus *107*
  Thomaskirche *107*
  Bach Museum *107*
Dresden *108*
  Introduction *108*
  Transport *110*
  Airport *110*
  Roads *110*
  Trains *110*
  Local Transport *110*

Travellers Information *111*
Tourist Offices 111
Financial and Currency *111*
Post Offices *111*
Consulates *112*
Emergency *112*
Hotel Reservations *112*
Leading Museums and Galleries *112*
Albertinum 112
Zwinger 112
Landmarks *112*
Katholische Hofkirche (Cathedral of St. Trinitatis) 112
Royal Dresden Palace 113
Taschenberg Palais 113
Zoo 113
Botanical Gardens 113
Tourist Offices in Other Major Cities *113*
German National Tourist Offices in the UK and USA *115*
Social Statistics *115*
Climate *116*
Language *117*
Constitution and Government *117*
National Anthem *120*
Recent Elections *120*
Current Administration *121*
Political and Financial Profiles *122*
Johannes Rau *122*
Gerhard Schröder *122*
Joschka Fischer *123*
Hans Eichel *124*
Wolfgang Schäuble *124*
Edmund Stoiber *125*
Ernst Welteke *125*
Oskar Lafontaine *125*
Helmut Kohl *126*
Konrad Adenauer *127*
Willy Brandt *128*
Helmut Schmidt *129*

Local Government *130*
Defence *130*
  Budget *130*
  Strength of Armed Forces *131*
  Paramilitary Forces *131*
  Conscription *132*
  Nuclear Capability *132*
  Policy *132*
International Relations *133*
Economy *133*
  Performance *134*
  Budget *134*
Currency *136*
Banking and Finance *137*
  Deutsche Bundesbank *137*
  Private Commercial Banks *138*
  Selected Commercial Banks *138*
  Central Bank of Co-operative Banking System *139*
  Public Law Credit Institutions *139*
  Bankers Organizations *140*
Stock Exchange *140*
Weights and Measures *141*
Energy and Natural Resources *141*
  Environmental Policy *141*
  Electricity *142*
  Oil and Gas *142*
  Minerals *142*
  Agriculture *142*
  Forestry *143*
  Fisheries *143*
Industry *144*
  Top Ten Companies *144*
  Labour *145*
  Trade Unions *145*
  Trade Union Organization *146*
International Trade *146*
  Imports and Exports *146*
Trade Fairs *147*

Communications *149*
    Roads *149*
    Rules of the Road *149*
    Rail *150*
    Civil Aviation *150*
    Shipping *151*
    Shipping Organizations 151
    Telecommunications *152*
    Postal Services *152*
Social Institutions *153*
    Justice *153*
    Religion *153*
    Religious Organizations *154*
    Education *155*
    Health *157*
    Welfare *157*
Culture *159*
    Broadcasting *159*
    Television 159
    Radio 160
    Foreign Radio Stations 160
    Theatre *160*
    Press *161*
    Daily Newspapers 161
    Sunday and Weekly Newspapers 162
    Periodicals 162
    News Agencies 163
    Foreign Bureaux 164
    Press and Journalists Associations 164
    Publishing in Germany 165
    Publishers *165*
    Libraries *170*
Sport *170*
    The Top Ten Sports *171*
Tourism *171*
    Tourist Headquarters *172*
    Central Hotel Reservations *172*
    Central Car Hire Reservations *173*

Etiquette *173*
    Social *173*
    Business *174*
Festivals and Millennium Events *175*
    Millennium Events *175*
    Annual Festivals *176*
    Public Holidays *176*
Diplomatic Representatives *177*
Other German Embassies in the EU *178*
Major German Embassies Worldwide *179*
EU Embassies in Germany *180*
Major non-EU Embassies in Germany *181*
Embassy Addresses *182*
Further Reading *183*
Tourist and Hotel Guides *185*

The Länder *186*
Baden-Württemberg *186*
    Key Historical Events *186*
    Territory and Population *188*
    Social Statistics *188*
    Constitution and Government *189*
    Recent Elections *189*
    Current Administration *189*
    Local Government *189*
    Economy *189*
    Performance *189*
    Banking and Finance *190*
    Energy and Natural Resources *190*
    Electricity 190
    Oil and Gas 190
    Agriculture 190
    Industry *191*
    Labour 191
    International Trade *191*
    Imports and Exports 191
    Trade Fair Organizers 191
    Communications *192*
    Roads 192

Rail 192

Civil Aviation 192

Shipping 192

Social Institutions *192*

Justice 192

Religion 193

Education 193

Culture *193*

Cinema 193

Tourism 194

Libraries 194

Theatre and Opera 194

Museums 194

Further Reading *194*

Bavaria *195*

   Key Historical Events *195*

   Territory and Population *196*

   Social Statistics *197*

   Constitution and Government *197*

   Recent Elections *197*

   Current Administration *198*

   Local Government *198*

   Banking *198*

   Energy and Natural Resources *198*

   Agriculture 198

   Industry *199*

   Labour 199

   Trade Fair Organizers *199*

   Communications *199*

   Metropolitan Railways 199

   Roads 200

   Social Institutions *200*

   Justice 200

   Religion 200

   Education 200

   Welfare 201

   Culture *201*

   Cinema 201

   Tourism 201

Festivals 202
Libraries 202
Theatre and Opera 202
Museums 202
Further Reading *202*
Berlin *203*
  Key Historical Events *203*
  Territory and Population *204*
  Social Statistics *204*
  Constitution and Government *205*
  Recent Elections *205*
  Current Administration *205*
  Banking *206*
  Industry *206*
  Labour 206
  Trade Fair Organizers *206*
  Communications *206*
  Metropolitan Railways 206
  Roads 207
  Civil Aviation 207
  Social Institutions *207*
  Justice 207
  Religion 207
  Education 208
  Culture *208*
  Cinema 208
  Tourism 208
  Libraries 208
  Theatre and Opera 208
  Museums 208
  Further Reading *209*
Brandenburg *209*
  Key Historical Events *209*
  Territory and Population *210*
  Social Statistics *210*
  Constitution and Government *211*
  Recent Elections *211*
  Current Administration *211*
  Local Government *211*

Economy *212*

Performance *212*

Energy and Natural Resources *212*

Electricity *212*

Agriculture *212*

Industry *212*

Labour *213*

International Trade *213*

Imports and Exports *213*

Communications *213*

Roads *213*

Social Institutions *213*

Education *213*

Culture *214*

Cinema *214*

Tourism *214*

Libraries *214*

Theatre and Opera *214*

Museums *214*

Bremen *214*

Key Historical Events *214*

Territory and Population *216*

Social Statistics *216*

Constitution and Government *216*

Recent Elections *216*

Banking *217*

Energy and Natural Resources *217*

Agriculture *217*

Industry *217*

Labour *218*

Communications *218*

Roads *218*

Shipping *218*

Social Institutions *218*

Justice *218*

Religion *218*

Education *219*

Culture *219*

Cinema *219*

Tourism 219

Libraries 219

Theatre and Opera 219

Museums 219

Further Reading *220*

Hamburg *220*

Key Historical Events *220*

Territory and Population *221*

Social Statistics *222*

Constitution and Government *222*

Recent Elections *222*

Banking *222*

Energy and Natural Resources *223*

Agriculture 223

Industry *223*

Labour 223

Trade Fair Organizers 224

Communications *224*

Roads 224

Shipping 224

Social Institutions *224*

Justice 224

Religion 225

Education 225

Culture *225*

Broadcasting 225

Cinema 226

Tourism 226

Libraries 226

Theatre and Opera 226

Museums and Galleries 226

Further Reading *226*

Hessen *227*

Key Historical Events *227*

Territory and Population *229*

Social Statistics *229*

Constitution and Government *230*

Recent Elections *230*

Current Administration *230*

Economy *230*

Performance 230

Banking *230*

Energy and Natural Resources *231*

Electricity 231

Oil and Gas 231

Water 231

Agriculture 231

Industry *232*

Labour 232

Trade Fair Organizers 232

Communications *232*

Roads 232

Civil Aviation 232

Shipping 233

Social Institutions *233*

Justice 233

Religion 233

Education 233

Culture *234*

Cinema 234

Press 234

Tourism 234

Libraries 234

Theatre and Opera 234

Museums 234

Further Reading *235*

Lower Saxony *235*

Key Historical Events *235*

Territory and Population *237*

Social Statistics *237*

Constitution and Government *238*

Recent Elections *238*

Current Administration *238*

Banking *238*

Energy and Natural Resources *239*

Electricity 239

Agriculture 239

Fisheries 239

Industry *239*

Labour 240

Trade Fair Organizers 240

Communications *240*

Roads 240

Rail 240

Civil Aviation 240

Social Institutions *241*

Justice 241

Religion 241

Education 241

Health 241

Culture *242*

Broadcasting 242

Cinema 242

Tourism 242

Libraries 242

Theatre and Opera 242

Museums and Galleries 242

Further Reading *242*

Mecklenburg-West Pomerania *243*

Key Historical Events *243*

Territory and Population *243*

Social Statistics *244*

Constitution and Government *244*

Recent Elections *244*

Current Administration *244*

Energy and Natural Resources *245*

Agriculture 245

Fisheries 245

Industry *245*

Labour 245

Communications *246*

Roads 246

Shipping 246

Social Institutions *246*

Justice 246

Religion 247

Education 247

Culture 247

Cinema 247

Tourism 247

Libraries 247

Theatre and Opera 248

Museums and Galleries 248

Further Reading 248

North Rhine-Westphalia 248

Key Historical Events 248

Territory and Population 250

Social Statistics 250

Constitution and Government 250

Recent Elections 251

Current Administration 251

Economy 251

Budget 251

Banking 251

Energy and Natural Resources 252

Agriculture 252

Industry 252

Labour 253

Trade Fair Organizers 253

Communications 253

Roads 253

Civil Aviation 254

Social Institutions 254

Justice 254

Religion 254

Education 254

Health 255

Culture 255

Cinema 255

Tourism 255

Libraries 255

Theatre and Opera 256

Museums and Galleries 256

Further Reading 256

Rhineland-Palatinate 256

Key Historical Events *256*
Territory and Population *258*
Social Statistics *258*
Constitution and Government *258*
Recent Elections *258*
Current Administration *259*
Banking *259*
Energy and Natural Resources *259*
Agriculture *259*
Forestry *260*
Industry *260*
Labour *260*
Communications *260*
Roads *260*
Social Institutions *261*
Justice *261*
Religion *261*
Education *261*
Culture *262*
Cinema *262*
Tourism *262*
Libraries *262*
Theatre and Opera *262*
Museums *262*
Further Reading *262*
Saarland *263*
Key Historical Events *263*
Territory and Population *264*
Social Statistics *264*
Constitution and Government *264*
Recent Elections *264*
Current Administration *264*
Energy and Natural Resources *265*
Electricity *265*
Oil and Gas *265*
Agriculture *265*
Forestry *265*
Industry *266*

Labour 266
Trade Fair Organizers 266
Communications 266
Roads 266
Shipping 267
Social Institutions 267
Justice 267
Religion 267
Education 267
Health 268
Culture 268
Cinema 268
Tourism 268
Libraries 268
Theatre and Opera 269
Museums 269
Further Reading 269
Saxony 269
　Key Historical Events 269
　Territory and Population 270
　Social Statistics 271
　Constitution and Government 271
　Recent Elections 271
　Current Administration 271
　Banking 272
　Energy and Natural Resources 272
　Agriculture 272
　Industry 272
　Communications 273
　Roads 273
　Social Institutions 273
　Religion 273
　Education 273
　Culture 273
　Cinema 273
　Tourism 274
　Libraries 274
　Theatre and Opera 274
　Museums 274

Further Reading *274*
Saxony-Anhalt *274*
Key Historical Events *274*
Territory and Population *275*
Social Statistics *276*
Constitution and Government *276*
Recent Elections *276*
Current Administration *276*
Energy and Natural Resources *277*
Agriculture *277*
Industry *277*
Labour *277*
Communications *278*
Roads *278*
Social Institutions *278*
Religion *278*
Education *278*
Culture *278*
Cinema *278*
Tourism *278*
Libraries *278*
Theatre and Opera *279*
Museums *279*
Further Reading *279*
Schleswig-Holstein *279*
Key Historical Events *279*
Territory and Population *280*
Social Statistics *281*
Constitution and Government *281*
Recent Elections *281*
Current Administration *281*
Energy and Natural Resources *282*
Agriculture *282*
Fisheries *282*
Industry *282*
Communications *283*
Roads *283*
Shipping *283*
Social Institutions *283*

Justice 283

Religion 283

Education 283

Culture 284

Cinema 284

Tourism 284

Libraries 284

Theatre and Opera 284

Museums 284

Further Reading 285

Thuringia 285

Key Historical Events 285

Territory and Population 286

Social Statistics 287

Constitution and Government 287

Recent Elections 287

Current Administration 287

Banking 288

Energy and Natural Resources 288

Agriculture 288

Industry 288

Labour 289

Communications 289

Roads 289

Social Institutions 289

Religion 289

Education 289

Health 290

Welfare 290

Culture 290

Cinema 290

Tourism 290

Libraries 290

Theatre and Opera 290

Museums 291

Further Reading 291

Colour maps fall between pages 164 and 165

GERMANY

Bundesrepublik Deutschland
(Federal Republic of Germany)

Capital: Berlin

Area: 357,022 sq. km

Population estimate, 2000: 82·69m.

Head of State: Johannes Rau

Head of Government: Gerhard Schröder

TERRITORY AND POPULATION

Germany is bounded in the north by Denmark and the North and Baltic Seas, east by Poland, east and south-east by the Czech Republic, south-east and south by Austria, south by Switzerland and west by France, Luxembourg, Belgium and the Netherlands. Area: 357,022 sq. km. Population estimate based on a microcensus of 1995: 81,538,603 (41,893,600 females); density, 228 per sq. km. In 1995 an estimated 86·5% of the population lived in urban areas. June 1997 estimate: 82,061,000, of which 66,652,000 live in the former Federal Republic of Germany and 15,409,000 in the former German Democratic Republic. There were 37·46m. households in April 1997; 13·26m. were single-person, and 11·37m. had a female principal breadwinner. 1996 density, 229 per sq. km.

The UN gives a projected population for 2000 of 82·69m.

On 14 Nov. 1990 Germany and Poland signed a treaty confirming Poland's existing western frontier and renouncing German claims to territory lost as a result of the Second World War.

The capital is Berlin; the Federal German government moved from Bonn to Berlin in 1999.

The Federation comprises 16 Länder (states). Area and population:

Länder	Area in sq. km	Population 1987 census	(in 1,000) 1997 estimate	Density per sq. km (June 1997)
Baden-Württemberg (BW)	35,753	9,286	10,393	291
Bavaria (BY)	70,551	10,903	12,057	171
Berlin (BE)[1]	891	· · ·	3,447	3,869
Brandenburg (BB)[2]	29,479	· · ·	2,562	87
Bremen (HB)	404	660	676	1,673
Hamburg (HH)	755	1,593	1,707	2,261
Hessen (HE)	21,114	5,508	6,031	286
Lower Saxony (NI)	47,611	7,162	7,832	164
Mecklenburg-West Pomerania (MV)[2]	23,170	· · ·	1,816	78
North Rhine-Westphalia (NW)	34,078	16,712	17,962	527
Rhineland-Palatinate (RP)	19,847	3,631	4,010	202
Saarland (SL)	2,570	1,056	1,083	421
Saxony (SN)[2]	18,413	· · ·	4,538	246
Saxony-Anhalt (ST)[2]	20,446	· · ·	2,715	133
Schleswig-Holstein (SH)	15,771	2,554	2,750	174
Thuringia (TH)[2]	16,171	· · ·	2,485	154

[1] 1987 census population of West Berlin: 2,013,000.

[2] Reconstituted in 1990 in the Federal Republic.

On 31 Dec. 1997 there were 7,365,800 resident foreigners, including 2,107,400 Turks, 721,000 Yugoslavs, 607,900 Italians and 363,200 Greeks. In 1997, 104,353 foreigners sought asylum (127,937 in 1995; 127,210 in 1994; 322,599 in 1993). Tighter controls on entry from abroad were applied as from 1993. 302,830 persons were naturalized in 1996, of whom 194,849 were from the former USSR. In 1996 there were 677,500 emigrants and 959,700 immigrants.

Populations of the 84 towns of over 100,000 inhabitants in 1996 (in 1,000):

Town (and Land)	Popula-tion (in 1,000)	Ranking by popu-lation	Town (and Land)	Popula-tion (in 1,000)	Ranking by popu-lation
Aachen (NW)	247·8	32	Fürth (BY)	108·7	76
Augsburg (BY)	258·8	28	Gelsenkirchen		
Bergisch Gladbach			(NW)	289·8	20
(NW)	105·7	79	Gera (TH)	122·5	62
Berlin (BE)	3,467·3	1	Göttingen (NI)	126·3	59
Bielefeld (NW)	323·7	18	Hagen (NW)	211·3	37
Bochum (NW)	399·3	16	Halle (ST)	280·1	22
Bonn (NW)	298·6	20	Hamburg (HH)	1,708·5	2
Bottrop (NW)	121·5	66	Hamm (NW)	182·8	43
Braunschweig (NI)	252·3	30	Hanover (NI)	522·7	12
Bremen (HB)	548·9	10	Heidelberg (BW)	138·7	52
Bremerhaven (HB)	129·8	56	Heilbronn (BW)	121·6	65
Chemnitz (SN)	263·3	27	Herne (NW)	179·2	44
Cologne (NW)	964·4	4	Hildesheim (NI)	106·1	78
Cottbus (BB)	122·4	63	Ingolstadt (BY)	112·5	72
Darmstadt (HE)	138·7	52	Jena (TH)	100·9	84
Dortmund (NW)	597·9	7	Kaiserslautern (RP)	101·9	81
Dresden (SN)	466·6	15	Karlsruhe (BW)	276·1	23
Duisburg (NW)	533·9	11	Kassel (HE)	201·4	39
Düsseldorf (NW)	570·8	9	Kiel (SH)	244·8	33
Erfurt (TH)	210·0	38	Koblenz (RP)	109·3	74
Erlangen (BY)	101·1	83	Krefeld (NW)	248·6	31
Essen (NW)	612·3	6	Leipzig (SN)	465·2	14
Frankfurt am Main			Leverkusen (NW)	162·3	49
(HE)	648·4	5	Lübeck (SH)	216·1	36
Freiburg im Breisgau			Ludwigshafen am		
(BW)	199·6	40	Rhein (RP)	167·0	47

Magdeburg (ST)	255·5	29	Recklinghausen		
Mainz (RP)	183·7	42	(NW)	126·9	58
Mannheim (BW)	311·7	19	Regensburg (BY)	125·4	61
Moers (NW)	106·9	77	Remscheid (NW)	121·8	64
Mönchengladbach			Reutlingen (BW)	108·9	75
(NW)	266·8	25	Rostock (MV)	224·0	35
Mülheim a. d. Ruhr			Saarbrücken (SL)	185·7	41
(NW)	176·1	45	Salzgitter (NI)	117·4	68
Munich (BY)	1,232·8	3	Schwerin (MV)	113·3	71
Münster (NW)	265·0	26	Siegen (NW)	111·1	73
Neuss (NW)	148·9	51	Solingen (NW)	165·4	48
Nuremberg (BY)	492·0	13	Stuttgart (BW)	585·4	8
Oberhausen (NW)	224·4	34	Ulm (BW)	116·1	70
Offenbach am Main			Wiesbaden (HE)	267·1	24
(HE)	116·6	69	Witten (NW)	104·5	80
Oldenburg (NI)	152·1	50	Wolfsburg (NI)	125·8	60
Osnabrück (NI)	167·7	46	Wuppertal (NW)	380·7	17
Paderborn (NW)	134·6	55	Würzburg (BY)	127·0	57
Pforzheim (BW)	118·8	67	Zwickau (SN)	101·9	81
Potsdam (BB)	135·9	54			

KEY HISTORICAL EVENTS

From the 8th century BC the Celtic peoples inhabited a vast propor-
tion of what we know as present day Germany, but by about 500 BC
warlike Germanic tribes had pushed their way north and settled in the
Celtic lands. The expanding Roman Empire tried to establish its
boundaries along the Rhine and the Danube rivers but attempts to
move further east had to be abandoned after the Roman provincial
Governor Varius was defeated in 9 AD in the Teutoborg Forest by the
Germanic forces under Arminius. For the next thousand years, the

towns of Trier, Regensburg, Augsburg, Mainz and Cologne, founded by the Romans, formed the main centres of urban settlement. Christianity was introduced under Emperor Constantine and the first bishopric north of the Alps was established in Trier in 314 AD.

At the start of the 5th century, the Huns overran the area and forced the indigenous Saxons north causing them to invade England. However the Franks, who came from the lowlands and were to become the founders of a civilized German state, gradually asserted themselves over all the other Germanic people. Towards the end of the 5th century a powerful Rhenish state was founded under King Clovis, a Salian Frank supposedly descended from a mythical hero named Merovech. The powerful Merovingian dynasty in time gave way to the Carolingians who held sway with Papal support. Charlemagne succeeded to the throne in 768 and began a reign that was later to be known as the First Reich (or Empire in German). The fortunes of the Franks continued to increase until their influence stretched from Rome in the south to the North Sea and from the Pyrenees to the River Elbe. Only Spain, Britain and southern Italy lay outside their control. The Pope in Rome crowned Charlemagne Emperor on Christmas Day 800 thus effectively creating what was to become known as the Holy Roman Empire. But the empire was too unwieldy to survive Charlemagne. On his death in 814 it began to break up. The Treaty of Verdun in 843 divided the French and German people for the first time creating a Germanic Eastern Europe and a Latin Western Europe. The first king of the newly formed eastern kingdom was Ludwig the German, and under him a specific German race and culture began to take shape. The last of Charlemagne's descendants died in 911 and with it the Carolingian dynasty. Rulership passed, via Conrad I, Duke of Franconia, to Henry I Duke of Saxony. Henry's son Otto proved to be such an able ruler that he became known as Otto the Great. He crushed the increasing power of the hereditary duchies and by making grants of land to the Church he strengthened his ties with Rome. His coronation as Emperor of the Romans in 962 confirmed him as the most powerful ruler in the Christian world.

In the next two hundred years, powerful dynasties emerged to threaten the position of the Emperor. After an intense feud, the Hohenstaufens gained supremacy over the Welfs and managed to keep the upper hand for well over a century. Best known as a crusader in the Holy Land, Frederick Barbarossa was their most successful leader. The Knights of the Teutonic Order set about converting Eastern Europe to Christianity and by the fourteenth century they had conquered much of the Baltic (now known as Prussia) and repopulated the area with Germanic peasants. By controlling the lucrative grain trade Germany grew rich.

The Golden Bull of 1356 established the method for electing an Emperor by setting up an Electoral College composed of seven Princes or Electors. Three of these were drawn from the church (the Archbishops of Cologne, Mainz and Trier), and four from the nobility (the King of Bohemia, the Duke of Saxony, the Margrave of Brandenburg and the Count Palatine of the Rhine), all of whom had the right to construct castles, mint their own coinage, impose taxes and act as judges. The title of Holy Roman Emperor nearly always went to an outsider and increasingly to members of the Austrian Hapsburg dynasty. The Great Schism of 1378–1417 which resulted in rival Popes holding court in Rome and Avignon effectively ended the church's residual power over German affairs.

The Hundred Years War between France and England helped to swell the prosperity of the rapidly growing number of Free Imperial Cities along the German trading routes, allowing them to snap up diverted trade to and from the Mediterranean. Merchants and craftsmen organized themselves into guilds, wresting control of civic life away from the nobility and laying the foundations for a capitalist economy. Founded as a defence and trading league at Lübeck, the

Hanseatic League successfully combated piracy and established Germanic economic and political domination of the Baltic and North Sea. They founded German communities in Scandinavia and all along the opposite coast as far away as Estonia.

In the 14th century the bubonic plague wiped out a quarter of the German population. Rather than blame their own tradesmen returning from Asia, it was the Jews who lived in tightly knit segregated communities who were blamed. Jews had been living in Europe since the tenth century. Excluded from guilds and trades they took to money lending, an occupation forbidden to Christians, and one which engendered envy and suspicion.

The first Hapsburg was elected King Emperor in 1273. Over two centuries, the Hapsburg dynasty became increasingly powerful, retaining the title of Holy Roman Emperor in the family from 1432 until its abolition nearly four hundred years later. Acceding to the title in 1493 Maximilian I gained the Netherlands by his marriage to Mary of Burgundy and control of Spain, Hungary and Bohemia by other marital alliances in his family.

In the early part of the 15th century, the unpopularity of the church was linked to tales of high level corruption coupled with a growing trade in the sale of indulgences. Huge land taxes were levied to pay for St. Peter's Church and other sacred buildings in Rome. In 1517, an Augustinian monk named Martin Luther, Professor of Theology at the University of Wittenberg, made his famous protest with 95 Theses or arguments against indulgence nailed to the door of Schlosskirche in Wittenberg. This was interpreted as a frontal assault on the Church of Rome and marked what is now seen as the beginning of the Reformation. Luther challenged the power of the Pope, the privileged position of the priests, and the doctrine of transubstantiation that had always been at the heart of Catholic dogma. But for the death of Maximilian I in 1519 and the subsequent power struggle for the title of Holy Roman Emperor, Luther might well have been executed as a heretic.

Following Maximilian's death, Francis I of France staked a claim to the succession in an attempt to avoid the concentration of power that would result in the election of the Hapsburg candidate, Charles I of Spain. To placate the Electors of Germany, the Pope named Luther's patron, Frederick the Wise of Saxony, as a compromise candidate. This gained Luther only a temporary reprieve as, after much political intrigue, the King of Spain was elected. Although Luther was excommunicated in 1520, he had the right to a hearing before an Imperial Diet (court). This was convened at Worms and although he was branded an outlaw and his books were ordered to be burned, he was given safe haven in Wartburg Castle where he translated the Bible into German. This was the first Bible to be made accessible to the common man. Thanks to the revolutionary system of printing invented by Johannes Gutenberg, Luther's ideas spread quickly throughout Germany. Luther's doctrine of 'justification by faith alone', with its apparent invitation to resist the authority of the church, was one of the main causes of the Peasants' War of 1524–25 which led to wholesale destruction of monasteries and castles. To the surprise of the rebels, Luther aligned himself with the authorities and so the uprising was brutally crushed. The Reformation thus gained a certain respectability. By 1555, so many of the small independent German states had joined the Protestant (as it was now known) cause that Charles V had to admit defeat and abdicated, retiring to a monastery in Spain. His brother Ferdinand succeeded him and signed the Peace of Augsburg. This agreement gave the secular rulers of each State the right to decide the form of their own religious practices, so dividing up Germany between Catholics and Lutherans.

Martin Luther died in 1546. The Catholics then launched a counter reformation following the reforms agreed at the Council of Trent. But Bavaria's annexation of the mostly Protestant free city of Donauwörth in 1608 led to the formation of the Protestant Union, an armed alliance under the leadership of the Palatinate. The Catholic League, set up by the Bavarians the following year, created a sharp division in Germany. Rudolf II, who reigned as Emperor for 36 years, chose Prague as his power base, thus weakening his wide territorial authority. After he was deposed in 1611, a series of dynastic and religious conflicts set in train what came to be known as the Thirty Years' War. Germany was devastated. The countryside was laid waste, towns were pillaged and mass slaughter reduced the population by as much as a third. Although the Catholics were the early victors, Denmark and Sweden as well as Catholic France (who preferred the Protestants to the Hapsburgs) backed the Protestants while Spain supported the Catholics. After repeated attempts to end the war, the Peace of Westphalia (signed in 1648), brought peace but deprived the Emperor of much of his authority. Power was divided between 300 principalities, and over 1,000 other territories. This weakened Germany to the point where it ceased to be a force to be reckoned with on the European scene.

During the seventeenth and eighteenth centuries, the German Princes consolidated their power, building vast palaces to bolster their claim to divine right. The Hanoverian branch of the Welf family even managed to gain the crown of Britain in 1714 – a royal union that was to last until 1837.

Meanwhile, the Hapsburgs were struggling to hold on to the title of Holy Roman Emperor. The Turks reached Vienna in 1683 but after they were repulsed, the Austrians pushed back eastwards and began to build up an Empire in the Balkans. This left their western borders vulnerable where the French, who had long regarded the Rhine as the natural limit of their territory to their east, annexed Alsace and Strasbourg in 1688 and 1697. To the north, the presence of Brandenburg-Prussia under the Hohenzollern family was beginning to be felt. Throughout the eighteenth century, Prussia was built up into a powerful independent state with its capital in Berlin. Strong militarism and a strict class-dominated society helped Prussia to become a major European power. When Frederick the Great came to the throne in 1740, he softened his country's military image by introducing reforms at home and by creating a cultured life at his court. His main preoccupation, however, continued to be expansion by force. His annexation of Silesia (under an old Brandenburg claim) provoked the Hapsburgs to retaliate and, backed by Russia and France, they launched the Seven Years' War. Frederick had only the tacit support of Hanover and Britain to fall back on and, within three years, the Prussian troops were seriously overextended. But Frederick engineered a dramatic change in his fortunes by swelling the ranks of his armies with fresh recruits and in 1772, helped by the collapse of the alliance between Austria and Russia, he annexed most of Poland and achieved his goal of establishing his version of Austria in north Germany.

Revolutionary France had expanded east and when the left bank of the Rhine fell under French control during the War of the first Coalition of 1792–97 the way was paved for the unification of Germany. After Napoleon Bonaparte defeated Austria in 1802 he decided to redraw the map of Germany. All but a few of the free German cities and all the ecclesiastical territories were stripped of their independence. In their place he created a series of buffer states – Bavaria, Württemberg and Saxony were raised to the status of kingdoms, with Baden and Hesse-Darmstadt as Duchies. In 1806, the Holy Roman Empire was officially abolished. The Hapsburgs promoted themselves from Archdukes to Emperors of Austria and set about consolidating their position in the Balkans. After the defeat of Prussia and the occupation of Berlin by Napoleon, the country was forced to sign away half its territory. In the aftermath, Prussia abolished serfdom and allowed the cities to develop their own municipal governments. Prussia played a vital role in the defeat of Napoleon at Waterloo in 1815, and the Congress of Vienna, which met to determine the structure of post-Napoleon Europe, established Prussian dominance in German affairs. Westphalia and

Rhineland were added to its territories and although there were still 39 independent states, much of Napoleon's original vision for the reorganization of the Holy Roman Empire was ratified. A German Confederation was established, each state was represented in the Frankfurt-based Diet and Austria held the permanent right to the presidency with Prussia holding the vice-presidency.

The dominant political forces in Germany after the Congress of Vienna were still extremely conservative, but the rapid advance of the industrial revolution brought about the emergence of a new social order with wage-earning workers and a growing bourgeoisie. The workers were quick to agitate for better working conditions and the middle classes for political representation. Adding to the social unrest was the peasant class whose poor living standards were made worse by the failed harvests of the late 1840s. By 1848 violence had erupted all over Europe, forcing the Prussian king to allow elections to the National Assembly in Frankfurt. Although this presented an opportunity for the electorate to introduce widespread liberal social reforms, the middle class members of the Assembly blocked all radical measures. When armed rebellions broke out in 1849, the National Assembly was disbanded and the Prussian army, backed by some of the other German kingdoms and principalities, seized power. From the 1850s, Prussia was in an unassailable position. Realizing the importance of industrial might, Prussia became the driving force for creating a single internal German market.

In 1862, Wilhelm I appointed Otto von Bismarck as Chancellor. Although a leading member of the Junker class, he set about introducing widespread reforms. In order to unite the liberal and conservative wings of the German political spectrum, he backed the demands for universal male suffrage and in return for the Chancellor's support for a united Germany, the liberals supported his plans for modernizing the army. Bismarck persuaded Austria to back him in a war against Denmark which resulted in the recapture of Schleswig and Holstein, and in a subsequent row with Austria over the spoils (the Seven Years' War) Austria was crushed by the superior strength of Prussian arms and military organization. Austria was forced out of German affairs and the previously neutral Hanover and Hesse-Kassel joined the other small German states under Prussia to form a North German Confederation. Bismarck still needed to bring the southern German states into the fold and, in 1870, he rallied all the German states to provoke a war with France. The outcome of the Franco-Prussian War of 1870–71 was the defeat of France and the creation of a united Germany (including the long disputed provinces of Alsace and Lorraine). Wilhelm I of Prussia was named Kaiser and the Empire was dubbed the Second Reich, commemorating the revival of German imperial tradition after a gap of 65 years.

At home, Bismarck continued with his liberal reforms. Uniform systems of law, currency, banking and administration were introduced nation-wide, restrictions on trade and labour movements were lifted and the cities were given civic autonomy. These measures were designed to contain the liberals while he set about trying to undermine the influence of the Catholic Church. Although he forced the Catholics to support his agricultural policies designed to protect the powerful interests of the Junker landowners, he had to back down on other issues. Despite the introduction of welfare benefits, opposition to Bismarck grew with the formation of the Social Democratic Party (SPD) in 1870.

Meanwhile, Bismarck was rivalling Britain and France with the acquisition of colonies. Closer to home, he managed a political balancing act, on one hand creating an alliance of the three great imperial powers of Germany, Russia and Austria and on the other a Mediterranean alliance with Britain to prevent Russia from expanding into the Balkans. When Wilhelm I died in 1888, he was succeeded after a brief reign by his son, Friedrich III – who died after only a few months – by his grandson Wilhelm II. 'Kaiser Bill' (as he came to be known in Britain) was a firm believer in the divine right of kings. After dismissing Bismarck from office in 1890, he appointed a series of 'yes men' to run his government, thereby seriously undermining the strength and stability that had been built up under Bismarck in the previous decade. Britain had long been an ally of Germany, bound by the ties of dynasty and common distrust of France but after the Kaiser came out in open support of the South African Boers with whom Britain was in conflict, relations between the two countries plummeted, and the European arms race accelerated. Bismarck's juggling of alliances collapsed and Europe was divided into two hostile camps. On one side, Germany was allied once more with Austria (who needed help in propping up her collapsing Eastern Empire) and with Italy. On the other, France and Russia, united in common mistrust of the German speaking nations, drew Britain closer to them. The European war that was brewing was set in motion in 1914 when a Bosnian nationalist assassinated the Austrian Archduke Franz Ferdinand at Sarajevo. Austria sent a threatening memo falsely accusing Sèrbia of causing the assassination. This led Russia to mobilize in defence of her Slavic neighbours. Seeing this as an excuse to strike first Germany attacked France. Belgium's neutrality (which had been guaranteed by Britain) was violated when the German armies marched through on their way to France and Britain declared war on Germany in 1914.

The German generals miscalculated the strength of the resistance from France and Russia. They had counted on a capitulation within a short time and when this did not happen, they found they were fighting a war on two fronts. A new form of warfare emerged with the digging of trenches all along Northern France and Belgium. The appalling injury and loss of life that was suffered by both sides during the next four years was to maim and destroy almost an entire generation of young men all over Europe. In 1917, the United States entered the war and although the revolution in Russia gained Germany a reprieve in 1917, allowing the transfer of vast numbers of troops from the eastern to western fronts, this respite was short-lived. Troops returning from Russia agitated against the war. At the same time, the German lines were weakened by over-extension. On 8 Aug. 1918 the German defences were finally broken and the armies routed. In 1916, the Kaiser had handed over military and political power to Generals Paul von Hindenburg and Erich Ludendorff. As the threat of defeat came closer, and in an attempt to minimize the potential damage of a harsh peace treaty, Ludendorff decided to leave the peace negotiations to a parliamentary delegation. He felt they would be more likely to gain lenient terms and this might serve to nip a possible Bolshevik style revolution in the bud. Two months of frenzied political activity followed which resulted in the abdication of the Kaiser and the announcement of a new German republic. World War I ended on 11 Nov. 1918.

The Elections that followed confirmed the Social Democratic Party as the new political force in Germany. Friedrich Ebert, leader of the SPD, was made President, with Philip Scheidmann as Chancellor. In 1919, a new constitution was drawn up at Weimar and a republican government under Chancellor Ebert attempted to restore political and economic stability. But the Treaty of Versailles had exacted painful losses. The rich industrial regions of Saarland and Alsace-Lorraine were ceded to France and Upper Silesia was given to a resurrected Poland. A corridor to the east effectively cut off East Prussia from the rest of the country and all Germany's overseas colonies were confiscated. The Rhineland was declared a demilitarized zone and the size of the armed forces was severely limited. The German economy was burdened with a heavy reparation bill.

Feeling betrayed by what they saw as a harsh settlement, the German military fostered the 'stab in the back' excuse for failure, which was readily accepted by a disillusioned public. Scheidmann was forced to resign and in the elections of 1920 the SPD withdrew from politics altogether leaving power in the hands of minorities drawn from the liberal and moderate conservative parties. The reparation payments were having such an effect on the economy that payments were withheld giving France the excuse to occupy the industrial region of the Ruhr in 1923. Passive resistance by the German workers meant that production ground to a halt and galloping inflation quickly ruined the middle class as the currency became worthless. Although the Weimar Republic seemed bound to fail, a new Chancellor, Gustav Stresemann, realised the danger of economic collapse and ended the passive resistance to the allies in the Ruhr. He also negotiated enormous loans from the United States to help rebuild Germany's economy. By Oct. 1924, the currency was re-established at more or less its former value and (very nearly) full employment and general prosperity ensued. Scheidmann went on to serve as Foreign Secretary during which time he negotiated a series of coalitions by which he re-established Germany as a world power. Reparation payments were scaled down and more US aid was negotiated. Even though the German people elected the ailing and aged Hindenburg in 1925, the German Republic seemed secure.

The National Socialist German Workers' Party had been founded in 1918 by a locksmith named Anton Drexler but he had been ousted almost at once by Adolf Hitler, a fanatical ex-corporal from Austria. The party attracted political extremists and misfits whose views mixed the extremes of right and left wing opinion. The party's constitution was based on a combination of Communism and Italian fascism. They adopted slogans and formed their own army, the Brown Shirts or Storm Troopers (SA), and Hitler's failed attempt at a Putsch in Bavaria in 1923 saw him arrested and convicted of high treason. He only served nine months of his sentence and emerged having used his time in prison to write his political manifesto 'Mein Kampf'. This collection of political thoughts and ideology was to form the blue print for his political programme. Initially, sales of Mein Kampf were negligible and Hitler's policies and views were seen as irrational and extremist and treated as something of a joke. Only the power of Hitler's personality sustained the National Socialists' position on the German political scene. In 1929, the Wall Street crash in America set in motion world-wide financial chaos and the newly found German economic stability collapsed with renewed unemployment and galloping inflation. The deteriorating situation proved fertile ground for Hitler's ideas which began to appeal to wounded national pride and seemed to offer an attractive solution to the rapidly growing economic crisis. Elections were held in 1930 and the Nazi party gained an astonishing 6·4m. votes, becoming the country's second largest party. The young people, the unemployed and the newly ruined middle classes were Hitler's main supporters but the right wing traditionalists still held power and their decision to back Hitler in order to gain control over his supporters backfired and the support of leading politicians only served to give him respectability. Considerable financial support from leading industrialists and giant corporations followed, enabling the Nazi party to fight a strong campaign in the 1932 presidential elections. Hindenburg, backed by the SPD and other democratic parties, just managed to win, and appointed Bruning as Chancellor. He introduced a series of economic measures, negotiated the end of reparation payments and regained Germany's right to arms equality. Bruning's attempt to introduce widespread reform of land ownership immediately lost him the support of the aristocracy. This proved to be the undoing of remaining efforts to make the Republic work. Two short term Chancellors followed – Franz von Papen and General Kurt von Scheicher. In 1932, one inconclusive election followed another. Hitler, greatly helped by a campaign of terror by his storm troopers, gained increased support. Von Papen plotted with Hitler, persuading Hindenburg to declare him Chancellor. Von Papen mistakenly believed that his party's majority in the

Reichstag would enable him to retain control. Hitler was sworn in as Chancellor on 30 Jan. 1933.

No sooner had Hitler assumed power than he set about destroying any and all opposition, stepping up the pre-election campaign of terror, which was now backed by the apparatus of the state. He was greatly helped by Hermann Goering, one of the new cabinet members, who was Prussian minister of the interior and thus had control of the police. A month later, the Reichstag was burned down and Hindenburg was obliged to declare a state of emergency giving Hitler the excuse to silence his opponents legally. Hitler was now the country's official dictator, declaring himself president of the Third Reich in 1934.

Hitler's policies involved a theory of Aryan racial supremacy by which, during the following decade, millions of Jews, gypsies, and other non-Aryan 'undesirables' were persecuted, used as slave labour, shipped off to concentration camps, murdered and their assets confiscated. Hitler's expansionism led to his annexation of Austria and German-speaking Czechoslovakia in 1938. The following year he declared all of Czechoslovakia a German protectorate and invaded Poland, attempting to restore the authority exercised there by Prussia before 1918. After the invasion of Czechoslovakia, Britain and France signed an agreement with Germany sacrificing Czech national integrity in return for what they believed would be world peace. Hitler interpreted this as a sign of weakness on the part of the allies and invaded Poland, signed a non-aggression pact with Russia and expected a similar collapse of resistance on the part of other western powers. However, by now Britain and France had realised that the Munich agreement was a humiliating sham and that Hitler's invasion of Poland on 1 Sept. 1939 meant that he was still hell bent on pursuing his policy of 'Lebensraum'. Two days after German tanks rolled into Poland, Britain and France declared war on Germany and World War II began.

Germany was extremely well prepared for this conflict and to begin with things went well for her. The fall of Poland was quickly followed by the Low Countries and in 1940 France was forced to sign an armistice with Germany and set up a puppet government in Vichy. Hitler bombarded Britain from the air but rather than invade, he turned his ground troops to the east, subduing the Balkans and, in 1941, planned an invasion of the Soviet Union. In Dec. 1941, Hitler's Japanese allies attacked the United States naval base at Pearl Harbour and America declared war on Germany. By this time, Germany was hopelessly overextended and defeat in North Africa was followed by the halt of German advance on Russia. The Allies invaded France in June 1944, liberating Paris in Aug. and Russian troops advanced from the east. Hitler was faced with certain defeat but refused to surrender, ordering the German people to defend every square inch of German territory to the death. On 30 April 1945, as Soviet forces marched into Berlin, Hitler committed suicide in his bunker. Germany surrendered unconditionally on 7 May 1945, bringing the Third Reich to an end.

The Allied forces occupied Germany – the UK, the USA and France holding the west and the USSR the east. By the Berlin Declaration of 5 June 1945 these governments assumed authority; each was given a zone of occupation, and the zone commanders-in-chief together made up the Allied Control Council in Berlin. The area of Greater Berlin was also divided into 4 sectors.

At the Potsdam Conference of 1945 northern East Prussia was transferred to the USSR. It was also agreed that, pending a final peace settlement, Poland should administer the areas east of the rivers Oder and Neisse, with the frontier fixed on the Oder and Western Neisse down to the Czechoslovak frontier.

By 1948 it had become clear that there would be no agreement between the occupying powers as to the future of Germany. Accordingly, the western allies united their zones into one unit in

March 1948. In protest, the USSR withdrew from the Allied Control Council, blockaded Berlin until May 1949, and consolidated control of eastern Germany, establishing the German Democratic Republic. A People's Council appointed in 1948 drew up a constitution, which came into force in Oct. 1949, providing for a communist state of five Länder with a centrally planned economy. In 1952 the government made a physical division between its own territory and that of the Federal Republic, in the form of a three-mile cordon fenced and guarded along the frontier. This left Berlin as the only point of contact; it was closed as a migration route by the construction of a concrete boundary wall in 1961. In 1953 there were popular revolts against food shortages and the pressure to collectivize. In 1954 the government eased economic problems, the USSR ceased to collect reparation payments, and sovereignty was granted. The GDR signed the Warsaw Pact in 1955. Socialist policies were stepped up in 1958, leading to flight to the West of skilled workers.

Meanwhile, a constituent assembly met in Bonn in Sept. 1948 and drafted a Basic Law, which came into force in May 1949. In Sept. 1949 the occupation forces limited their own powers and the Federal Republic of Germany came into existence. The occupation forces retained some powers, however, and the Republic did not become a sovereign state until 1955 when the Occupation Statute was revoked.

The Republic consisted of the states of Schleswig-Holstein, Hamburg, Lower Saxony, Bremen, North Rhine-Westphalia, Hessen, Rhineland-Palatinate, Baden-Württemberg, Bavaria and Saarland, together with West Berlin.

The first chancellor, Konrad Adenauer (1949–63), was committed to the ultimate reunification of Germany and would not acknowledge the German Democratic Republic as a state. The two German states did not sign an agreement of mutual recognition and intent to co-operate until 1972, under Chancellor Willy Brandt.

The most marked feature of the post-war period was rapid population growth and the restoration of industry. Immigration from the German Democratic Republic, about 3m. since 1945, stopped when the Berlin Wall was built in 1961; however there was a strong movement of German-speaking people back into Germany from German settlements in countries of the Soviet bloc. Industrial growth also attracted labour from Turkey, Yugoslavia, Italy and Spain.

The Paris Treaty, which came into force in 1955, ensured the Republic's contribution to NATO, and NATO forces were stationed along the Rhine in large numbers, with consequent dispute about the deployment of nuclear missiles on German soil.

Even before sovereignty, the Republic had begun negotiations for a measure of European unity, and joined in creating the European Coal and Steel Community in 1951 and the European Economic Community in 1957. In Jan. 1957 the Saarland was returned to full German control. In 1973 the Federal Republic entered the UN.

In the autumn of 1989 movements for political liberalization in the GDR and re-unification with Federal Germany gathered strength. Erich Honecker and other long-serving Communist leaders were replaced in Oct.–Nov. The Berlin Wall was opened on 9 Nov.

Following the reforms in the GDR in Nov. 1989 the Federal Chancellor Helmut Kohl issued a plan for German confederation. The ambassadors of the 4 wartime allies met in Berlin in Dec. After talks with Chancellor Kohl on 11 Feb. 1990, President Gorbachev said the USSR had no objection to German re-unification. The Allies agreed a formula ('two-plus-four') for re-unification talks to begin after the GDR elections on 18 March. 'Two-plus-four' talks began on 5 May 1990. On 18 May Federal Germany and the GDR signed a treaty transferring Federal Germany's currency, together with its economic, monetary and social legislation, to both the Federal Republic and the GDR as of 1 July. On 23 Aug. the Volkskammer by 294 votes to 62 'declared its accession to the jurisdiction of the Federal Republic as from 3 Oct. according to article 23 of the Basic Law', which provided for the Länder of pre-war Germany to accede to the Federal Republic. On 12 Sept. the Treaty on the Final Settlement with Respect to Germany was signed by the Federal Republic of Germany, the GDR and the 4 war-time allies: France, the USSR, the UK and the USA.

The Federal Assembly (*Bundestag*) moved from Bonn to the renovated *Reichstag* in Berlin in 1999.

A UNITED GERMANY

The single most important event in German post-war history was the reunification of the Federal Republic with the former East Germany. That it happened at all was remarkable enough but that it was achieved without major social and political disruption was a huge tribute to the strength of a still young democracy. That is not to say that reunification has been trouble free. Notwithstanding the injection of billions of Deutsche Marks of public subsidy which has transformed the infrastructure and restored urban areas, the easterners have found the transition from communism to capitalism more painful than they had anticipated. Part of the problem has been the adoption of the Deutsche Mark which, by virtue of its strength as an international currency, inspires confidence while at the same time making it harder for export markets in central and eastern Europe to afford to buy German. The collapse of much traditional industry in the east has been hastened by wage equalization deals which have pushed up labour costs. As a result, unemployment has soared.

But there are signs that an economic revival may not be far off. The automotive and information technology sectors are doing well and the chemicals industry, which contracted sharply after reunification, is beginning once more to expand. Of the eastern Länder, Saxony and Thuringia are the most advanced.

As a psychological factor, the government move to Berlin is calculated to do much to bring eastern Germany back into the centre of national life as an equal part of the country.

CHRONOLOGY

The Romans and Celtic Tribes

8th century BC

Celtic peoples inhabit most of present day Germany.

1st century BC

Germanic tribes settling in the north. Roman Empire expanding.

1st century AD

Emperor Constantine introduces Christianity. First German Bishopric established at Trier.

The Frankish Empire

6th century

King Clovis of the Franks converts to Christianity.

8th & 9th centuries

768   Emperor Charlemagne succeeds to the throne.

The First Reich

800   Charlemagne was crowned Emperor by Pope Leo III in Rome.

843   Treaty of Verdun divides Charlemagne's Empire into East (Germanic) Empire (later to become Germany) and West (Latin) Empire (later to become France).

10th century

911   Conrad, Duke of Franconia, becomes King of Germania and is succeeded by Henry, Duke of Saxony. The Slav peoples east of the Elbe are converted to Christianity.

Holy Roman Empire

962   Henry's son Otto ('The Great') crowned Emperor combining the kingdoms of Germany, Italy and Burgundy.

11th century

Pope Gregory VII questions the supremacy of the Emperors and their hereditary rights are ended. The Hohenstaufen family establish themselves as rulers of Germany.

12th century

1122   Concordat of Worms releases the territory of the Holy See in Rome from the sovereignty of the Emperor Frederick I ('Barbarossa'); he renounces the right to appoint bishops and abbots.

13th century

1273   Hapsburg family become rulers of Austria (they retain the throne until 1918).

14th century

Bubonic Plague spreads throughout Europe.

1337   Start of the Hundred Years' War between France and England. Trade prospers along the German trade routes. The Hanseatic League (and other similar economic and trade organizations) is formed.

1356   The Golden Bull enacted by Charles IV decrees that henceforth the Emperors should be elected by an Electoral College of seven Electors (three from the church and four nobles). The foundations of a modern state are also laid out in the Golden Bull. First constitution in Europe.

1386   Heidelberg University (oldest in Germany) is founded.

Hapsburg Dynasty

15th century

1438   Albert II, Duke of Austria and Count of Hapsburg elected Emperor, taking the title Holy Roman Emperor. The Hapsburg

family goes on to dominate the line of succession of the Holy
Roman Empire until 1806.

1450   Invention of the movable type printing press by Johannes
Gutenberg in Mainz.

1477   The future Maximilian marries Mary of Burgundy.

The Reformation

16th century

The hereditary principle is restored to the Empire by the
Hapsburgs.

1517   Martin Luther (1483–1546) attacks the church with his 95
'Theses' nailed to the door of Wittenberg Church. He refuses to
retract, is summoned before the Diet (Court) of Worms, and is
exiled. Protected by the Duke of Saxony, he translates the Bible
and via the printing press his ideas spread rapidly.

1530   Confession of Augsburg drawn up and becomes the charter of the new 'Protestantism'.

1555   The Peace of Augsburg establishes Protestantism as the
official religion of the northern states of Germany.

17th century

1618   Start of the Thirty Years War consisting of a series of religious and dynastic struggles for power.

1648   Peace of Westphalia sees German cities sacked, the
economy in ruins and the countryside laid waste.

1685   Massive emigration of French Huguenots (Protestants) to
Prussia.

1688/89   War of the House of Orleans breaks out. French troops
sack the Palatinate.

Rise of Prussia

18th century

1700   Frederick I, Elector of Brandenburg and Duke of Prussia,
is made King of Prussia by the Emperor. Prussia begins to emerge

as the strongest German State, with a permanent army, centralized administration and a new sense of national pride.

1713   Emperor Charles VI secures his succession with the Pragmatic Sanction.

1740   War of the Austrian Succession. Frederick the Great comes to the throne of Prussia and consolidates Prussia's position in Germany. He is revered as an enlightened despot bringing culture and order to his court.

1756   The Seven Years War between Prussia (backed only by England and Hanover) and the Hapsburgs (backed by France and Russia).

1772   Frederick annexes Poland.

1792   Beginning of the Revolutionary Wars. The Prussians are defeated at Valmy.

Fall of the Holy Roman Empire

19th century

1802   After taking control of France and defeating Austria, Napoleon enters Berlin and decides to redraw the map of Germany. The Holy Roman Empire is officially abolished.

Towards German Unification

1815   Prussia re-establishes dominance in German affairs by playing a key role in the defeat of Napoleon at the Battle of Waterloo. The Congress of Vienna establishes a confederation of 35 autonomous German states represented by a National Assembly sitting in Frankfurt.

1840   Failed crops and poverty result in unrest.

1849   Armed rebellion breaks out. The National Assembly is disbanded and Prussia gains pre-eminence.

The Bismarck Era

1862   King Wilhelm I appoints Otto von Bismarck Chancellor of Germany.

1866   Bismarck defeats the Austrians at Sadowa and creates a northern German Federation uniting Prussia with Hanover, Hesse, Schleswig-Holstein and all the states north of the Main. Bismarck introduces liberal reforms, with uniform systems of currency, law, banking, and administration. Restrictions on trade and labour movements are lifted and universal male suffrage introduced.

The Second Reich (1871–1918)

1871   Prussia defeats France and a unified Germany (including Alsace-Lorraine) with Wilhelm I at its head is declared at Versailles.

1888   Wilhelm II succeeds his father.

1890   Wilhelm (The Kaiser or Emperor) forces the resignation of Bismarck. He provokes England and France.

The First World War

20th century

1914   Germany declares war on France and Russia, invades Belgium and Great Britain declares war on Germany.

1917   Russia, in the grip of the Bolshevik revolution, asks for an armistice. The United States of America declares war on Germany.

1918   Wilhelm II abdicates (9 Nov.). Armistice signed on 11 Nov.

The Weimar Republic

1919   Germany adopts a republican constitution. The Kaiser Wilhelm goes into exile. Post war inflation begins to spiral out of control. Adolf Hitler joins the German National Socialist Party and becomes its leader. He tries to seize power, is imprisoned (released in 1924) and starts to write Mein Kampf – his political manifesto (first published in 1925).

1923   The French occupy the Ruhr in protest at non-payment of war reparations by Germany.

1929 Germany becomes a member of League of Nations and recognizes western frontiers imposed at the Treaty of Versailles in 1919.

1929 Wall Street crash heralds the collapse of economic confidence.

1932 Backed by paramilitary organizations, National Socialists profit from widespread discontent and financial hardship and gain ground in the general election.

1933 The middle classes see Hitler as a rampart against the threat of Communism and allow him to accede to the title of Chancellor.

The Third Reich

1934 Hitler declares himself President of the Third Reich. He becomes dictator of Germany.

1938 Hitler's expansionist policies lead to invasion and annexing of Austria and Czechoslovakia. He pursues policies of Aryan supremacy, casting as the enemy Jews, Gypsies and other 'undesirables'.

1939 Czechoslovakia, France and England sign an agreement sacrificing Czech national integrity in exchange for German promises of European peace. Hitler invades Poland. Two days later France and England declare war.

The Second World War

1940 France signs an armistice with Germany. Hitler bombards England from the air, subdues the Balkans and plans to invade Russia.

1941 Japanese air attacks on American naval forces at Pearl Harbour lead to a US declaration of war on Japan and then Germany.

1944 In June, the Allies invade France and in Aug. take Paris. From his bunker in Berlin Hitler refuses to surrender.

1945   Russian troops take Berlin and Hitler commits suicide
(30 April). Germany surrenders unconditionally on 7 May.

Post-War Germany and the Cold War

1945   Britain, USA and USSR meet in Potsdam to divide Germany
into four zones of occupation (France occupying the fourth). Berlin
is also divided into four sectors.

1946   Beginning of the Cold War between USSR and the West
over occupation policies.

1948   USSR withdraws from the Allied Control Council, and
blockades Berlin (until 1949).

1949   USSR consolidates control of eastern Germany by setting
up the German Democratic Republic (East Germany) with five
communist controlled Länder and a centrally planned economy.
The three western zones are amalgamated to form the Federal
Republic of Germany (West Germany) under the leadership of
Konrad Adenauer.

The Federal Republic

1951   Creation of European Coal and Steel Community.

1955   Birth of NATO (North Atlantic Treaty Organization). Troops
of occupation stationed along the Rhine. Disputes over deployment of nuclear weapons on German soil.

1957   Creation of the European Economic Community. Saarland
returns to full German control.

1961   The Berlin Wall is built, dividing the eastern sector from the
west. Cold War reaches crisis point.

1972   Chancellor Willy Brandt signs a Treaty with East Germany
confirming a policy of openness toward the East (Ostpolitik).

1973   Both Germanies enter the United Nations.

1989   Government of East Germany opens the frontier
between East and West Germany and the Berlin Wall is
destroyed.

1990   First free elections in East Germany. On 3 Oct. Parliament
ratifies the reunification treaty and the national day is moved to
3 Oct.

1991   Parliament votes for Berlin to become capital of Germany.

1994   By Sept., all Soviet troops have been withdrawn from the
old East Germany and all occupying allied forces have left Berlin.

1999   Government, Parliament and president move to Berlin.

CULTURAL BRIEFING

Architecture and Design

Romanesque

9th–12th centuries

German Romanesque architecture, as elsewhere in Europe, owes
its roots to the heritage of the occupying Romans, and the remains
of Roman buildings can often be found, mostly in the foundations
of churches and cathedrals.

10th and 11th centuries

Ottonian Architecture

The revival of religious architecture during the reign of Otto I
produced enormous churches with wide aisles interspersed with
columns and piers but as yet no stone vaulting.

Rhineland Romanesque

Typical of this period are the churches with trefoil apses in the form
of cloverleaves to be found around Cologne. Towards the end of
the 11th century, ribbed stone vaulting over the nave marked the
transition from Romanesque to Gothic.

Gothic

(13th–16th centuries)

Cologne Cathedral is perhaps the most famous example of
German Gothic architecture. Influenced by French Gothic style,

two slender towers frame the façade and the interior has soaring pointed vaulting.

1150–1250   Cistercian Monasteries also influenced German monastic building. Their churches were usually built without towers, with squared off chancels and rectangular side chapels. Most of these monastic complexes were later adapted in the Baroque style but an example of a monastic complex that has remained intact can be seen at Maulbronn. East of the Elbe, most important buildings were brick-built ('Backsteingotik' – Brick Gothic).

Late Gothic style (Spätgotik) dominated church architecture for three centuries and was responsible for the Hall-Churches usually with decorative rib vaulting. The growth of trade and commercial prosperity gave rise to the building of impressive town halls, covered markets and half-timbered private houses.

Renaissance

(1520–1620)   Germany was in the grip of the Reformation and so the influences of the Italian Renaissance were limited to southern Germany. The architecture (both lay and church) of Northern Germany was more influenced by Flemish and Dutch designs.

Baroque and Rococo

(17th and 18th centuries)

Catholic Southern Germany was most influenced by Baroque style and many abbots rebuilt their abbeys, with masons, painters, sculptors and stucco-workers creating complex and elaborate intricate interiors. Much of the blossoming of German baroque is due to a group of architects – the Vorarlberg School – who were working in Swabia, Bavaria, Switzerland and Alsace between 1680 and 1750. Many princely palaces and castles also date from this period and usually have monumental staircases at their hearts with arcaded galleries and painted ceilings leading to staterooms and libraries on the first floor.

Neo-Classicism

(18th and 19th centuries)

The court at Versailles built for Louis XIV inspired a new style of court building and many French architects were employed by local German rulers (or Electors) to build their palaces and country mansions. Meanwhile, excavations at Pompeii gave rise to a fashion for church designs based on classical Graeco-Roman style, with colonnaded façades and symmetrical interiors and decorative motifs drawn from Greek and Roman friezes (garlands, urns, vases etc.).

1830   A revival of Gothic style which many Germans saw as representing the 'Old Germany' and was a reaction to the simplicity of the neo-classical style. The simple graceful furniture produced during this period – known as Biedermeier – probably inspired the Edwardian style of furniture in England in the early 20th century.

1850   The Founders Period (Gründerzeit) describes the heavy pretentious reproductions of medieval and renaissance furniture favoured by wealthy industrialists. Government and public buildings were also furnished in this style during this period.

Modern and Contemporary Movements

20th century

Style 1900 or Jugendstil (or Art Nouveau) swept Germany in the early years of the twentieth century, largely due to the availability for the first time of mass-produced good quality furniture. With the growth of industry came the concept of practical household items which were attractive to look at. Architects such as Peter Behrens, Mies van der Rohe and Walter Gropius were the pioneers.

1920s   Gropius was director of the Bauhaus School of architecture and applied arts. Founded in Weimar and then moved to Dessau, the school broke down the divisions between monumental and decorative elements in architectural design and it attracted many talented avant-garde painters and sculptors, as well as architects.

The Third Reich

Adolf Hitler appointed Albert Speer as his architect and commissioned government buildings in the neo-classical style intended to last 1,000 years. Many were intended for public rallies, such as the stadium in Nuremberg.

Post World War II

German cities were extensively bombed during World War II, and in the post war period some cities had to be almost completely rebuilt. The damaged churches and cathedrals were painstakingly rebuilt by such architects as Dominikus Böhm and Rudolf Schwartz.

East and West Germany

Following World War II communist controlled GDR (East German) architects like Hermann Henselmann (a former Bauhaus member) were producing heavy functional 'Stalinist' architecture, while in the west, municipal and cultural buildings were being designed by a new generation of innovative architects among them Hans Scharoun, Otto Frei, Oswald Mathias Ungers and J.P. Kleihuis. The influence of the style and philosophy of the Bauhaus school is still felt in the design of many of Germany's modern buildings, and modern German design is known for its purity of line, lightness of materials and functionality. With the reunification of Germany, the capital has been moved back from Bonn to Berlin, and the Reichstag (parliament building) has been entirely renovated.

Painting and Sculpture

9th–15th century

Two art forms dominate from the Carolingian (9th century) period – frescoes and illuminated manuscripts. Among the few frescoes that have survived, examples can be found in the crypt of St. Maxim's church in Trier and Stiftskirche St. Georg on the island of Reichenau in Lake Constance – also a centre for the illumination of early Christian Manuscript.

10th century

Stained glass dating from the 10th century in Augsburg Cathedral is some of the earliest in Europe. The Bishops Throne, carved from stone set on two lions, is also 10th century.

c. 1200   Ceiling paintings in Michael's Kirche in Hildesheim.

Gothic

12th century

Stained glass played an important part in Gothic cathedrals but gothic architecture left little room for frescoes. Good examples of early gothic stained glass can be found in Cologne cathedral.

13th–15th century

The Cologne School of Painting. Early examples of landscapes and religious painting on panels.

c. 1340   Meister Bertram-Erschaffung der Tiere (Creation of the animals).

c. 1432   Die Meerfahrt der Heiligen (sea voyage of Mary Magdalene) by Lukas Moser.

Renaissance

15th and 16th centuries

German Renaissance often referred to as Dürerzeit (the age of Albert Dürer, 1471–1528). He was a humanist, deeply affected by the reformation, and the first German artist to deal with the theory and practice of Italian Renaissance art. His intense religious scenes and woodcuts and drawings of animals in nature can be found in the Alte Pinakothek in Munich and in museums and collections over the world.

Dürer influenced Lucas Cranach the Elder – the central figure in the South German School of Mannerism, a movement idealizing beauty. Also influenced by Dürer was Hans Holbein, whose realistic portraits often depicted stylized figures detached from their environment.

Other notable artists of the 15th and 16th century: Stefan Lochner (d. 1451), Master Painter of the Cologne School, Veit Stoß, painter sculptor, woodcarver and engraver, Tilman Riemenschneider (1460–1531) sculptor and woodcarver, Master of Severinus, painter (late 15th century), The Master of the Life of the Virgin, painter (late 15th century), and Friedrich Herlin, painter (d. 1500).

Baroque and Rococo

17th century

During the 17th and 18th centuries, the style became much more elaborate and ornate. Frescoes, sculptures and paintings were integrated into the architecture. Elaborate stone and woodcarving ornamented the churches and sculpture was incorporated into the palaces and gardens of the day. Frescoes became important once again – this time in palaces rather than in churches. Two of Germany's most important painters, Adam Elsheimer (1578–1610) and Johann Liss (1597–1630), were both working in Italy and many of the frescoes and paintings in the palaces were done by Italian or French painters.

Other notable artists of the 17th century: Andreas Schlüter (1660–1714), sculptor working in northern Germany; the Medrians, a family of engravers specialising in plates illustrating German towns; Johann Baptist Zimmermann (1680–1758), fresco painter working in pastels in Rococo style.

Neo-Classicism

18th century

Buildings in the 18th century reverted back to Graeco-Roman styles, and in painting and sculpture the human figure came back into fashion. Johann Winkelmann (1717–68) published works on classical painting and sculpture and a history of classical art. This influenced many of the artists of the time including Anton Mengs

(1728–79) who became painter of the Royal Court at Dresden. Johann Heinrich Tischbein (1751–1829) painted still lifes and animals and, his friend, Goethe. His most famous painting, Goethe in der Campagna di Roma, shows Germany's most famous author in a classical Italian landscape (now in the Städel Art Institute in Frankfurt am Main).

Other notable artists of the 18th century: Johann Gottfried Schadow (1764–1850), sculptor whose four horse chariot adorns the Brandenburg Gate in Berlin; Balthasar Permoser (1651–1732), sculptor to the Court of Dresden; the Asam Brothers, baroque sculptors.

19th century

Romanticism

The Romantic Movement represented a return to more conventional religious themes with the emphasis on spirituality. Caspar David Friedrich (1774–1840) was perhaps the most famous German romantic painter who not only painted intensely mystical religious picture but wild romantic landscapes. Otto Runge (1777–1810) was the founder of the German Romantic Movement and his work typifies the Dresden School. Raphael influenced the intensely religious work of a group of artists known as the 'Nazarener'.

Realism and Naturalism

By the middle of the 19th century artists began to paint outdoors whether in the countryside or in urban settings and the early beginnings of impressionism began to be felt.

Impressionism

Late in the 19th century the German impressionist movement emerged headed by Max Liebermann (1847–1935) and Fritz von Uhde (1848–1911). To start with the new style was not popular in Germany and the Romantic Movement continued longer here than in France or Italy.

Other notable artists of the 19th century: Wilhelm Leibl
(1844–1900) realist painter, Adolf von Hildebrand (1847–1921)
monumental sculptor, Johann Overbeck (1789–1869) 'Nazarener'
painter, Hans Thoma (1838–1924) portrait painter and lithograph-
er, Adolph Menzel (1815–1905) realist painter known for his works
on the life of Friedrich I.

20th century

Expressionism

The expressionist movement owed much to the influences of
Edvard Munch and to Van Gogh and presented a vision of the
world that was intense, violent and often tragic.

Die Brücke

(The Bridge Group) emerged in Dresden and brought together
painters like Erich Heckel, Ernst Ludwig Kirchner and Karl
Schmidt-Rott-Luff. The artists often lived in communes and
used their studios as exhibition space. Emil Nolde led the expressionist movement in Germany even though he only belonged
briefly to Die Brücke. (The Nazis banned Nolde from painting
in 1941).

Der Blaue Reiter

(Blue Rider) was an association of Expressionist painters working
in Munich, founded by Wassily Kandinsky and Franz Marc (later
joined by August Macke and Paul Klee). The group was united by a
desire to free art from the constraints of reality, paving the way to
abstraction.

Neue Sachlichkeit

(New Objectivity) was a movement that affected all the arts and
reached its height with the Bauhaus movement. Although architecture formed the basis of the Bauhaus movement, it also brought
together a large number of avant-garde artists and designers

(see architecture above). George Grosz was co-founder of the German Dadaist movement and later the Rote Gruppe (the Red Group) with John Heartfield. Of the women artists, Käthe Kollwitz had worked through the naturalist and expressionist movements to reach social realism.

Early 1950s

The respected German artists that had been exiled from Nazi Germany during the war returned and German art began the revival. Of the post war expressionists, Willi Baumeister and Ernst Nay led the way.

1960s

Gruppe Zero, based in Düsseldorf and led by Otto Piene and the sculptor, Heinz Mack, carried on the legacy of the Bauhaus. Josef Beuys created the School of Constructivist Sculpture in Düsseldorf. His interactive 'Happenings' and 'Performances' made him one of the most influential post-war modern German artists.

1970s to the Present
Neue Wilde

(The New Wild) movement of the late 1970s and early 1980s combined new wave music and the visual arts and was mainly centred in Cologne, Berlin and Hamburg.

The Germany of today places great importance on the arts, and new galleries and museums are constantly being built. Modern and contemporary art is thriving and many artists are developing work using the latest technological advances – video, laser technology etc. There is an enormous summer long exhibition of German contemporary art (the Documenta) as well as work from around the world that takes place every 5 years in Kassel. The next one is due to be held in the summer of 2002.

Music

Middle Ages

12th and 13th centuries

The Minnesänger (minstrels and troubadours) were travelling court musicians who drew inspiration from Moorish and Gregorian chants and French lyric poetry for their songs.

14th and 15th century

The Meistersingers formed themselves into guilds (based on the tradesmen's guilds) and followed the tradition of the troubadours. To join you had to pass a test and produce a new melody or lyric. (In the 19th century, Richard Wagner wrote an opera about a famous Meistersinger, Hans Sachs).

Renaissance

16th century

In the wake of the reformation, the new liturgy of Martin Luther's Protestantism gave rise to different forms of church singing. Chorales, or hymns, were sung in German rather than Latin (and gave rise eventually to the German Cantatas and oratorios).

Notable composers: Michael Praetorius, Johann Pachelbel, Heinrich Schutz, Dietrich Buxtehude, John Walther (Luther wrote the words for Walther's 'Eine Feste Burg').

Baroque

17th century

The Baroque style was epitomised by Johann Sebastian Bach (1685–1750) but the movement had started at the turn of the century with the music of composers like Buxtehude. The century was dominated by the work of two composers – Johann Sebastian Bach and Georg Händel. Bach was immensely prolific and his long creative life produced an enormous legacy of concerti, cantatas, and works for keyboard and oratorios. Georg Friedrich Händel was born in Germany although he spent most of his working life in England and his music is greatly influenced by his travels in Italy. Georg Philipp Telemann, who was heavily influenced by French and Italian music, was the first composer/performer to give public concerts.

18th century

Musicians of the School of Mannheim modernized the symphonic form. The sonata became popular (largely through Carl Phillipp Emmanuel Bach). The Singspiel – popular operetta with dialogue interspersed with Lieder (songs) – appeared in Germany for the first time. In 1743 Berlin's first opera house was built. Christoph Willibald Gluck staged his first operas in Paris.

The Viennese School

The late 18th century was dominated by Austrian composers – Joseph Haydn and Wolfgang Amadeus Mozart. Although not German, their involvement with and influence on German music was immense. Haydn preceded Mozart and was a considerable influence on him, but in his short lifetime Mozart transformed European music with operas, concerti, 41 symphonies, chamber music, and works for solo instruments and keyboard. Musical instruments were also going through a period of technological advancement and the first modern flutes, clarinets and oboes appeared. Mozart and Haydn were Austrians who worked in Germany. Ludwig van Beethoven, on the other hand, was a German born in Bonn who went to Vienna where he was taught by Haydn. His work reflects the Age of Enlightenment. Towards the end of his life, Beethoven became profoundly deaf but continued to compose and his 9th symphony and many of his late string quartets were written after he had lost all his hearing.

The Romantics

18th and 19th centuries

Franz Schubert was most famous for his revival of the 'Lied' (song) and he wrote several famous song cycles drawing on the lyric

German poets, including Heine and Goethe, for his words. Carl Maria Weber wrote Germany's first Romantic opera 'Der Freischutz'. Felix Mendelssohn-Bartholdy, although using classical musical forms, was a true Romantic in inspiration. Robert Schumann started life as a pianist but continued the tradition of Schubert and wrote many songs as well as chamber works and symphonies, and Johannes Brahms combined the classical German style with passionate lyricism. The late 18th century saw the arrival of Richard Wagner, who revolutionised German opera. He introduced the idea of using 'Leitmotifs' – signature tunes – to introduce and identify his characters to the audience and these were interwoven with elaborate orchestration to produce a continuous work. The stories were drawn, for the most part, from early Nordic and Germanic myths and legends (this made his work very popular with the Nazis in the 1930 and 1940s). Also in the late 19th century, Gustav Mahler was the inventor of the 'Orchesterlieder' – symphonic sung poems.

Other notable composers of the late 19th century: Hugo Wolf, Franz Liszt (who was at the centre of a group of composers in Weimar between 1844 and 1860) and Richard Strauss (who was married to Richard Wagner's daughter).

20th century

Richard Strauss really belongs to the 20th century although he wrote in the Romantic style and followed the tradition of Mahler, writing Orchesterlieder as well as symphonies and song cycles. During the early part of the 20th century Alban Berg, Anton von Webern and Paul Hindemith were, like Richard Strauss, writing music in the romantic tradition while Arnold Schönberg led an innovative school of atonal music – a system of music using the twelve-tone scale. Although Austrian, Schönberg exerted an enormous influence on 20th century music in general and musical developments in Germany in particular. Carl Orff, who was a pupil of Schönberg, introduced new ideas about musical education and his theatrical productions combined drama and speech and song. In the 1930s the influence of jazz and American music began to be felt and Kurt Wiell, who had originally been influenced by the atonal composers, wrote the Three Penny Opera in collaboration with Berthold Brecht.

In the years after World War II, Germany saw the rise of modal twelve-tone serial music and the beginning of the use of electronics in the composition of serious music. Wolfgang Fortner used electronic elements in some of his mature works. Another notable post-war composer, Bernd Alois Zimmermann, perceived past, present and future techniques as one in his work (including in his opera 'The Soldier'). After 1950, a new generation of musicians using electronic techniques, led by Karlheinz Stockhausen, emerged, including Hans Werner Henze, who writes operas combing modernity and tradition, atonality and tonality. Wolfgang Rihm, who like Henze was a pupil of Fortner, writes in an extremely complex musical language made up of combinations of traditional and modernistic techniques.

Music in Modern Germany

In Germany today, there are many thriving orchestras, both amateur and professional, all over the country. As well as the Berlin Philharmonic, the Gewendhaus Orchestra Leipzig and the Bamberg Symphony Orchestra, three of the biggest radio stations have their own resident orchestras. The most important musical centres in Germany today are Berlin, Hamburg, Dresden, Leipzig and Stuttgart for opera and ballet, Nuremberg for organ music, Stuttgart for choral singing and Munich for the music of Bach and Richard Strauss. Bayreuth has an internationally famous annual festival devoted entirely to the operas of Richard Wagner.

Literature and Theatre

Middle Ages

9th century

The earliest form of German literature was the oral tradition of handing down tales of heroic deeds from one generation to the next.

c. 800   During the reign of Charlemagne educated clerics recorded what they could of the narratives, and the 'Lay of Hildebrand', together with 'Ludwigslied' and 'Heiland', were written down for posterity.

12th century

The literature of the royal court moved away from clerical influences to tell the tale of the 'Nibelungen' (Richard Wagner later based his operas on these Germanic myths and legends).

13th century

Walther von der Vogelweide, the greatest of the Minnesänger, was writing lyric poetry in finest Middle High German. Wolfram von Eschenbach published 'Parzifal' – the story of the quest for the Holy Grail (also used by Wagner for his opera Parsifal). Tristan und Isolde was also written during this period.

14th century

Writing in Germany during this period had strong mystical themes. Among contemporary authors writing between 1275 and 1361 were Meister Eckhard, Heinrich Scuse and Johannes Tauler.

15th century

1450   This century saw the arrival of the movable type printing press (invented by Johannes Gutenberg in Mainz) and although initially the new books were for the most part religious (the first Bible was printed in 1453) the invention went on to revolutionize literary tradition.

16th century

> 1534   Martin Luther completed his translation of the Bible into Modern German. It was printed on the new Gutenberg press and widely circulated. For the first time the scriptures were accessible to non-Latin speaking people.

Baroque

17th century

> Much of the literature of this period reflects the Thirty Years' War and the Reformation. Language societies were established to formalise German grammar and usage. Martin Opitz published his 'Buch der Deutschen Poeterey' ('Book of German Poetry') and Andreas Gryphius wrote plays and poems dwelling on the Baroque ideals of earthly transience and the meaninglessness of life.
> 1669   Grimmelshausen published his 'Simplicissimus' – the account of the ups and downs of a loveable rogue – considered to be the greatest 'Schelmenroman' (picaresque novel) of the period.

The Age of Enlightenment (Aufklärung)

18th century

> This era of European literature was inspired by the French philosopher Descartes and his German counterpart, Gottfried Wilhelm Leibniz. Leibniz – a philosopher, linguist and mathematician – published 'Theodicy', in French and Latin, and, without any knowledge of Newton's work on the subject, invented differential calculus. The literature of the day dispensed with superstition and relied on the triumph of human reason. Johann Christian Gottsched became Professor of Poetry at Leipzig and set about remodelling German theatre along French lines.
> Christoff Wieland wrote 'Geschichte des Agathon' – believed to be Germany's first 'Bildungsroman' (a novel showing the development of the hero). Gotthold Ephraim Lessing wrote critical works,

fables and legends. He rejected the French theatre reforms of Gottsched, favouring Shakespearean dramatic forms. He wrote the first German tragedies in domestic (non-aristocratic) settings.

Sturm und Drang

'Storm and Stress' (literally) describes a golden age of literature dominated by two giants of German literary history, Johann Wolfgang von Goethe and Friedrich von Schiller. Their arrival marks the start of the flowering of Modern German national literature. In reaction to the Enlightenment, this new movement exalted freedom, emotion and nature although Goethe eventually tempered this with proposals for more discipline and a classical ideal of noble, serene and harmonious humanity.

1759–1805   Schiller published historical dramas, which are undisguised songs of liberty.

1774   Goethe published 'The Sorrows of Young Werther', a novel that made his reputation.

Neo-Classicism

1788–1832   Goethe published classical dramas, novels, and 'Faust', a two part drama in verse considered to be the greatest work in German literature.

1770–1831   Hegel defined the historical conscience and dialectic.

The Romantic Movement

18th century

The Romantic Movement in Germany was part of a Europe-wide one that embraced the Greek and Roman ideals but took the reader deep into the realms of the imagination.

19th century

1812   First publication of the book of Fairy Tales by the Brothers Grimm.

Naturalism and Realism

1788–1860   The works of Arthur Schopenhauer advocated pity as the only antidote to life's suffering.

1797–1856   Start of Junges Deutschland (Young Germany) – a movement that grew up as a reaction to the non-political Romanticism. In response to the censorship prevalent at the time, Heinrich Heine wrote scathing satirical works. His book of poems (Buch der Lieder) is today considered to be Germany's best collection of love poems – his work was banned in 1835.

1848   Karl Marx and Freidrich Engels published their 'Communist Manifesto'.

1862–1946   Gerhardt Hauptmann developed naturalist, socially critical dramas (e.g. 'The Weavers').

20th century

1844–1900   Friedrich Nietzsche denounced the decadence of humanity in 'Also Sprach Zarathustra' (Thus Spoke Zarathustra).

1875–1955   Thomas Mann published his novels Buddenbrooks, Dr. Faustus, the Magic Mountain and Death in Venice.

1877–1962   Hermann Hesse published Der Steppenwolf, Narziß und Goldmund and The Glass Bead Game – novels preoccupied with psychoanalytical issues.

1883–1924   Franz Kafka wrote novels of nightmarish confusion and absurdity – 'The Trial', 'Metamorphosis', 'The Castle' and 'America'.

1883–1924   Bertolt Brecht, one of the first German dramatists to experiment with radical new forms of theatre, published, among other things, two of Germany's most popular dramatic works 'Leben Galilei' (life of Galilei) and 'Die Dreigroschenoper' (The Three Penny Opera – which was set to music by Kurt Weil). Brecht went into exile during the Nazi years and wrote scripts in Hollywood and, after the McCarthy witch-hunts of the 1950s, ended up in East Berlin.

1900–1930   Publication of Rainer Maria Rilke's 'Das Stundenbuch' (The Book of Hours) confirmed him as Germany's greatest lyric poet.

Existentialist Movement

1920–1950   Husserl, Heidigger and Jaspers were among the German existential writers.

National Socialism

1933–1945   National Socialism forced many writers into exile, especially Jewish authors. On 11 May 1933 crowds of students threw books by non-German authors onto a bonfire. (Heinrich Heine wrote, 'Wherever books are burnt, men will eventually be burnt'). Among the authors whose work was incinerated were Marx, Heinrich Mann, Sigmund Freud, and many more.

Post-War Period

1945–present   The post war period saw the return of many writers from exile. Heinrich Böll and Günter Grass both emerged as new influential authors. They were both members of Gruppe 47, a circle of writers focussing on post-war social problems. Christa Wolf, who had grown up in East Germany, is generally accepted as one of the best, if controversial, writers in post war Germany. Sarah Kirsch, who emigrated to the West, has gained a reputation as a highly respected poet. Stefan Heym, who was exiled during the war years, settled in East Germany and has written widely about the situation of East Germans in the 1990s. Since the 1980s, Patrick Süsskind has been one of Germany's most popular young writers. His novel 'Das Parfum' (Perfume), as well as being a best seller in his own country, has been translated into many languages all over the world.

Cinema
Silent Films

1880s–1930s   Germans saw their first public film show in Berlin in 1895 and early films were shown all over Germany in booths at town fairs or shops. By 1917, the government had set up a body to raise production standards. Early silent films were highly melodramatic and the influence of Freud could be strongly felt in the psychological story lines of films like Stellan Rye's 1913 classic 'Der Student von Prag' (The Student from Prague). By 1920, a period of intense creativity in the film business was producing films like G.W. Pabst's 'Die freudlose Gasse' (The Joyless Street) 1925, and Joe May's 'Asphalt' (1929). Fritz Lang's 'Metropolis', made in 1926, stands out as a cinema classic and is still shown regularly today.

Sound Films of the 1930s

In 1927 the German film business was privatized and passed into the hands of the Hugenberg group. Marlene Dietrich appeared for the first time in Der blaue Engel (The Blue Angel) made in 1940 and directed by Joseph von Sternberg. It was the first of her many films. In 1931 a film appeared loosely based on the Three Penny Opera (play by Brecht with music by Kurt Weil). Made in 1932, 'Das Testament des Dr. Mabuse' (The Testament of Dr. Mabuse) was Fritz Lang's first talkie. The story of a psychiatric patient who tries to take over the world, the Nazis prevented its premier and Lang had to show it in Austria. When Hitler came to power financial problems at Ufa (Universum-Film AG) allowed the Nazis to take over 99% of the shares. All films made from 1937 had to be approved by Goebbels' 'Reichskulturkammer' (Chamber of Culture) and a combination of censorship and bans forced more than 500 actors and directors to leave the country to avoid internment or worse. Many went to Hollywood and although some got work playing German parts, many were unable to leap the language barrier. Peter Lorre (born László Loewenstein, an ethnic-German Hungarian) was successful both in Hollywood and then back in Germany after the war. During the 1930s and 1940s, Leni Riefenstal made documentary films for the government including her famous 1938 film of the Berlin Olympic Games.

Post-War Film

Most of the films made in Germany just after the war deal with Nazism and the war, and are known as Trümmerfilme (literally, rubble films). A film corporation was set up in the Soviet Zone of eastern Germany. Konrad Wolf was probably East Germany's best director and his film 'Sterne' (Stars) won him an award at the Cannes Film Festival.

1960s–1970s   The sixties produced the Oberhausener Gruppe, a group of directors who published a manifesto in 1962 rejecting the old ways of making films and declaring that 'Papa's Cinema is Dead'. Der junge deutsche Film emerged around 1965 as a sort of German version of the French 'Nouvelle Vague' (New Wave) with directors like Volker Schlöndorff, Alexander Kluge and Edgard Reitz producing some fine films.

1970s–1980s   Werner Herzog, Rainer Werner Fassbinder, Margarethe von Trotta, Wim Wenders and Doris Dorrie emerged as the most significant directors of the 70s and 80s. With the collapse of the Berlin Wall, the GDR's film lot was sold to a French corporation and it has now been upgraded to a tourist attraction. Schlöndorff regards the place as 'sacred' ground and continues to produce films there.

1990s   The German films of the 1990s have the emphasis on relationships, and directors like Sönke Wortmann and Katja von Garnier have both made successful films about love and work crises from the female perspective while Doris Dorrie created a film with black humour about a single woman in the 1990s. Germany has also produced a 'road movie' – Detlev Buck's 1993 'No More

Mr. Nice Guy' is probably the best film to emerge from Germany since reunification.

A huge new museum of the cinema has been opened on the 'Museum Bank' in Frankfurt with a film, video and book library as well as screenings of German and International films.
1996   There were 4,035 cinemas with a total seating capacity of 760,282 in 1996. A total of 132·9m. visits to the cinema were made in the course of the year. 64 feature films were made.

MAJOR CITIES

(The international code for telephoning or faxing Germany is the code required to dial out of your own country followed by 49.)

BERLIN:

Berlin is the Capital of a reunified Germany. It is situated in the east of Germany on the Spree and Havel rivers. It is within, but administratively not a part of, Brandenburg,

Formed from two villages chartered in the 13th century, Berlin was a leading member of the *Hanseatic League* and became prominent as a commercial, cultural, and communications centre of Central Europe. It was the capital of *Prussia* and of the German Empire after 1871 and the Weimar Republic after World War I. In World War II it was badly damaged by allied bombing and a Soviet artillery attack. In 1945 it was divided into British, American, and French occupation zones (West Berlin) and a Soviet zone (East Berlin). The status of divided Berlin became a major *Cold War* issue and in 1948–49 the Western powers carried out a large-scale airlift to supply West Berlin during a Soviet land and water blockade. In 1949 East Berlin was made the capital of the German Democratic Republic; in 1950 West

Berlin was established as a state within, and the de jure capital of, West Germany, with *Bonn* as the de facto capital. In Aug. 1961 East German authorities erected the 29-mile (47-km) Berlin Wall along the line of partition to halt the exodus of refugees to the West. As the East German Communist regime collapsed (1989–90), the Wall was breached in Nov. 1989. In West Berlin, the formal supreme authority of the Western Allies endured until 1990. Upon German reunification in Oct. 1990, East and West Berlin were amalgamated, Berlin was declared the national capital and the new, all-German parliament held a symbolic session in Berlin in the old Reichstag building. In 1991 Parliament voted to move the federal government to Berlin.

With the move of the parliament (Bundestag) and the federal organ of the Länder (Bundesrat) in 1999, Berlin once again fulfils the functions of a capital city. Although some government offices, diplomatic missions etc. are still in Bonn, the move will be completed by the end of the year 2000.

Berlin is Germany's largest city, its historic capital, and a major cultural centre. The city's manufactures include electrical equipment, chemicals and clothing. Among its many cultural institutions are the renowned Berlin Philharmonic, the gallery of the Charlottenburg Palace, with its collection of Rembrandts, and the Pergamon Museum, known for classical art. See also Berlin, page 203.

TRANSPORT

Airports
Berlin has three international airports.

Flughafen Tegel (Otto Lilienthal Airport): Tel: (0)30 41-01-23-06. Most scheduled and charter flights arrive and depart from this airport. Connected by express bus X9 to the Bahnhof Zoologischer Garten (Zoo Station), or by bus (#109) or #128 to the centre of Berlin.

Flughafen Tempelhof: Tel: (0)30 69-51-22-88.

Some domestic flights arrive and leave from this airport. It is nearer the city centre and is linked by bus #119 to the Zoo Station or by U-Bahn.

Flughafen Schönefeld: Tel: (0)30 60-91-51-66.

South-east of Berlin, most intercontinental flights and flights to and from the former Soviet Union arrive and depart from this airport. Linked by S-Bahn and bus to central Berlin.

Trains

Deutsche Bahn Information (Train information telephone line)

Tel: (0)30 29-74-92-77.

There are two main railway stations in Berlin. Most trains stop at both.

Zoologischer Garten

Main train station in the west of Berlin. Services to and from the north and west and other European countries.

Ostbahnhof (formerly Hauptbahnhof)

Main train station in the east of Berlin. Most trains stop at both the stations but some trains to the former GDR stop only at Ostbahnhof.

Roads

Connected by Autobahnen (motorways) A10 (circles Berlin and links with all other Autobahnen), A11 (north), A12 (east), A13 (south), A2 (west), A24 (north-west), A9 (south).

Buses

ZOB (Central bus station)

(by the Funkturm near the Kaiserdamm). Tel: (0)30 301-80-28.

Long distance inter-Europe buses arrive and depart from this station.

Local Transport
Berliner Verkehrsbetriebe (BVG)
Berlin has what is probably the most efficient public transportation system in the world, consisting of surface rail (S-Bahn), tram (Straßenbahn), bus and underground (U-Bahn). Tickets are available from tourist offices, machines, bus drivers, or ticket windows at the U and S-Bahn stations. There are also 1-day, 7-day and longer term passes available. Maps and information available from tourist offices.

Ferries
Stern- und Kreis Schiffahrt: Puschkinallee 16–17.
Tel: (0)30 536-36-00. Fax: (0)30 53-63-60-99.
Operates ferry services along the River Spree.

Taxis
Taxis operate 24 hours and may be hailed, found at ranks or ordered by telephone (women may request a female driver).

Radio-taxi: Tel: (0)30 21-02-02, 26-10-26 or 690-22.

Velotaxis: Tel: (0)30 304-66-55.
These are Pedicabs that seat two people following limited routes in the city centre.

Car Hire
See central reservation numbers under general information.

Bicycle Hire
Bicycles can be rented at the Bahnhof Zoo (next to lost and found) or at
Herr Beck: Goethestr. 7. Tel: (0)30 312-19-25.

TRAVELLERS INFORMATION

Tourist Offices

Berlin Tourismus (headquarters of Tourist Offices):
Tel: (0)30 25-00-25. Fax: (0)30 25-00-24.

Europa Centre Office: Budapester Str. Tel: (0)30 25-00-25.

Info-point Dresdner Bank: Unter den Linden 17.
Office also at the Brandenburg Gate (Brandenburger Tor Office) and
at the airport (Flughafen Tegel. Tel: (0)30 41-01-34-26).

Financial and Currency

American Express (Main Office): Uhlandstr. 173.
Tel: (0)30 88-45-88-21.

Thomas Cook (Main Office): Friedrichstr. 56. Tel: (0)30 20-17-220.
There are currency exchange offices, banks, and banks with ATM
cash machines all over Berlin.

Post Office

Bahnhof Zoo (most central and has one counter open until midnight):
Tel: (0)30 311-00-20.
Offices also at airports and other major stations.

Consulates

UK Consulate: Unter den Linden 32–34. Tel: (0)30 20-18-40.
Fax: (0)30 20-18-41-58.
US Consulate: Neustädtische Kirchstr. 4–5. Tel: (0)30 238-51-74.
Fax: (0)30 238-62-90.
US Citizens' service: Clayallee 170. Tel: (0)30 832-92-33.
Fax: (0)30 831-49-26.
For more information on consulates, embassies etc., see under
'Diplomatic Representatives'.

Emergency
Police: Platz der Luftbrücke 6. Tel: 110 or (0)30 69-95.
Ambulance and fire: Tel: 112.

Medical Emergency
Emergency doctor: Tel: (0)30 31-00-31.
Emergency dentist: Tel: (0)30 89-00-43-33.
American and British Embassies have lists of English-speaking doctors.

Pharmacies
For late night information: Tel: (0)30 011-41.
Europa-Apotheke. Tauenzienstr. 9-12. Tel: (0)30 261-41-42.
(By Europa Centre close to Bahnhof Zoo).
Münz-Apotheke: Münzstr. 5. Tel: (0)30 241-10-83 (just off Alexanderplatz).
After hours, closed pharmacies have a sign indicating the nearest open one.

Internet Access
Website: Joachimstaler Str. 41, 10623 Berlin.
Tel: (0)30 88-67-96-30.
Web site: www.vrcafe.de
Internet-Café Hai Täck: Brünnhildestr. 8, 12159 Berlin-Friedenau.
Tel: (0)30 85-96-14-13.
Web site: www.haitaeck.de

Hotel Reservations
See central reservations on page 172.

Leading Museums and Galleries
Tiergarten-Kulturforum: Matthäikirchplatz. Tel: (0)30 20-90-55-55 (for all museums).

Houses the **Kunstbibliothek** and the **Kupferstichkabinett**, a collection of lithographs and drawings by old masters from the 14th–18th centuries including Dürer, Breughel the Elder, Rembrandt and Botticelli, and from the 19th and 20th centuries, Goya, Daumier, Menzel, Kollwitz and Picasso. The library has a richly stocked art section and also hosts special exhibitions in its public reading rooms.

Kunstgewerbemuseum (Museum of Applied Arts)

A new building also in the Kulturforum complex, the museum houses an enormous collection of decorative arts and crafts. There are 16th century chalices made of gold and silver in Nuremberg, medieval reliquaries, The Guelph Treasure, Italian Majolica from the 14th to the 16th century, municipal plate from Lüneburg and gothic jewellery from Nuremberg, porcelain and lacquer cabinets from China, Biedermeier and Jugendstil objets d'art, glass from Franconia and Art Nouveau and Art Deco porcelain, earthenware and glass.

The basement houses Germany's largest permanent collection of international design (furniture, appliances etc.).

Neue Nationalgalerie: Potsdamerstr. 50.
Mies van der Rohe designed this steel and glass structure in 1968 to house important collections of paintings and there are many examples of 19th and 20th century painting and sculpture, including works by such artists as Renoir, Klee, Munch, Miró, Max Ernst, Juan Gris, Kokoschka, Barlach, Kirchner, Bechmann and Henry Moore. Two thirds of the museum is devoted to special exhibitions.

Musikinstrumenten-Museum. Tiergartenstr. 1. Tel: (0)30 25-48-10.
This museum, right next door to the Philharmonic, houses an enormous collection of musical instruments from 14th century virginals to Pianolas.

Museumsinsel (Museum Island)

In addition to the treasures of the former GDR, many other collections have moved here recently from other museums in Berlin, and are housed in four separate museums.

Pergamon Museum: Kupfergraben. Tel: (0)30 20355-504 or 20355-00.

One of the world's largest museums of ancient history. The museum houses extensive collections of Greek, Assyrian, Islamic and Far Eastern art as well as such important archaeological treasures as the entire Babylonian Ishtar Gate from 575 BC, the Roman Market Gate of Miletus and the Pergamon Altar of Zeus (180 BC).

Alte Nationalgalerie. Bodestr. 1–3. Tel: (0)30 20-35-52-57.

This 17th century building houses paintings and sculptures from the 19th century. There are large canvasses representing life at the court of Frederick and also the worlds of industry, the Prussian army and the poor of the times. French painting from this period is also well represented with paintings by Rousseau, Corot, Courbet, Renoir, Pissaro, Cézanne and many others. The sculpture gallery contains works by German sculptors Johann Gottfried Schadow and Christian Daniel Rauch as well as Rodin, Degas and Maillol.

Bodemuseum: Monbijoubrücke. Tel: (0)30 20-35-55-03. Fax: (0)30 200-46-31.

Exhibitions of Egyptian art share this museum with late-Gothic wooden sculptures, early Christian art, Byzantine masterpieces and 15th–18th century paintings by Lippi, Cranach the Elder, and other German, Italian and Dutch renaissance and baroque artists. There are also three galleries devoted to the history of medals from the Renaissance to the present. The Kindergalerie contains interactive exhibits for children.

Altes Museum (Old Museum): Klustgarten.

Recently converted into a museum that mounts special exhibitions including exhibitions of 20th century avant-garde art.

Dahlem-Museen (Dahlem Museums): Tel: (0)30 83011.

The largest complex of museums in Berlin is situated in the suburb of Dahlem, and includes a museum of ethnology, art gallery, sculpture collection and museums of Indian, Islamic and Oriental art.

Landmarks

The Reichstag: Tel: (0)30 22-73-21-31.

This imposing grey stone neo-Renaissance style palace was once the seat of the parliaments of the German Empire and the Weimar Republic. During the civil unrest that preceded World War II, the Reichstag was burned down, an act that gave Adolf Hitler the excuse to declare a state of emergency and call for the elections that would return him to power. In the years after the war, Berlin was divided into zones (French, Soviet, American and British) and the capital of Germany moved to Bonn. After the reunification of Germany it was decided to renovate and rebuild the Reichstag and a British architect, Norman Foster, won the commission. In 1995, before work began, the American artist Christo wrapped the still ruined building in shimmering silvery metallic fabric. After only three weeks the wrapping came off and the scaffolding went up. The work, which includes a giant glass dome, will be completed in time for the first parliamentary session of the new millennium.

Brandenburger Tor (Brandenburg Gate)

The Brandenburg gate was once the symbol of divided Germany and once formed part of the Berlin Wall that formed the boundary between the east and west sectors of the city. It was designed by Karl Gotthard Langhans in 1791. Six Doric columns within the structure of the arch support an antique style entablature. The arch is crowned by the winged Goddess of Victory in a two-wheeled chariot drawn by four prancing horses (by Gottfried Schadow). Inside the gate are two chambers. One is the Raum der Stille (Room of Silence) where the visitor can sit in silence and reflect on peace and the other, more prosaically, has a branch of the Tourist Office.

Schloß Charlottenburg: Spandauer Damm. Tel: (0)30 32-09-11. This palace was built as a summer residence for Queen Sophie-Charlotte, wife of King Frederick I. Building started in 1695, and the original palace was quite small. It was soon enlarged and in 1710 the dome was added. Frederick II later added a new east wing, and the Castle was lived in by Queen Louise, the wife of Friedrich-Wilhelm III.

The palace complex houses several museums and royal apartments and there are extensive gardens. The **Apartments of Frederick I and Sophie-Charlotte (Historische Räume)** contain portraits of the royal family, a huge courtroom, tapestries, richly carved furniture, consoles, fire screens etc. The **Knobelsdorff Wing – eastern or new wing (Neuer Flügel)** was built between 1740 and 1748 to balance the west wing. It houses two Chinese rooms and the Etruscan Room on the garden side, and on the street side the apartments of Friedrich-Wilhelm III contain works dating from the Napoleonic Wars including David's 'Napoleon Traversing the Great St. Bernard Pass'. The **Gallery of Romanticism (Nationalgalerie)** houses works by Romantic painters of the early 19th century including Caspar David Friedrich, Karl Friedrich Schinkel and Carl Blechen. The **Royal Apartments** are a good example of 'Frederician Rococo' and contain masterpieces of the 18th century collected by Frederick II. The Principal Apartments of Frederick II give a vivid impression of the life of a monarch. While the Golden Gallery – a superb example of Prussian Rococo – is surrounded by gilded mirrors with representations of cherubs, the elements and four seasons are entwined with scrolls, garlands and cornucopia.

The **Park (Schloßpark)** was landscaped in the English fashion under Friedrich-Wilhelm II and a yew and cypress walk leads to a small mausoleum in the form of a temple containing the tombs of Friedrich-Wilhelm III, Queen Louise, the Emperor Wilhelm I and Queen Augusta.

Nearby is the Ägyptische Museum und Papyrussammlung (Egyptian Museum and Papyrus Collection) where it is possible to trace the historical and artistic evolution of the Egyptian civilization. The world famous exquisite bust of Nefertiti dating from approximately 1350 BC, an ebony head of Queen Teje (18th Dynasty) and a green head of a priest from 300 BC are the highlights of the collection. (The other half of the Egyptian collection can be seen in the Bodemuseum on the Museumsinsel – see above).

Potsdamer Platz

Since reunification Berlin has become Europe's biggest building site and much of this construction has gone on at Potsdamer Platz. Before the First World War it was the busiest junction in Europe and the first ever traffic light was situated there. When the Berlin Wall went up in 1961 it became a part of no-man's land, but now huge building projects by Sony and Daimler aim to make it the focal point of the city once more. Shopping centres, cinemas, hotels, embassies, restaurants, offices and apartments are still being constructed although large parts are already completed.

Alexanderplatz

Originally named to commemorate the visit of the Russian Tsar, Alexanderplatz is now an unimaginative open space surrounded by concrete buildings designed in the communist era to be the centre of East Berlin. Its main attraction is the Fernsehturm (TV tower), Berlin's tallest structure with an observation floor and unparalleled views. Much to the dismay of communist officials, sunlight reflecting off the top of the tower forms a cross visible all over Berlin, considered by many to be a form of divine retribution.

Performing Arts

Philharmonie: Matthäikirchstr. 1. Tel: (0)30 25-48-81-32.

Fax: (0)30 25-48-81-35.

(Ticket booking: Email: karten-buero@philharmonc.sireco.de) (There are no concerts between June and Sept.)

This concert hall is the home of the Berlin Philharmonic Orchestra (the legendary Herbert von Karajan was Director from 1954–89; Claudio Abbado is the present Director) and was built in 1963 by the architect Hans Scharoun. The roof is in the shape of a giant wave and the musicians play in near perfect acoustics in the centre of the auditorium surrounded by the audience in tiered rows of seats.

Opera

Staatsoper: Unter den Linden 7, Mitte, Berlin. Tel: (0)30 20354555.

The first Königliches Opernhaus (Royal Opera House) was inaugurated in 1742 during the reign of Frederick II. After the First World War the Royal Opera House was renamed the Staatsoper. The Staatsoper building on Unter den Linden was bombed and destroyed on 9 April 1941 and it was not until 1955 that it was rebuilt, according to the original plans. Danile Barenboim was appointed Musical Director with effect from 1993 with a view to transforming the Staatsoper once again into a glittering international house employing the world's leading directors and singers.

Deutsche Oper: Bismarckstr. 35, Berlin. Tel (0)30 3410249.

The Deutsches Opernhaus opened in Charlottenburg on 7 November 1912. The city of Berlin took it over in 1925, renaming it the Stadtische Oper. In 1961, the same year that the Berlin Wall went up, the new opera house in the Bismarckstrasse opened with a production of Mozart's *Don Giovanni* and was henceforth known as the Deutsche Oper Berlin. After the fall of the wall the Deutsche Oper's position has remained essentially unchanged.

FURTHER READING

Taylor, R., *Berlin and its Culture*. Yale University Press, 1997

Tusa, A., *The Last Division – A History of Berlin, 1945–1989*. Perseus Books, Reading, Mass., 1997

HAMBURG:

Hamburg is Germany's largest and busiest port, situated on the Elbe and Alster rivers. It is also capital of Hamburg State, in the north of Germany, and the second largest city in Germany. Founded in the 9th century, it formed, in the 13th century, an alliance with Lübeck that became the basis of the Hanseatic League and the city is known to this day as the 'Free and Hanseatic City of Hamburg', abbreviated to 'HH' even on many roadsigns. At no time in its history – except for a brief occupation by Napoleon in the early 18th century – has Hamburg been subject to foreign rule. In 1189, Hamburg gained the right to navigate the Elbe and held off pirates and trade rivals to emerge as the leading light of the Hanseatic League. Its geographical location at the confluence of several rivers made it a hub for overland trade from the Baltic and the shipbuilding trade led to prominence in other financial concerns. Hamburg is home to Germany's first stock exchange, founded in 1558, and the bank of Hamburg dates back to the early 1600s. Hamburg was declared a Free Imperial City in 1618 enabling it to wield considerable power both locally and nationally. By the start of the First World War, Hamburg had become one of the world's wealthiest cities. The Hamburg-Amerika shipping line was the largest shipping firm in the world. Although the city suffered badly in World War II, the city's wealth assisted in an extensive post-war rebuilding programme and most of the copper-roofed brick architecture has been restored to its former glory. As well as shipbuilding and other related industries, manufactures include copper and machinery and it is a major centre for publishing. Felix Mendelssohn and Johannes Brahms were born in Hamburg where Germany's first opera house saw the earliest performance of Händel's first opera.

TRANSPORT

Airport

Fuhlsbüttel Airport: Tel: (0)40 507-50 (flight information).
The airport was among the first in Europe and is located north of the city centre serving many cities in Europe and within Germany as well as connections to international destinations. The main airlines flying in and out of Hamburg are Lufthansa, the German national carrier (Tel: 01803-80-38-03), Air France (Tel: (0)40 50-75-24-59) and British Airways (Tel: (0)40 30-96-63-63 or 01803-340-430 for reservations).

Trains

Deutsche Bahn Information: (Train Information Line)
Tel: (0)40 39-18-43-13.
    Hamburg has four train stations – Hauptbahnhof, Dammtor, Altona and Harburg. Hauptbahnhof handles most of the traffic with frequent connections to Berlin, Munich, Frankfurt and Copenhagen although most of the long distance trains stop at both Hauptbahnhof and Dammtor stations.
    Most of the trains from Kiel, Schleswig, Flensburg and Westerland stop only at Altona station.

Roads

Hamburg has three ring roads that control the flow of traffic through the city and is connected by Autobahnen (motorways) to the rest of

Germany and Europe – A7 (north/south), A24 (from Hamburg east), A1 (north-east/south-west).

Buses

Long distance and international buses arrive and depart from the ZOB across the Steintorplatz from the Hauptbahnhof.

Local Transport

Transport around the city is operated by HVV and consists of U-Bahn (underground), S-Bahn (surface trains) and buses. Tickets are available from orange Automaten (automatic machines). Tourists can buy a 'Hamburg Card' that is valid for all public transport and also offers free admission to most museums and discounts on boat trips and bus tours. It is available from tourist offices.

Ferries

Scandinavian Seaways: Van-der-Schmissenstr. 4. Tel: (0)40 38-90-30. Fax: (0)40 38-90-31-20.
Regular ferries to England, Ireland, Copenhagen, Oslo and Amsterdam leave from about 1 km west of the Fischmarkt.

Taxis

There are taxi stands outside the stations and taxis can be hailed.
Radio taxi: (0)40 211-211 or 221-122.
Taxiruf: (0)40 44-10-11.

Car Hire

See central reservation numbers on page 173.

Bicycle Hire

O-Niel Bikes, Beethovenstr. 37. Tel: (0)40 53-11-77-44.

Boat Hire

Sail boats, paddleboats and rowing boats can be hired on the
Außenalster by the Kennedy Bridge.
Segelschule Kpt. Pieper. An der Alster. Tel: (0)40 24-75-78.

TRAVELLERS INFORMATION

Tourist Offices

Hauptbahnhof Office: near Kirchenallee exit. Tel: (0)40 30-50-12-01.

Fax: (0)40 30-05-13-33.

Email: info@hamburg-tourism.de Web: www.hamburg-tourism.de

St. Pauli Landungsbrücken: Between Piers 4 and 5.

Tel: (0)40 30-05-12-00.

Hotline for information and reservations: Tel: (0)40 30-05-13-00.

Financial and Currency

ReiseBank in the Hauptbahnhof will cash travellers cheques and
currency and arrange Western Union money transfers. There are also
many banks and cash ATM machines all over the city.
American Express: Ballindamm 39. Tel: (0)40 30-90-80. Refund
service 0130-85-31-00.
Fax: (0)40 30-90-81-30.
Thomas Cook: Thomas Cook Reisebüro, Mittelweg 126.
Tel: (0)40 41-46-110.

Post Offices

Main office at Gr. Burstah 3.
Also an office in the Hauptbahnhof (Kirchenallee exit).

Consulates

UK. Harvestehuder 8a. Tel/fax: (0)40 448-03-20.

USA. Alsterufer 27. Tel: (0)40 41-17-10.

Emergency

Police: Tel: 110.

Police stations (BGS/Bahnpolizei) near the Kirchenallee exit of the Hauptbahnhof and on the Reeperbahn (corner of Davidstr. and Spielbudenplatz).

Fire: Tel: 112.

Medical Emergency

Ambulance: Tel: 112.

Medical emergency service: Tel: (0)40 228-02-2.

24 hours first aid service: Tel: (0)40 248-28-11.

Emergency dental service: Tel: (0)40 115-00.

Private medical and dental emergency service:

Tel: (0)40 331-155.

Pharmacies

Senator-Apotheke. Kirchenallee near the Hauptbahnhof.

For late at night, see the windows of closed pharmacies for nearest one open.

Internet Access

Staat- und Universitätsbibliothek. Von Melle Park 3.

Tel: (0)40 41-23-22-33. Http://www.sub.uni-hamburg.de

Cyberb@r. On the third floor of the Karstadt department store, Mönckebergstrasse 16.

Hotel Reservations

See central reservation numbers on page 172.

Leading Museums and Galleries

Hamburger Kunsthalle (Fine Arts Museum): Glockengiesserwall 1.
Tel: (0)40 24-86-26-12.

This museum houses one of the largest art collections in Germany.
The first part of the museum consists of German and Dutch art from
the medieval age to the 19th century including works by Master
Bertram of Minden, Master Francke, Rembrandt, Van Goyen, the
Ruysdaels, Van der Velde and Pieter de Hooch. The next section has
paintings by French painters such as Courbet, Manet and Monet. The
Galerie der Gegenwart is a newly built extension to the museum (by
Oswald Mathias Ungers) and was built to house post-1960s art. There
are works here by most of the famous names of the 20th century –
Oldenburg and Warhol among others. However, the museum's main
strength lies in its collection of 19th century German paintings with an
entire room devoted to Caspar David Friedrich's hunting landscapes.

Museum für Kunst und Gewerbe (Museum of Decorative Arts)
Steintorpl. 1. Tel: (0)40 24-86-26-30.

This large yellow building houses a large collection of handcrafts,
china, and furnishings displayed chronologically starting with artefacts from ancient Egypt and progressing through Roman times right
up to the present. Among the most notable exhibits are medieval stat-
uary, gold and silver plate (including the reliquary of St George by
Berndt Notke), sumptuous renaissance furniture, fine examples of
German clock making and delicate 18th century porcelain. There are
also a number of fine examples of ornaments, furniture and artworks
from the Jugendstil as well as works from China, Japan and the world
of Islam.

Landmarks

Außenalster

This beautiful stretch of water right in the city centre offers the
visitor an opportunity to rent boats. A boat trip will allow the visitor to

appreciate the city's skyline punctuated by Hamburg's famous five towers, all of them over 100 metres high. The towers crown the city's four main churches and the Rathaus (town hall).

Hamburg Hafen (Port of Hamburg)
Harbour cruises
Kapitän Prüsse: Tel: (0)40 31-31-30.

Hadag: Tel: (0)40 311-70-70. Fax: (0)40 31-17-07-10.
Hamburg docks comprise 60 basins, and more than 68 km of quays. The basins are accessible to ocean going vessels and thanks to the relatively small tides no locks are necessary to allow the ships to navigate the Elbe. Three hundred and forty shipping lines call regularly at the port and transport merchandise and passengers to a thousand ports all over the world. There are boats trips which allow the visitor an opportunity to witness the bustling activity of this enormous port with its variety of vessels, cargo ships, tankers, tugs, lighters, refrigerator ships, container ships, police craft and customs launches as well as the ferry boats that carry workers to and from the south bank of the Elbe all day. Some of the ships can be visited including the Rickmer Rickmers (Tel: (0)40 35-69-31-19), a three masted steel windjammer from 1896 that has been converted into a museum ship with old navigation equipment and modern maritime technology. It is also possible to visit the Cap San Diego, a 10,000 tonne freighter built in Hamburg and launched in 1962. The lively Fischmarkt (fish market) functions before 10 am on Sundays and on public holidays.

Große Michaelskirche: Tel: (0)40 37-67-81-00.
Built in the 18th century, this brick church is one of the finest examples of the baroque tradition in northern Germany. It was built for the Lutheran sect to a design by the architect Sonnin and is spacious, well proportioned and well lit. The tower (one of Hamburg's famous

five and the only one you can climb) rises high above the Elbe with a lantern turret in the form of a rotunda, and is known by the local people simply as 'der Michael'. It has become the emblem of the city. At weekends, the tower acts as a screen on which a multimedia presentation about Hamburg's millennial existence is projected.

Fernsehturm (Television Tower): (in the Planten un Blomen Park to the west of the Alster).

It is possible to ascend this slender steel and concrete plinth to the observation platform at the top (132 metres). The platform revolves, taking 55 minutes, allowing the visitor to see a slowly moving panorama of the entire city of Hamburg below.

MUNICH (MÜNCHEN):

Situated on the River Isar, Munich is the capital of Bavaria, in the south of Germany. Founded in 1158 by *Henry the Lion*, in 1255 it became the residence of the *Wittelsbach* family who predominated until the 20th century. The city was greatly enlarged, and areas that had been destroyed by the great fire of 1328 were rebuilt by Ludwig the Bavarian during the 14th century. By 1503 Munich was established as a wealthy trading centre, had 13,500 residents and was the capital of the duchy of Bavaria. Continued outbreaks of plague forced the city authorities to make improvements in the sewage and sanitation systems but the population was decimated. Despite the Protestant reforms of Martin Luther that swept through Germany in the 16th century, Munich remained resolutely catholic and Protestants were viciously persecuted. During the thirty years' war, Munich was invaded by Swedish troops and in 1632 surrendered to King Gustav

Adolphus. The city's freedom was bought from the Swedes only to fall to the Hapsburgs from 1705 to 1714. However, the 18th century saw Munich's Golden Age with an explosion of Baroque and Italianate architecture. During the 19th century, the Golden Age was enhanced when Napoleon's conquest of the territories and reorganizing of Europe elevated Bavaria to the status of a Kingdom with Munich as its capital. The marriage of the Bavarian Crown Prince Ludwig I to the Saxon-Hildburghausen Princess Therese marked what later turned into the Oktoberfest (an annual Bavarian festival). In 1818, Bavaria became the first German state with a written constitution. Under King Ludwig, it expanded rapidly into a major cultural and artistic centre. Most of the city's most famous landmarks – among them, Königsplatz, Alte Pinakothek, Ludwigstrasse and the Königsbau and Festsaalbau sections of the Residenz – were built at this time. Ludwig I's son was the 'mad' King Ludwig whose obsessive programme of building castles and palaces all over Bavaria depleted the city's coffers so seriously that eventually he was declared mentally unfit to rule. He and his doctor were found drowned in mysterious circumstances in Lake Starnberg. His brother Otto's regent, Prince Luitpold, embarked on another programme of enlargement and expansion. By the turn of the 20th century, Munich had 500,000 inhabitants and had become Germany's second city. After World War I, runaway inflation and political in-fighting provided Adolf Hitler with a fertile breeding ground for his extreme political views and in the 1920s National Socialism was founded in Munich and had its party headquarters there. *The Munich Pact of* 1938 was signed in the city. Badly damaged during World War II, it was largely rebuilt after 1945. Munich today is a thriving city with a strong local economy based on such major industrial giants as BMW, Bayer pharmaceuticals and MAN (automotive and truck producers). Other important industries include processed food, beer and precision instruments. Franz-Josef Strauss airport is the country's second most important air transport centre after Frankfurt.

TRANSPORT

Airport

Flughafen München (Franz-Josef Strauss Airport): (0)89 97-52-13 13
(General flight information).
International and continental flights by most international carriers.

Connected to the city centre by either trains to and from the
Hauptbahnhof or Air shuttle bus to and from Arnulfstr. on the north side
of the railway station.

Trains

Hauptbahnhof: (0)89 22-33-12-56.
Munich is the transportation hub of Southern Germany with
connections to all the major cities of Germany as well as all over
Europe.

Roads

Munich is surrounded by Autobahnen (motorways) A9 (north/south), A8
(north-west/south-east), A92 (north/east) and A96 (south/west).

Buses

Long distance and international buses arrive and depart from the north
side of the Hauptbahnhof.
Enquiries from Deutsche Touring: Tel: (0)89 59-18-24.
Web: www.munich-tourist.de
Email: 100711.1505@compuserve.com

Local Transport

Munich has an efficient zone-based transport system run by the MVV.
Tickets are valid on S-Bahn (surface trains), U-Bahn (underground) and
trams and buses. There is also a network of night buses.
Maps and schedules from any tourist office.

Taxis

Can be found at stands in front of the station, can be hailed in the
street or telephoned.

Radio-taxi: Tel: (0)89 216-11 or (0)89 194-10.

Women may request a female driver.

Car Hire

See central reservation numbers on page 173.

Bicycle Hire

Radius Bikes: at the Hauptbahnhof. Tel: (0)89 59-61-13.

Aktiv-Rad: Hans-Sach-Str. 7. Tel: (0)89 26-65-06.

TRAVELLERS INFORMATION

Tourist Offices

Fremdenverkehrsamt. East side (front) of the Hauptbahnhof.
Offices also at the airport and inside the entranceway to the Neues
Rathaus, Marienpl.
Tel: (0)89 23-33-01-56 or 23-33-02-57. Fax: (0)89 23-33-02-33.
Email: Munich_Tourist_Office@compuserve.com
Web: www.munich-tourist.de
Euraide. Near platform 11, Hauptbahnhof. Tel: (0)89 59-38-89.
Fax: (0)89 550-39-65. Email: euraide@compuserve.com.
Web: www.cube.net/kmu/euraide.html

Financial and Currency

ReiseBank: Main entrance of Hauptbahnhof or on platform 11 at the
Hauptbahnhof. Tel: (0)89 55-10-80.

American Express: Promenadepl. 6. Tel: (0)89 29-09-00. (Hot line: 01430 85-31-00).

Thomas Cook: Petersplatz 10. Tel: (0)89 23-50-920.

There are currency exchange offices, banks and ATM cash machines all over the city.

Post Office

Main Post Office: Arnulfstrasse 32, 80074 Munich. (Behind the Hauptbahnhof.)

Tel: (0)89 54-54-23-36.

Consulates

UK. Bürkleinstr.10, 4th floor. Tel: (0)89 21-10-90.

USA. Königstr. 5. Tel: (0)89 288-80; 0190-91-50-00; (0)89 88-72-2. US citizens' and passport services.

Emergency

Police: Hauptbahnhof. Tel: 110.

Fire: Tel: 112.

Medical Emergency

Ambulance. Tel: (0)89 192-22.

Emergency medical service. Tel: (0)89 55-1771.

Poison control. Tel: (0)89 192-40.

For English speaking doctors contact the consulate.

Pharmacies

Bahnhof Apotheke. Bahnhofpl. 2. Tel: (0)89 59-41-19 or 59-81-19.

After hours, closed pharmacies have a sign indicating the nearest one that is open.

Internet Access

The Internet Café. Altheimer Eck 12. (Near Marienplatz.)
Tel: (0)89 260-78-15.
Internet Café. Nymphenburger Strasse 145. Tel: (0)89 129-11-20.

Hotel Reservations

See central reservation numbers on page 172.

Leading Museums and Galleries

Residenz: Max-Joseph-Pl. 3. Tel: (0)89 29-06-71.
The Residenz was the home of the most powerful family of Munich –
the Wittelsbachs. Building began in 1385 but continued into the
19th century creating a Palace that traces 400 years of Bavarian
royal architectural history. The Palace and grounds contain several
museums. The **Residenz Museum** has more than 100 rooms display-
ing the treasures accumulated by the Wittelsbach family over 7 centuries. Among them the Ancestral Gallery, which was rebuilt in the
18th century with gilded stucco and carvings, houses family paintings and portraits. The **Porcelain Chambers** display 19th century
porcelain from Berlin, Meissen and Nymphenburg while there are
impressive collections of Chinese and Japanese lacquerware,
tapestries, carpets, furniture and jewellery to be found in the Asian
Collections. The State Apartments are elaborately decorated in
French Rococo style by Effner and Cuvilliés.

The **Schatzkammer (Treasury)** has a magnificent collection of
jewels and precious objects from the 10th century onwards. Crowns,
diadems, illuminated prayer books, ciboria, cameos, portable jewel
encrusted altars and reliquaries reflect the prosperous past of the
Ruling House of Bavaria. There is a superb 11th century crucifix
made for Queen Gisela of Hungary as well as many exotic works of art
from Turkey, Persia and Mexico.

Altes Residenztheater (Old Residence Theatre) is also known as the Cuvilliés Theatre after the man who created it between 1751 and 1753. This enchanting ornate Rococo masterpiece was badly damaged by bombing in 1944 but the furnishings had been removed so what you see is original. The tiers of Court boxes are all different with the 'Prince-Elector's Box' the most magnificent.

Schloß Nymphenburg: Tel: (0)89 179-08.
The Italian architect Barelli built the palace as a villa for the Electress Adelaide of Savoy. The Prince Elector Emmanuel added two lateral pavilions on either side linked to the main palace with arcaded galleries. Subsequent rulers constructed a semicircle of outbuildings, which resulted in a strong similarity to the Palace of Versailles. The surrounding park was enlarged and laid out by two pupils of Le Nôtre, Carbonet and Girard, during the 18th century. Today, in addition to the rooms on the main building, the palace houses several museums. The main palace rooms include a splendid banqueting hall in pale green, white and gold with a musician's gallery overlooking the park. The apartments of Queen Caroline in the south pavilion contain the Schönheitengalerie (Gallery of Beauties) created by King Ludwig I to house portraits of any and all the women from all walks of life that caught his eye.

The **Marstallmuseum** is housed in the former stables and contains collections of 18th and 19th century harnesses, broughams, coaches, carts, sledges and sedan chairs used by the Wittelsbach family. Above the stables is the **Nymphenburger Porzellan Sammlung Bäuml,** spanning 250 years of porcelain manufacture. In the north wing of the palace is a natural history museum (**Museum Mensch und Natur**), especially designed to be of interest to children. The **Botanical Garden (Botanischer Garten)** is located in the grounds of the palace and the enormous greenhouses and gardens are reputed to be among the finest and best stocked in Europe.

Alte Pinakothek: Barerstr. 27. Tel: (0)89 23-80-52-15.

This colossal building was originally designed to house the collections of the Wittelsbach family. It is now Munich's most important art gallery and contains masterpieces dating from the 14th to the 18th centuries including works by artists such as Titian, Leonardo da Vinci, Raphael, Dürer, Rembrandt and Rubens.

Neue Pinakothek: Barerstr. 29. Tel: (0)89 23-80-51-95.

This post-modern building is next door to the Alte Pinakothek and houses works of art from the 18th to the 20th centuries including works by such artists as Van Gogh, Klimt, Cézanne, Manet etc.

Deutsches Museum: Museumsinsel 1 (near Isartor). Tel: (0)89 217-91.

Considered to be the world's largest museum of science and technology, the exhibitions are set out in 46 departments on 6 floors. The basement is devoted to mining and automobiles, the ground floor to tunnel construction, railway and aeronautics, the first floor has physics and chemistry and musical instruments and the whole of the second floor is taken up with an exhibition of the Altamira caves. The third floor contains geodesy, weights and measures, microelectronics and telecommunications while the fourth to sixth floors are dedicated to astronomy and amateur radio. There are numerous interactive exhibits and many scale models of working apparatus, and many of the exhibits are accompanied by demonstrations and film commentaries.

BMW Museum: Petuelring 130. Tel: (0)89 38-22-33-07.

Munich is home to BMW (Bayerische Motoren Werke) and the museum is located directly behind the headquarters building – which was built in 1970–73 and, with its distinctive steel cylinders, is itself an architectural attraction. The exhibits include many BMW cars, motorcycles, plates, concept cars, simulators and interactive displays, all immaculately presented.

Landmarks

Marienplatz and the Old Town

The square of Marienplatz is the heart of Munich and serves as a stepping off point for a tour of the old town. At the centre of the square is the Mariensäule (Mary Column) which was erected in 1590 to celebrate the removal of the Swedish forces. On the very top is a golden figure of the Virgin Mary. The Neues Rathaus (New Town Hall) is a late gothic building which surrounds six courtyards where festivals and events take place throughout the year. The blackened façade of the building is covered with grotesque gargoyles and statues and the famous Glockenspiel (carillon). The Glockenspiel is active at 11 a.m. and 5 p.m. during the summer months only. The old Town Hall is at the other end of the square and was completely rebuilt after World War II. It now contains a toy museum (**Spielzeugmuseum**). Tel: (0)89 294-00-1.

There are several important churches in or near the square – Alter Peter (St Peterskirche) was the city's first parish church in the 11th century but the gothic building of today was begun in the 13th century. Behind the Altes Rathaus, the Heiliggeistkirche is Munich's largest Gothic hall church with an amazing Rococo ceiling. The Frauenkirche (Church of Our Lady) is the metropolitan church of the Archbishopric of Munich-Freising and is built in a simple style in typical Bavarian red brick. The church contains the tomb of Ludwig the Barbarian and a magnificent altarpiece.

COLOGNE (KÖLN):

Cologne (in German, Köln) is located in North Rhine-Westphalia, in the west of Germany, on the River Rhine. Founded in the 1st century BC by the Romans (hence the name Köln – 'colony'), it flourished from the 4th–13th centuries under powerful archbishops. Throughout the

Middle Ages, Cologne's position at the crossroads of many international trade routes made it a thriving centre for commerce and the arts. With 40,000 people living within the walls of Cologne, it was the biggest and most densely populated city in the country. The power of Cologne during the Middle Ages derived not only from trade; it was also a powerful bishopric and the Archbishops of Cologne exerted considerable power over the affairs of the city. By the beginning of the 14th century, Cologne had become a centre for religious, intellectual and artistic life attracting many eminent scholars to preach and teach there. This led in 1338 to creation of Cologne University by the lay Burghers of the city. In 1475, Cologne became a free imperial city and in the 15th century, a member of the *Hanseatic League*. In later centuries, Cologne remained one of Germany's most important cities and steady expansion continued until, in the late 19th century and early 20th century, industrialization accelerated this expansion into rapid growth. Cologne became one of the principal engines of Germany's economy. The city was badly damaged in World War II when most of the city was destroyed. However, miraculously, a few buildings such as the great Gothic cathedral, started in 1248, and the Romanesque Church of St. Andreas, still stand and others have been meticulously restored to their former glory. Cologne is a thriving river port and an industrial centre producing electronic equipment, chemicals and other manufactures including, of course, the famous Eau de Cologne perfume. Cologne is the centre of the Roman Catholic Church in Germany and a cultural centre with many museums, art galleries and theatres. There have always been publishing houses in Cologne, and now the city has become the media centre of Germany. It has eight television stations including WDR (Westdeutscher Rundfunk) and five radio stations including Deutsche Welle, Deutschland Radio and Westdeutscher Rundfunk. There are many sound studios, a media park and an Academy of Media Arts. The media business yields an annual turnover in Cologne of around 20bn. DM.

TRANSPORT

Airport

Cologne shares its airport with Bonn and has non-stop flights to more than 50 destinations (including a shuttle service to Berlin that leaves 24 times a day) with connections all over the world.

Köln-Bonn Flughafen: Tel: (0)2203 40-25-38 (Information).
The airport is linked to the bus station at the Hauptbahnhof (railway station) in the city by a bus service (bus number 170) that leaves every 15 minutes during the day and every 30 minutes at night.

Trains

Deutsche Bahn Central Information Line: Tel: (0)221 194-19.
Cologne is a major hub of rail traffic and trains to all over Germany and Europe arrive and depart from the Hauptbahnhof. Cologne is linked to Bonn by both main-line trains and S-Bahn with departures every 20 minutes.

Roads

Cologne is surrounded by the immense Kölner Ring that has exits to Autobahnen (motorways) A1 (north-east), A3 (north-south), A4 (east), and A57, A555 and A559 for all other directions.

Buses

Long distance and international buses arrive and depart from the bus station at the Hauptbahnhof. (Deutsche Touring's Eurolines buses depart for Paris six times weekly and for Prague three times).

Local Transport

The city's transport system is run by VRS (Verkehrsverbund Rhein-Sieg: Tel: (0)221 208-08-8) with a mix of buses, S-Bahn and U-Bahn trains and trams. Tickets are available from orange ticket machines and need to be validated upon boarding. Transport schedules and maps are available from any VRS station and tourist offices.

Boats

Rheinseilbahn: Tel: (0)221 76-20-06.
A pleasant way to cross the Rhine from the zoo to the Rheinpark

KD River Cruises: Tel: (0)221 208-83-18.
Day river cruises up and down the River Rhine.

Taxis

Taxis may be hailed in the street, found at taxi stands (there is one outside the Hauptbahnhof) or by telephone.
Radio Taxis: (0)221 28-82

TRAVELLERS INFORMATION

Tourist Offices

Verkehrsamt. Unter Fettenhennen 19 (opposite the Cathedral entrance). Tel: (0)221 221-33-45. Fax: (0)221 21-33-20.
Email: koelntourism@koeln.org Web: www.koeln.org/koelntourismus www.germany-tourism.de
The office has a public phone-fax, a cash ATM as well as maps etc.

Financial and Currency

The main tourist office has a cash ATM (see above) and there is an office at the Hauptbahnhof. There are banks and cash ATM machines all over the city.

American Express: Burgmauerstr. 14. Tel: (0)221 925-90-10.

Thomas Cook: Komödienstr. 7/Burgmauer 4. Tel: (0)221 925-25-96.

Post Office

Main Office: Breite Str. 6–26 WDR Arkaden (inside the shopping mall).

Consulates

For consulate representation see Bonn below.

Emergency

Police: Tel: 110.

Police Headquarters: corner of Nord-Süd-Fahrt and Blauback.
Tel: (0)221 229-1.

Fire: Tel: 112.

Medical Emergency

Ambulance: Tel: 112.

Emergency doctor: Tel: (0)221 192-92.

Pharmacy: Dom Apotheke. Komödienstr. 5. Tel: (0)221 257-67-54.

24-Hour Pharmacies: the Dom Apotheke has a list of after hours pharmacies posted outside.

Internet Access

FuturePoint: Richmodstr. 13. Tel: (0)221 206-72-06.

Hotel Reservations

See central reservation numbers on page 172.

Leading Museums and Galleries

Römische-Germanisches Museum: Roncallipl. Tel: (0)221 44-38.
This museum contains an impressive and very thorough collection of
Roman artefacts found along the Rhine. It is built on the site of a

Roman Villa and highlights of the exhibits include the Mausoleum of
Poblicius (30–40 AD) and the Dionysius Mosaic, made of millions
of fragments of stone and measuring 14·5 metres by 7 metres.
Many everyday objects such as toys, tweezers, lamps and jewellery
show that some design has changed little over the centuries.

Heinrich-Böll-Platz: Bischofsgartenstr. 1. Tel: (0)221 48-02.
This spectacular modern building houses three museums:

Wallraf-Richartz Museum: Tel: (0)221 23-72.
This museum ranks as one of Germany's finest. One floor is complete-
ly taken up with an exhibition of the works of the Cologne Masters
from the 14th to 16th century. Other exhibits include works by
Rembrandt, Rubens and Dürer. The Italian renaissance is represent-
ed by, among others, Martini and Lorenzetti and 16th century Italy by
Titian and Tintoretto. 19th century romantics include Caspar David
Friedrich and Lovis Corinth and French impressionists include
Renoir, Monet, Sisley, Cézanne, Van Gogh and Gauguin. There are
also sculptures in this section by Degas and Rodin.

Museum Ludwig: Tel: (0)221 23-70.
The collection takes up at the point the ones in the Wallraf-Richartz
Museum left off – namely with modern and contemporary art of the
20th century. The Blauer Reiter movement is represented by Macke,
Marc and Kandinsky, expressionism by Kokoschka and Beckman
and there is a special section for German art between the wars –
Constructivism, the Bauhaus, New Objectivity and the Cologne
progressives. The museum also has an impressive collection of
Russian avant-garde art. The section devoted to the surrealist
movement shows that the Dada movement owes its origins to
Cologne. There are oils, gouaches and collages by Max Ernst. French
modern art is represented by Modigliani and Maillol and the cubists
by Braque, Léger, Delauney and Juan Gris.

There are sections devoted to Post-war German painting, pop art (with works by Warhol, Rauschenburg and Segal) and contemporary German, American, Japanese and Chinese art. There is a sculpture collection on the terrace and a fine view of the cathedral.

Agfa-Foto-Historama: Tel: (0)221 24-11.
This collection has been compiled from the archives of the Agfa company and the Stengler Collection, as well as other private collections, and chronicles the advances made in photography over the last 150 years. There is a rotating exhibition of works by Manray.

Beatles Museum: Heinsbergstr. 13. Tel: (0)221 21-25-98.
For light relief, this cheery museum is crammed with nostalgic memorabilia of the 'Fab Four' and has a large '60s style café.

Landmarks

The Kölner Dom (Cathedral)

Dedicated to St. Peter and St. Mary, the cathedral miraculously survived the heavy bombing of World War II almost entirely intact. The vast gothic edifice was begun in 1248, work was suspended in 1560 for lack of money and it lay half-finished for 300 years. Under Napoleon it was used as a horse stable and prison by the troops but in 1880 after almost six centuries it finally reached completion thanks to an infusion of money from King Friedrich Wilhelm IV. The cathedral is the largest and most perfect example of high Gothic of its kind in the world. Despite the enormous size of the cathedral (it rises to 157 metres) the impression is of lightness and grace, thanks to the lacy spires and flying delicate buttresses. The interior is just as impressive with a phalanx of pillars and arches supporting the lofty central nave. The stained glass windows illuminate numerous treasures including the Garo Crucifix which dates from 970, the largest choir stalls in Germany and the Shrine of the Three Magi behind the altar, which is said to contain the bones of the kings who followed the Star to the stable in Bethlehem to worship the baby Jesus. The richly ornate bejewelled and gilt sarcophagus was brought from Milan in 1164 by Frederick Barbarossa as spoils of war, thus instantly turning Cologne into a major pilgrimage site. It is possible to ascend the South Tower by means of a very steep staircase with 529 steps but the astounding panorama of Cologne and the surrounding countryside might make it worth the climb of 98·25 metres. St. Peter's Bell, the world's largest swinging bell (24 tons), is known affectionately as der große Peter. Cast in the 19th century, it is known as 'Germany's Bell on the Rhine' and bears an inscription calling for national unity.

The Old Town:
In the shadow of the cathedral, the Hohenzollern Brücke crosses the Rhine and opens out into a promenade guarded by equestrian statues of the royal family. A piece of modern architecture balances the ornate gothic beauty of the cathedral – Heinrich Böll Cultural Centre houses three museums (see below).

The **Rathaus (Town Hall)** is surmounted by a Gothic tower, and the 1570 Renaissance arcade and loggia (the only section that survived the war) is decorated with flights of Baroque cherubs. On the façade, a glockenspiel rings every day at noon and at 5 p.m. Nearby, the Romanische Praetorium und Kanal hark back to Cologne's Roman past and visitors can see the excavated ruins of a former Roman Governor's Palace. The Roman sewer is still visible and was used as an air raid shelter during World War II.

Romanesque Churches
Cologne had such enormous wealth between 1150 and 1250 that a large number of Churches were built during this period of the city's heyday. Many survived until the bombardment of World War II when many were destroyed. About a dozen have since been restored and they are scattered around the medieval town. The most remarkable

include: **Groß St. Martin** (Tel: (0)221 257-79-24) which looks down on the Fischmarkt with its four slender turrets grouped around a central spire and a handsome interior with a cloverleaf choir; and **St. Maria im Kapitol** (Tel: (0)221 46-15), which also has a cloverleaf choir (the one in Groß St. Martin was modelled on this one), and a carved door that predates its consecration date of 1065 by a few years. The choir screen is richly carved with wooden panels depicting the life of Christ. **St. Gereon** on Christophstr. has a staggering four storey decagonal dome – an amazing feat of engineering for the early 13th century.

FRANKFURT AM MAIN:

Frankfurt am Main is the largest city of the State of Hesse. It has a population of nearly 650,000 and lies on the River Main. The name Frankfurt, which derives from 'ford or crossing of the Franks', probably originated around 500 AD but the first written mention of the city is to be found in the writings of Charlemagne's biographer, Einhard, in the late 8th century. In 1152, Frederick Barbarossa was elected ruler of Germany in the town and in the 13th century the Hohenstaufen family built a new imperial castle to replace the original Pfalz (imperial castle) and walled the town. In 1356 the Golden Bull, which gave a constitution to the Holy Roman Empire, designated Frankfurt as the election and coronation place of the Emperors – a privilege it retained until 1806. Frankfurt was also an Imperial Free City until 1806 when Napoleon made it the seat of government for the prince primate of the Confederation of the Rhine and, in 1810, the capital of the Grand Duchy of Frankfurt. After the fall of Napoleon in 1815, Frankfurt had a brief period as a free city again and the

Frankfurt National Assembly was held there in 1848–49. From 1816 to 1866, the city was the seat of the German Bundestag and thus the capital of Germany. After the Seven Weeks War in 1866, Prussia annexed the city and it was only after Frankfurt was integrated into a unified Germany that the city began to develop into the major industrial and commercial centre that it is today. Frankfurt has long been a key stopping off point for river, road and rail trade traffic from Switzerland and southern Germany northward along the Rhine to the Ruhr region and across the Main River to north central Germany. Frankfurt is still a major hub of German traffic and since the Main River was canalized in the late 19th century, the city has an important inland shipping port. The old town of Frankfurt was the largest intact medieval town in Germany until it was badly damaged in World War II. Although many of the historical landmarks remain, it has largely been restored and rebuilt with many fine modern buildings. Today, Rhein-Main airport is the largest in Germany and one of the busiest in the world. Frankfurt is a major centre for banking and the stock exchange was established in 1585. Trade fairs have been held in some form since 1240 and today Frankfurt is host to many trade fairs – a motor show, computer and, most famously, the book fair (the world's largest, drawing 9,500 companies from over 100 countries). The city's manu-factures include machinery, pharmaceuticals, chemicals, printing materials, leather goods and foodstuffs (including high quality sausages – hence 'frankfurter'). Frankfurt is the birthplace of the German poet Goethe and the city's university, which is named after him, is one of the largest institutions of higher education in Germany. The Frankfurt Zoo is known all over the world and there are many fine museums.

TRANSPORT

Airport

Flughafen Rhein-Main: Tel: (0)69 69-01.

Web site: www.frankfurt-airport.de

The airport is one of Europe's busiest with the second highest freight and passenger turnover after Heathrow, with flights to and from destinations all over the world.

Situated 9 km to the south-west of the city, the airport is linked to Frankfurt by tram or bus. The S-Bahn runs every 15 minutes to the Hauptbahnhof (railway station) and tickets are available from the green automatic machines marked 'Fahrkarten'.

Trains

Deutsche Bahn Central Information Line: Tel (0)69 26 53 45 81.

The main station, the Hauptbahnhof, handles more trains than any other station in Germany with frequent connections to destinations all over Germany and Continental Europe.

Roads

Frankfurt is linked to other German cities by Autobahnen (motorways) A5 (north-east), A45 (north-west/south-east), A3 (east-west) and A67 (south) with a linking road to the A61 (north-south to the west).

Buses

Long distance and international buses arrive and depart from the south side of the Hauptbahnhof.

Europabus: Deutsche Touring. Römerhof 17. Tel: (0)69 790-30.

Local Transport

The city's transport system is run by RMV (Rhein-Main-Verkehrsverbund) and consists of S-Bahn, U-Bahn, buses and Straßenbahn (trams).

RMV. Tel: 0130-235-14-15.

Web site: www.rmv.de

Tickets (including a 24-hour pass) are available from machines in the stations and a zone system of fares applies. Tickets, maps and schedules are available at the tourist offices.

Taxis

Taxi ranks are all over the city; you can hail them or telephone.

Radio Taxis: Tel: (0)69 23-00-01 or 25-00-01.

Car Hire

See central reservation numbers on page 173.

Bicycle Hire

Holger's Rad-Laden: Eschersheimer Landstr. 470.

Tel: (0)69 52-20-04.

Per Pedale: Leipzigstr. 4, Tel: (0)69 707-23-63.

TRAVELLERS INFORMATION

Tourist Offices

Main office is in the Hauptbahnhof. (0)69 212-38-80-0.

Fax: (0)69 212-37-88-0.

There is also an office at Römerberg 27 (borders Römerplatz)

Tel: (0)69 21-23-87-08.

The German National Tourist Board. Beethovenstr. 69.

Tel: (0)69 974-64-0.

The Goethe Institute (for cultural information concerts etc.):

Hedderichstr. 108-110. Tel: (0)69 961-22-70.

Email: TCF-Info@frankfurt-main.de

Web: www.TCF.frankfurt-main.de www.germany-tourism.de
www.goethe.de/

Financial and Currency

Exchange facilities are available at the airport, in the Hauptbahnhof
and at banks in the city. There are cash ATM machines all over the
city.

American Express: Kaiserstr. 8. Tel: (0)69 21-05-01-11.
Fax: (0)69 28-33-98. Hotline: 0130-95-31-00.

Thomas Cook: Kaiserstr. 11. Tel: (0)69 13-47-33.

Post Office

Main Branch: Zeil 90 (inside Hertie's department store).
Tel: (0)69 21-11. Fax: (0)69 29-68-84.
Post Code: 60313.

Consulates

UK. Bockenheimer Landstr. 42. Tel: (0)69 170-00-20.
Fax: (0)69 72-95-53.
USA. Siesmayerstr. 21. Tel: (0)69 753-50. Fax: (0)69 74-89-38.

Emergency

Police: Tel: 110.

Frankfurter Rechtshilfekommittee für Ausländer (legal help for foreigners): Tel: (0)69 729-16-1.

Fire: Tel: 112.

Medical Emergency

Ambulance: Tel: 112.
UK and US Consulates have lists of English-speaking doctors.

24-hour routine medical queries: Tel: (0)69 192-92.

Emergency Clinic: Friedberger Landstr. 430. Tel: (0)69 475-0.

Pharmacies: There is a pharmacy in the basement of the Hauptbahnhof. Tel: (0)69 23-30-47.
Fax: (0)69 24-27-19-16.
For out of hours check windows of closed pharmacies for the nearest one that is open. For recorded lists, Tel: (0)69 11500.

Internet Access

CyberRyder Internet Café: Töngesgasse 31. Tel: (0)69 92-08-40-10.
Email: info@cyberder.de
Web: www.cyberder.de

Cyber's: the Internet-n-Active Café: Zeil 112-114. Tel: (0)69 29-49-64.
Email: cybers@internet.de

Hotel Reservations

See central reservation numbers on page 172.

Leading Museums and Galleries

Museumsufer: This stretch of the south bank of the River Main between Eiserner Steg and the Friedensbrücke is home to seven museums. The area is interspersed with green spaces and residential districts.

Städelsches Kunstinstitut und Städtische Galerie: Schaumainkai 63.
Tel: (0)69 605-09-80.
One of Germany's most important art collections with exhibits of paintings and graphics. The Italian renaissance and the Old Masters are most notably represented by works by Fra Angelico, Botticelli, Tintoretto, Veronese, Dürer, Van Eyck, Rembrandt, Rubens, Vermeer and Heironymus Bosch and the French impressionists by Renoir and

Matisse. There is a collection of German Expressionists including works by Beckman, Kirchner and Marc. Picasso and Braque herald in the cubists while Max Ernst, Paul Klee and Fieninger represent surrealism and the Bauhaus. There are examples of contemporary art and part of the museum is given over to an extensive graphics collection.

Museum für Kunsthandwerk (Museum of Applied Arts): Schaumainkai 17. Tel: (0)69 21-23-40-37 or (0)69 21-23-85-30.

The Museum building was designed in 1985 by the New York architect Richard Meier (a pupil of Marcel Breuer at the Bauhaus). Meier integrated an existing classical building, Villa Metzler, into the museum. Purity of line and richness of materials and colour fill this airily spacious building. The museum contains arts and crafts from Europe (from the middle ages to the present), the Near East (9th to 19th centuries) and the Far East (Neolithic to the present). As well as 16th century folding chairs, carved renaissance and baroque furniture, jewel-encrusted commodes and cabinets, and Jugendstil items, there is a particularly fine collection of 15th and 16th century Venetian glassware. The Islamic section contains carpets, furniture, weapons and glassware and faience. A porcelain collection from the European manufacturers includes work from Meissen, Berlin, Fürstenburg, Nymphenburg, Vienna, Höchst and Sèvres.

Deutsches Filmmuseum (German Museum of Cinema): Schaumainkai 41. Tel: (0)69 21-23-88-30.

Film buffs will enjoy looking at the different inventions relating to the discovery of animation. Emile Reynaud's 1882 praxinoscope, Edison's Kineto-scope and a copy of the Lumière Brothers' Cinematograph (1894) are among the historical exhibits. There are reproductions of silent and talking studios where visitors can compose their own shots, and drawings, designs, and working models for special effects – among them, King Kong. There is also a small cinema showing shorts and newsreels.

Museum für Post und Kommunikation (Museum of Post and Communications): Schaumainkai 53. Tel: (0)69 606-00.
Web: www.museumsstiftung.de
This innovatively designed building traces the history of German travel and communication with interactive video displays. The displays follow the development of German communications systems from the earliest prototypes to state-of-the-art modern technology, each in historically appropriate settings.

Deutsches Architektur-Museum (German Architecture Museum)
Schaumainkai 43. Tel: (0)69 21-23-88-44.
The museum was designed by Oswald Mathias Ungers as an extremely original complex containing not only the museum, but incorporating an existing magnificent villa of the Bismarck period into his ultra-modern design. The museum, which was opened in 1984, houses a collection of architects' plans, models and examples of European architecture from the last 10 years. There are also examples of interior design and a series of tableaux illustrate human development from various civilizations with examples of their dwellings.

Landmarks
Römerberg (Old Town)
The Römerberg is the old central square of Frankfurt and since the old town was almost entirely destroyed during World War II, most of the buildings that originally date from the 14th and 15th centuries have been sympathetically rebuilt or restored. The square derives its name from the **Haus zum Römer** (the **old Town Hall**) – the oldest and most richly decorated of three houses has a 19th century façade with statues of Emperors above a balcony balustrade with Imperial Eagles. A small inner courtyard has a graceful Renaissance stairway. To the east of the square, the **Dom (Bartholomäuskirche)** was designated a cathedral after it had been chosen as the election and coronation site of the Emperors in 1356 and 1562. A Gothic church with three naves

and a wide transept, its outstanding feature is the west tower (Westturm) with its gabled polygonal crown, cupola and lantern. Inside the cathedral the choir stalls were richly carved by master craftsmen from the Upper Rhine in the 14th century and the mural paintings are the work of a master of the Cologne School. The Cathedral Museum has been installed in the remains of the cloister and contains elaborate ornaments worn by the ecclesiastic Electors at the coronation ceremonies. The **Kaisersaal (Imperial Hall)** is the former banqueting hall and is adorned with the portraits of 562 German Emperors from Charlemagne to Franz II, 13 of whom were crowned here. The **Paulskirche (St. Paul's Church)** is opposite the Römerberg and once served as the meeting place for Germany's first Democratic National Assembly after the 1848–49 revolution. It is now used as a political memorial and conference centre.

Goethe Haus (Birthplace of Goethe): Großer Hirschgraben 23-25 (a few blocks north-west of the Haus der Römer) Tel: (0)69 13-88-00. The house was described by Goethe as 'Spacious, light and tranquil with free-standing staircases, large vestibules and several windows with pleasant views of the garden'. Visitors are able to picture the home life of the family as they wander through the rooms with paintings of the Goethe family and friends hanging on the walls. Some of the original furniture remains and adjacent to the house there is a small museum and library where there are displays of literary memorabilia.

Zoo: Alfred-Brehm-Platz. Tel: (0)69 21-23-37-35.
The zoo is on the eastern side of town and is world famous for its rare species (there are over 5,000 examples of over 600 species) and for its highly successful breeding programme. The animals live in habitats as close to their natural homes as possible and the birds are free to fly around the visitors in an enormous aviary. There is a huge beehive with thousands of bees at work and nocturnal animals can be observed in a special dark house.

BONN:

In 1949 Bonn was made the de facto capital of Germany. In 1991 the German parliament voted to move the federal government to Berlin. The move is to be completed by the end of the century, and although the newly renovated Reichstag was officially opened in 1999, some government offices will remain in Bonn and many of the embassies will take some years to complete the move to Berlin.

Bonn, a thriving university town, is located in the region of North Rhine-Westphalia, in the West of Germany, on the River Rhine. The city was settled by the Romans and celebrated its 2000th anniversary in 1989. From the 16th to the 18th century, Bonn was the residence of the prince-Electors and archbishops of Cologne and was the capital city of the see of Cologne. Some of the fine baroque architecture from this period has survived despite heavy bombing in World War II. Bonn has been designated the federal city for science and communication and is home to Deutsche Telekom and the Centre for Advanced European Studies and Research (CAESAR).

Manufactures include ceramic and metal goods, chemicals, and pharmaceuticals as well as Haribo's money-spinning Gummi-Bears (Gummibärchen) which generate two billion Deutsche Marks per year. Bonn is the birthplace of Beethoven.

TRANSPORT

Airport

Köln-Bonn Flughafen: Tel: (0)2203 404-00-1 (flight information). Bonn shares the airport with Cologne. There are international and continental flights. The airport is linked to the centre of Bonn by shuttle buses (Express Bus 670) that arrive and depart from the train station.

Local Transport

Deutsche Bahn Information: (General Train Information, Cologne)
Tel: (0)221 194-19.

The city of Bonn is linked to Cologne and other Rhine cities by
the VRS (Verkehsrverbund Rhein-Sieg) S-Bahn, U-Bahn and
Bundesbahn network which is divided into tariff zones – the further
you go the more you pay. The system also serves as the public
transportation system for the city itself.

Tickets are available from automatic machines (Automaten) and
at designated vending stations.

Roads

Bonn stands at the crossroads of several Autobahnen (motorways)
– A3 (north/south to the east), A61 (north/south to the west) and A4
(east/west to the north), and the city is bisected by the B9 highway.

Buses

International and long distance buses arrive and depart from the
Hauptbahnhof.

Taxis

Taxis may be hailed in the street or found at taxi stands.
Radio Taxi (Funkzentrale) Tel: (0)228 55-55-55.

Car Hire

See central reservation numbers on page 173.

Bicycle Hire

Kurscheid. Roerstr. 4. Tel: (0)228 63-14-33.

TRAVELLERS INFORMATION

Tourist Offices

Headquarters: Münsterstr. 20. Tel: (0)228 77-34-66 or 19-44-33.
Fax: (0)228 77-31-00.
(in a passage way in the Cassius Bastei arcade north of the
Hauptbahnhof.)
Email: eurade@compuserve.com
Web: www.cube.net/kmu/euraide.html www.bonn-regio.de
Email: info@tourcon-bonn.de

Financial and Currency

The Bank at the Hauptbahnhof (railway station) will exchange
currency and travellers cheques. There are cash ATM machines all
over the city.

Post Office

Main Post Office. Münsterplatz 17. Postal code 53111.

Consulates

(For information regarding Embassies, see under Berlin)
UK. Friedrich-Ebert-Allee 77. Tel: (0)228 916-70.
Fax: (0)228 916-72-00.
USA. Deichmanns Aue 29. Tel: (0)228 33-91. Fax: (0)228 339-20-53.

Emergency

Police: Tel: 110.
Fire: Tel: 112.

Medical Emergency

Ambulance 112.
Medical emergency. Tel: (0)228 192-92.
Emergency dentist. Tel: (0)228 115-00.

Pharmacies

Bahnhof Apotheke: Next door to the tourist office.

Hotel Reservations

See central reservation numbers on page 172.

Leading Museums and Galleries

Beethoven Geburtshaus (Birthplace of Beethoven): Bonngasse 20.
Tel: (0)228 63-51-88.

Beethoven was born and spent the first years of his childhood here.
The house contains memorabilia of all kinds related to Beethoven
including an early violin of his and some of his primitive hearing aids.
There is an annual festival of his works (at the first Beethoven festival,
Franz Liszt fought with Hector Berlioz while King Ludwig's mistress,
Lola Montez, danced on the tables).

Münster Basilika (Collegiate Church): Münsterpl.

This splendid example of late Rhineland Romanesque architecture
was originally a triple-aisled basilica built on the site of a roman
necropolis. The present building was constructed after the fire of
1239. The Romanesque cloister has graceful arcades supported by
rows of columns.

Haus der Geschichte der Bundesrepublik Deutschland: Adenauerallee
250. Tel: (0)228 916-50.

This is the first museum in Germany to be devoted to contemporary
history. Exhibitions and displays make use of modern audio-visual
techniques, interactive control panels and electronic buttons.
Among the exhibits are antique Volkswagen cars, Konrad Adenuaer's
official Mercedes, the rough wooden seats that Mikhail Gorbachev
and Helmut Kohl sat on during the 1990 summit in Kaukasus Platz
and an area of darkness with the continuously scrolling names of
holocaust victims. During construction work, a Roman cellar was

uncovered and it has been incorporated into the museum on the basement level.

Kunstmuseum Bonn (Bonn Museum of Art): Freidrich-Ebert-Allee 2. Tel: (0)228 77-62-60.
A stunning modern building by the architect Axel Schulter houses a large and impressive collection of expressionists and modern German painting.

Deutsche Museum Bonn: Ahrstr. 45.
This museum is an offshoot of the more famous museum of science and technology in Munich and has as its theme 'Research and Technology in Germany since 1945'. Modern media presentations, video and videophones show technological developments from both east and west Germany since World War II.

Landmarks
Poppelsdorfer Schloß
This fine 18th century building has a French style façade and Italian courtyard and was built between 1715 and 1753 by the French architect Robert de Cotte. It is linked with Bonn's other great castle, Kurfürstliches Schloß, by an elegant carriageway bordered by rows of chestnut trees. At the back of the palace are the university's botanical gardens. The Kurfürstliches Schloß, which was built in the 18th century, now serves as the centre of Bonn's Friedrich-Wilhelms-Universität.

DÜSSELDORF:

As the finding of the bones of Neanderthal man would suggest, the area around Düsseldorf has been inhabited for at least 52,000 years. Düsseldorf, literally meaning 'the village on the Düssel', is the capital of Germany's North Rhine-Westphalia region and has long played an important role in European trade and travel. Situated on the banks of the Rhine it is one of Germany's most prosperous cities due to its role as a banking centre, and is Germany's centre of fashion. Düsseldorf owes its prominence to the large Ruhr bituminous coalfield which allowed the area to develop as the centre of the most important industrial, mining and energy-generating area of Germany.

Düsseldorf was first chartered by the Count of Berg in 1288 and became the capital of the duchy of Berg. This dynastic line ended with the assassination of Engelbert I.

The region succeeded to the Limburg and Jülich dynasties from the 14th century until the 17th century. It then became the capital of the Palatinate-Neuberg line.

Düsseldorf suffered terribly during the Thirty Years' War (1618–48) and during the War of the Spanish Succession (1701–14) but was restored by elector palatine Johann Willhelm II. The town became part of Prussia in 1815.

During the Second World War Düsseldorf was pounded and a large portion of the city was reduced to ruins as a result of some 200 air raids which occurred between 1942 and the end of the war. After the war many of the city's older buildings were repaired and many new buildings were built.

TRANSPORT

Airport

Düsseldorf's Lohhausen Airport is 8 km north of the city. Trains depart to the city every 20 minutes and return from Hauptbahnhof every 30 minutes. An S-Bahn connection (S7) every 20–30 minutes and bus no. 727 are available as well. Taxis run a 24-hour service to Düsseldorf. Tel: (0)211 4210.

Trains

The main railway station (Hauptbahnhof) is located at Konrad Adenauer Platz. Being part of the S-Bahn network, it is well connected with trains regularly departing to and arriving from cities such as Munich, Hamburg, Berlin and Frankfurt. Direct lines from Amsterdam and Moscow also run to Düsseldorf.

Local Transport

Düsseldorf has an all-encompassing network of trains, trams, buses and U-Bahn. All of these are operated by the Rheinishe Bahngesellschaft. Tel: (0)211 58228.

For purposes of local transport the city is divided into zones and one simply buys a ticket for the number of zones expected to travel through.

Taxis are plentiful in Düsseldorf. Tel: (0)211 33333 or (0)211 19410.

TRAVELLERS INFORMATION

Tourist Offices

The German National Tourist Office is located at Konrad Adenauer Platz. Tel: (0)211 17202. Fax: (0)211 161071.

The Office of Publicity and Economic Development is at Mühlenstr. 29.

Tel: (0)211 8991. Fax: (0)211 8929061.

E-mail: tourist@dusseldorf.de

Financial and Currency

American Express

Königsallee 98a.

Tel: (0)211 386910.

Thomas Cook Foreign Currency Services
Schlüterstr. 3, Im Metro Markt.
Tel: (0)211 9660909.
There are currency exchange offices, banks and ATM cash machines all over the city.

Post Office
The main Post Office is located at Immermannstrasse 1, just off Konrad Adenauer Platz and near the Hauptbahnhof. This is also the sight of the post restante or **Hauptpostlagernd**.

Consulates
UK: British Consulate-General / Directorate General for Trade and Investment Promotion
Yorck Str. 19.
Tel: (0)211 9448-0.
Web: www.british-dgtip.de/
USA: U.S. Consulate General
Kennedydamm 17.
Tel: (0)211 470610. Fax: (0)211 431448.
Web: www.us-botschaft.de/

Emergency
Police Tel: 110.
Fire Tel: 112.

Medical Emergency
During the night Tel: (0)211 19292.
For dental emergencies Tel: (0)211 666291.

Hotel Reservations
See central reservation numbers on page 172.

Leading Museums and Galleries

The **Kunstsammlung Nordrhein-Westfalen** at Grabaplatz 5 on the east bank of the Rhine houses a particularly interesting display of 20th Century artists, including Picasso, Matisse, Klee and Braque.

This is close to the **Hochschule für bildende Künste** or Academy of Art, which houses many galleries and students. This is worth a visit for a look at the architecture. It was designed by Hermann Riffart after the example of Italian renaissance buildings.

The **Kunstmuseum**, just north of the Altstadt at Ehrenhof 5, has three floors of displays including a fine collection of Art Nouveau and Art Deco glass. The Kunstmuseum also houses Rubens' altarpiece of 'The Assumption' and 'Venus and Adonis'.

The **Schloß Jägerhof**,which houses the **Goethe Museum**, is situated at the northeasterly corner of the Hofgarten. The building was completed in 1772, and was in those days situated far away from the city gates. It was the residence of the 'Bergische Oberjägermeister' or local gamekeeper. Its history is a troubled one and it has seen much renovation over the years as a result of bombings and burnings.

Theatres

The futuristic looking **Düsseldorf Schauspielhaus**, built between 1968 and 1970 and nicknamed 'the cheese-box', is situated at:
Gustaf-Gründgens-Platz 1, 40211 Düsseldorf.
Tel: (0)211 369911.

The Deutsche **Oper am Rhein**, which can house 1,342 people, is situated at:
Heinrich-Heine-Allee 16a.
Tel: (0)211 890 8211.

LEIPZIG:

Leipzig was the second largest city in the former German Democratic Republic and is located 182 km south-west of Berlin, on a flat plain in Western Saxony called the Leipzig basin.

Leipzig started life as a small Slav village near the confluence of the rivers Elster and Parthe. Its name is derived from the name 'Lipsk' which means 'the place where the lime trees grow'. Its history is a prestigious one. It was the birthplace of Richard Wagner, the home of Felix Mendelssohn, and it welcomed Johann Sebastian Bach as organist and choirmaster of St. Thomas' Church and City Musical Director. Leipzig University was where Johann Wolfgang Goethe studied. It witnessed, however reluctantly, the victory of allied Austrian, Prussian, Russian, and Swedish troops over Napoleonic forces in 1813 at the Battle of The Nations. It was the first city in the world to produce a daily newspaper. Leipzig was first mentioned in 1015, in the 'Urbs Libzi' in the chronicles of Bishop Thietmar von Merseburg. Leipzig has long been known as an important intellectual and cultural centre. The University of Leipzig was established in 1409. Leipzig has many museums, and its musical, dramatic and bookmaking academies are internationally renowned.

Leipzig's early prosperity and consequent cultural flowering was based on trading success. Leipzig people owe much of their success to the trade in furs, books, textiles and yarns. During the 16th century silver was found in the nearby 'Ore Mountains.'

Leipzig was hit hard during World War II and much of its old architecture was lost to allied bombing. The reconstruction of the city was pursued under the communist policy of East Germany. When citizens of the former German Democratic Republic began calling for a reunified Germany it was to Leipzig that the country turned. It was one of the leading centres in the democratic revolution.

TRANSPORT

Airport

Leipzig's **Flughafen Leipzig-Halle** is situated is 13 km north-west of Leipzig and is midway between Leipzig and Halle.

Tel: (0)341 2240. Fax: (0)341 2242526.

Flight Information Tel: (0)341 2241155.

Buses to and from the airport alight at the Hauptbahnhof every 30 minutes.

Trains

The huge Hauptbahnhof, the largest of its kind in the world, is at the northern edge of the ring road, which encircles Leipzig's city centre, at Willy-Brandt Platz. From here trains can be boarded for all major cities in the country, including Munich, Dresden, Berlin, Hanover, Hamburg and Stuttgart.

There is also a smaller Bayerischer Bahnhof, which is located just south of the ring road and which services more local journeys.

Local Transport

Trams are the easiest way to get around Leipzig. An extensive system of 40 tram routes service most areas of the city. The fares are time-based rather than distance-based and although the system sounds confusing it soon becomes self-explanatory.

For further information about trams in Leipzig visit: www.leipzig.com/(eng)/verkehr/ovm/bahn/

Taxis can be found outside the Hauptbahnhof and at other taxi ranks throughout the city. Tel: (0)341 982222.

TRAVELLERS INFORMATION

Tourist Offices
The Leipzig Tourist Office is at: Richard Wagner Str. 1.
Tel: (0)341 7104260. E-mail: lipsia@aol.com Web: www.leipzig.de/

Financial and Currency
American Express has an office at the Hotel Maritim Astoria on Platz der Republik 2. Tel: (0)341 7224721.

Thomas Cook Foreign Currency Services can be found on Geithainer Str. Tel: (0)341 6517337.

There are other currency exchanges and ATM cash machines across the city.

Post Offices
The main Post Office is located at Augustusplatz 1 near the Opernhaus. Another branch is situated in the Hauptbahnhof.

Consulates
UK: British Trade Office
Gohliser Str. 7. Tel: (0)341 5649672 or
(0)341 5649674. Fax: (0)341 5649673.

USA: Consulate General of the United States
Wilhelm-Seyfferth- Str. 4. Tel: (0)341 213840.

Emergency
Police: 110.
Fire/Ambulance: 112.
Emergency Call for Women: (0)341 3065246.
Traffic police: (0)341 9663015.

Medical Emergency

Medical Emergency/Ambulance: 115.

Medical Emergency (0)341 19292.

Hotel Reservations

See central reservation numbers on page 172.

Leading Museums and Galleries

The **Ägyptisches (Egyptian) Museum** has one of Europe's most impressive collections of Egyptian artefacts and antiques. The 9,000 piece collection includes sarcophagi and stone vessels from the 3rd Century BC. The museum, like all others in Leipzig, is closed on a Monday.

Schillerstr. 6. Tel: (0)341 9737010.

The **Grassi Museum Complex** consists of three museums:

The **Musikinstrumenten-Museum** has a vast collection of musical instruments from all over the world.

Täubchenweg 2c. Tel: (0)341 2142120. Fax: (0)341 2142135.

The **Museum für Völkerkunde (Museum of Ethnology)** has a huge collection of cultural artefacts from around the world. Its permanent exhibitions include Australia – dreamtime and presence – African nations and cultures and Indians – the aborigines of America.

Johannisplatz 5–11. Tel: (0)341 21420.

The **Museum für Kunsthandwerk (Museum of Arts and Crafts)** has a permanent exhibition of applied arts from the Middle Ages to the first part of the 20th century.

Johannisplatz 5–11. Tel: (0)341 21420.

Landmarks

Battle of Leipzig/Battle of the Nations Monument

To the south-east of the city centre on Prager Strasse is the memorial to the victory of the allies (English, Austrians, Prussians, Russians, and Swedish) over Napoleon at the Battle of Leipzig in Oct. 1813.

The memorial was opened in 1913. There is an impressive view of the city from the platform of the 91-metre high monument, if you can climb its 500 steps.

The **Opernhaus** is situated off Goethestrasse at the northern side of Augustusplatz and near the Swan Pond. The opera performed here is a mixture of modern and traditional.
Augustusplatz 12. Tel: (0)341 12610. Fax: (0)341 1261300.

The **Neues Gewandhaus** stands on the Augustusplatz and houses the orchestra once led by Mendelssohn; the oldest established orchestra in Europe. The **Gewandhausorchester (Gewandhaus Orchestra)** is still considered one of the best in the world.
Augustusplatz 8. Tel: (0)341 12700. Fax: (0)341 1270200.

Thomaskirche (St. Thomas Church) was built in 1212 and was where Johann Sebastian Bach was cantor for the last 27 years of his life. The choir that he led is still going strong. Inside and outside the church there are memorials to Bach. Bach's tomb has been in St. Thomas' Church since 1950. Every Monday evening there is a free concert in front of the Bach Memorial Statue.

Opposite the church is the **Bach Museum**, which documents the great man's life in Leipzig.

DRESDEN:

Dresden is the capital city of Saxony. It was the third largest city in the former German Democratic Republic and is 160 km south of Berlin.

Dresden began life as 'Drezdzany', a Slavonic fishing village on the banks of the Elbe River. It seems to have grown as two distinct settlements on opposite sides of the river. A German colony was established on the south bank of the Elbe opposite a Slav settlement on the north bank. Ironically the most recent of these settlements became known as 'Altstadt' (Old Town) whereas the older Slav settlement became known as 'Neustadt' (New Town). During the 11th century, Dresden became the centre of the domain of Margrave Henry the Illustrious of Meissen and began to grow. After his death it passed to the King of Bohemia. From the 15th century onwards it became the residence of the Saxon Dukes and as such Dresden became not only the capital of one of the most important Protestant territories but the centre of the most powerful German state after the Hapsburg territories. It was during this period that Dresden underwent a period of redevelopment.

Dresden's 'heyday' came with the help of the Elector Augustus the Strong who gathered around him brilliant artists, sculptors and architects who transformed the city into what became known as 'The Florence of the North', a masterpiece of Baroque architecture.

Dresden was targeted during the Seven Years War and her rulers fled to Warsaw. Prussian troops occupied the city and there was widespread destruction of the city's suburbs. Another period of upheaval came with the Napoleonic wars. In a bloody battle before the gates of the city in Aug. 1813 Napoleon achieved one of his last victories, against 170,000 Austrians, Prussians and Russians under Prince Karl Philipp, before moving his attention towards Leipzig and the Battle of the Nations.

Dresden, although stripped of her finery, became an important city during the 19th century. Railway connections and a port development on the Elbe served to attract business to the city. This coupled with a lively and rich cultural life meant that Dresden became a popular tourist destination. By the turn of the century Dresden had become the fourth largest city in the German Empire, with a population of more than half a million inhabitants.

The city suffered greatly from deprivation and political upheaval in the aftermath of the First World War. But it seemed, as the Second World War came to an end, that Dresden had been spared the wholesale destruction that had befallen Berlin. Indeed the enigma surrounding the events of Feb. 1945 is that nobody really knows why Dresden should have been targeted. On the nights of 13 and 14 Feb., and 2 March and 17 April, Dresden was destroyed by joint Anglo-American 'saturation' bombing raids. Figures suggest that 35,000 to 135,000 people perished in the attacks or under the rubble that was Dresden. In May 1945 Soviet troops occupied Dresden.

Reconstruction of Dresden could only begin with the clearing of huge amounts of rubble. This done, buildings of architectural, cultural or administrative importance were rebuilt. A policy of rejuvenation was continued under the socialist control of the German Democratic Republic.

Situated in a valley, Dresden was the only major town in the former German Democratic Republic unable to receive any Western TV or radio broadcasts, giving rise to the nickname 'Valley of the Unknowing'.

Since the peaceful democratic revolution and the reunification of Germany, Dresden has once again become an important regional capital and cultural centre. In 1998 Dresden welcomed over 6·9m. visitors. Four bridges connect the northern and southern sections of the city.

TRANSPORT

Airport

Flughafen Dresden (Dresden Airport) is situated 9 km from Dresden city centre in the northern city district of Klotzsche.

Tel: (0)351 881-0. Fax: (0)351 881-3665.

There are regular bus services to and from the city centre.

Roads

The A13 motorway connects Dresden to Berlin and the A4 motorway in the west and south provides a link with Leipzig, Bavaria and Hessen. A further motorway to Prague is currently under construction.

Trains

Dresden has two railway stations. The main railway station, **Hauptbahnhof**, is on the southern side of the town at the end of Prager Strasse and **Dresden-Neustadt** is on the north of the river, just 500 metres north-west of Albertplatz. There are daily connections to all major German and many other European cities. Before embarking on a journey from Dresden it is worth establishing which station one should start from as some trains only stop at one of the two stations.

Local Transport

Dresden has a network of 18 tram routes and 26 bus routes which cover most of the city. Fares are time-based rather than zone-based. This extensive system of tram and bus routes is operated by Dresden Public Transport Corporation. Tel: (0)351 857-0. Fax: (0)351 857-1010.

The **Dresden Suburban Railway** system connects Dresden with important communities in the Upper Elbe valley region, including Schöna, Arnsdorf , Meissen and Tharandt. It too is operated by the Dresden Public Transport Corporation.

Tel: (0)351 857-0. Fax: (0)351 857-1010.

The **Saxon Steamship Company** operates a number of historical paddle steamers and modern motor ships along the Elbe River. The route runs from Decin in the Czech Republic through Dresden and as far north as Meissen.

TRAVELLERS INFORMATION

Tourist Offices

Dresden has two very good tourist offices. The Dresden Information Office is at:

Prager Strasse 10, near the smaller of the two post offices.

Tel: (0)351 491-920. Fax: (0)351 310-5247.

The second is the Information Neustadter Markt Office which is at the southern end of Haupstrasse.

Tel: (0)351 535-39.

An English language tourist information web site is under construction at:

www.dresden-tourist.de/eng/homepage.html

The German edition already exists at:

www.dresden-tourist.de/homepage.html

Financial and Currency

Thomas Cook Travel Services have an office at

Marie Curie Str. 9. Tel: (0)351 8584356.

There are currency exchanges and ATM cash machines across the city.

Post Offices

The main Post Office in Dresden is situated in the northern part of the city at Königsbrücker Strasse 21. A smaller post office can be found on Prager Strasse on the southern side of the city.

Consulates

For Diplomatic Missions of the United Kingdom and the United States of America in Saxony see Leipzig.

Emergency

Police: 110.
Fire/Ambulance: 112.

Hotel Reservations

A list of Dresden hotels and online booking forms can be found at:
www.lodging-germany.com/dresden/hotels.htm

Leading Museums and Galleries

The **Albertinum**, on Brühlscher Garten, was named after the art-loving Saxon King Albert and was once the city's Armoury. It now houses the **Sculpture Collection**, the **New Masters Gallery**, the **Green Vault** with its world renowned collection of jewels and jewellery, and the **Coin Collection**.
Tel: (0)351 495-3056.

The **Zwinger** derives its name from its position between the inner and outer walls of the old city. Zwinger means 'keep'. Built in the early 18th century by Daniel Pöppelmann and the sculptor Balthasar Permoser, it is considered the height of Baroque architecture. The Zwinger houses the **Old Masters Gallery**, the **Armoury Museum**, the **Porcelain Collection**, the **Zoological Museum** and the **Mathematical-Physical Salon**.

Landmarks

Katholische Hofkirche. The **Cathedral of St. Trinitatis**, south across the Augustusbrücke, is a beautiful Catholic cathedral in the Baroque style finished in 1754 by the Italian architect Gaetano Chiaveri. Many Saxon Kings lie beneath the cathedral in the crypt, as does a vessel containing the heart of Augustus the Strong.

The **Royal Dresden Palace** was the home and seat of government of the Saxon princes and kings from the 13th until the early part of the 20th century. It suffered greatly during the allied bombing campaigns of 1945 and has only now begun to be properly restored. A stone bridge connects the south wing of the palace with the **Taschenberg Palais**, now a hotel. Friedrich August I had this Baroque palace built between 1707 and 1711 for his mistress Countess Cosel.

Dresden **Zoo** and **Botanical Gardens** are situated in Grosser Garten to the south-east of Altstadt along Bergerwiese Park Strasse. These fine gardens are home to many well-kept animals and plants. Tel: (0)351 478-060.

TOURIST OFFICES IN OTHER MAJOR CITIES

Essen
Essen Central Tourist Office
Touristikzentrale Essen, C/o Essen Marketing GmbH, Im Handelshof, Am Hauptbahnhof 2, 45127 Essen.
Tel (0)201 19433. Fax (0)201 88-72044.
www.essen.de/emg/

Dortmund
Verkehrsverein Dortmund
Königswall 18, 44137 Dortmund.
Tel (0)231 502-2666 or (0)231 140341. Fax (0)231 163596.
www.dortmund.de/

Stuttgart
Stuttgart Marketing GmbH, Königstr. 1A, 70173 Stuttgart
(Centre, directly opposite the main railway station).
Tel (0)711 2228-240. Fax (0)711 2228-217.
www.stgt.com/stuttgart/marketie.htm

Bremen

Bremer Touristik Zentrale GmbH (Bremen Central Tourist Office),
Findorffstr. 105, 28215 Bremen.

Tel (0)1805 101030. Fax (0)421 30 800-30.

www.bremen–tourism.de/

Duisburg

Duisburg Agentur GmbH, Königstr. 53, 47051 Duisburg.

Tel (0)203 28544-11. Fax (0)203 28544-44.

www.duisburg-agentur.de/

Hanover

Hannover Tourist Information, Ernst-August-Platz 2, 30159 Hannover.

Tel (0)511 3014-20/21/22.

www.hannover.de/

Nuremberg

Nürnberg Tourist Office, Frauentorgraben 3, 90443 Nürnberg
(Tourist Information in main station).

Tel (0)911 2336-0. Fax (0)911 2336-166.

www.nuernberg.de/

Heidelberg

Heidelberg Convention and Visitors Bureau, P.O. Box 10 58 60, 69048
Heidelberg (Tourist Information Office, Main Station, Willy Brandt-
Platz, Heidelberg).

Tel (0)6221 19433. Fax (0)6221 1388111.

www.heidelberg.de/

Bochum

Verkehrsverein, Postfach 102830, Kurt-Schumacher-Platz, 44728
Bochum (Tourist Information in the main railway station).

Tel (0)234 963020 or 19433. Fax (0)234 9630255.

www.bochum.de/

Wuppertal

Tourist Information Wuppertal, Pavillon, Döppersberg, 42103 Wuppertal.

Tel (0)202 563-22-70. Fax (0)202 563-80-52.

www.wuppertal.de/

German National Tourist Office in the UK

PO Box 2695

London W1A 3TN.

Tel: (0)20 7317-0908.

Fax: (0)20 7495-6129.

German National Tourist Office in the USA

122 East 42nd Street

Chanin Building

52nd Floor

10168–0072 New York

Tel: 212 661-7200.

Fax: 212 661-7114.

SOCIAL STATISTICS

Calendar years	Marriages	Live births	Of these to single parents	Deaths	Divorces
1992	453,428	809,114	120,448	885,443	135,179
1993	442,605	798,447	118,284	897,270	156,646
1994	440,244	769,603	118,460	884,661	166,496
1995	430,534	765,221	122,876	884,588	169,425
1996	427,297	796,013	135,700	882,843	175,550

Of the 427,297 marriages in 1996, 27,907 were between foreign males and German females, and 29,637 vice-versa. The average age of bridegrooms in 1996 was 33·4, and of brides 30·5.

Rates (per 1,000 population), 1996: Birth, 9·7; marriage, 5·2; death, 10·8; infant mortality (per 1,000 live births): 5·0; Stillborn rate, 4·5 per 1,000 births. Expectation of life, 1996: Men, 73·3 years; women, 79·7. Suicide rates over 1990–95, per 100,000 population, 17·5 (men, 24·9; women, 10·7). Fertility rate, 1990–95, 1·3 births per woman.

Legislation of 1995 categorizes abortions as illegal, but stipulates that prosecutions will not be brought if they are performed in the first 3 months of pregnancy after consultation with a doctor.

CLIMATE

Oceanic influences are only found in the north-west where winters are quite mild but stormy. Elsewhere a continental climate is general. To the east and south, winter temperatures are lower, with bright frosty weather and considerable snowfall. Summer temperatures are fairly uniform throughout. Berlin, Jan. 31°F (−0·5°C), July 66°F (19°C). Annual rainfall 22·5" (563 mm). Dresden, Jan. 30°F (−0·1°C), July 65°F (18·5°C). Annual rainfall 27·2" (680 mm). Frankfurt, Jan. 33°F (0·6°C), July 66°F (18·9°C). Annual rainfall 24" (601 mm). Hamburg, Jan. 31°F (−0·6°C), July 63°F (17·2°C). Annual rainfall 29" (726 mm). Hanover, Jan. 33°F (0·6°C), July 64°F (17·8°C). Annual rainfall 24" (604 mm). Köln, Jan. 36°F (2·2°C), July 66°F (18·9°C). Annual rainfall 27" (676 mm). Munich, Jan. 28°F (−2·2°C), July 63°F (17·2°C). Annual rainfall 34" (855 mm). Stuttgart, Jan. 33°F (0·6°C), July 66°F (18·9°C). Annual rainfall 27" (677 mm).

LANGUAGE

The official language is German. 'High German' as spoken today evolved from the 16th century when Luther's translation of the Bible into Modern High German became the accepted form of the language. Prior to this Old and Middle High German were spoken, the latter becoming standard form in 1100 AD and the language of medieval literature.

High German is generally spoken today, although various regional dialects exist, and Low German, derived from Old Saxon and Middle Low German, is still spoken in the northern lowlands.

The Gothic script favoured by the Nazis and often associated with them no longer appears in print.

An agreement between German-speaking countries in Vienna on 1 July 1996 provided for minor orthographical changes and established a Commission for German Orthography in Mannheim. There have been considerable objections within Germany, particularly in the North, and many Länder are to decide their own language programmes for schools. Generally, both old and new spellings are acceptable.

CONSTITUTION AND GOVERNMENT

The Basic Law (*Grundgesetz*) was approved by the parliaments of the participating Länder and came into force on 23 May 1949. The Federal Republic is a democratic and social constitutional state on a parliamentary basis. The federation is constituted by the 16 Länder (states). The Basic Law decrees that the general rules of international law form part of the federal law. The constitutions of the Länder must conform to the principles of a republican, democratic and social state based on the rule of law. Executive power is vested in the Länder, unless the Basic Law prescribes or permits otherwise. Federal law takes precedence over state law.

Legislative power is vested in the *Bundestag* (Federal Assembly) and the *Bundesrat* (Federal Council). The Bundestag is currently composed of 669 members and is elected in universal, free, equal and secret elections for a term of 4 years. A party must gain 5% of total votes cast in order to gain representation in the Bundestag, although if a party gets 3 candidates elected directly, they may take their seats even if the party obtains less than 5% of the national vote. The electoral system combines relative-majority and proportional voting; each voter has 2 votes, the first for the direct constituency representative, the second for the competing party lists in the Länder. All directly elected constituency representatives enter parliament, but if a party receives more 'indirect' than 'direct' votes, the first name in order on the party list not to have a seat becomes a member – the number of seats is increased by the difference ('overhang votes'). Thus the number of seats in the Bundestag varies, but is usually around 670. The Bundesrat consists of 69 members appointed by the governments of the Länder in proportions determined by the number of inhabitants. Each *Land* has at least 3 votes.

The Head of State is the Federal *President* who is elected for a 5-year term by a *Federal Convention* specially convened for this purpose. This Convention consists of all the members of the Bundestag and an equal number of members elected by the Länder parliaments in accordance with party strengths, but who need not themselves be members of the parliaments. No president may serve more than 2 terms. Executive power is vested in the Federal Government, which consists of the Federal *Chancellor*, elected by the Bundestag on the proposal of the Federal President, and the Federal Ministers, who are appointed and dismissed by the Federal President upon the proposal of the Federal Chancellor.

The Federal Republic has exclusive legislation on: (1) foreign affairs (2) federal citizenship; (3) freedom of movement, passports, immigration and emigration, and extradition; (4) currency, money and coinage, weights and measures, and regulation of time and calendar; (5) customs, commercial and navigation agreements, traffic in goods and payments with foreign countries, including customs and frontier protection; (6) federal railways and air traffic; (7) post and telecommunications; (8) the legal status of persons in the employment of the Federation and of public law corporations under direct supervision of the Federal Government; (9) trade marks, copyright and publishing rights; (10) co-operation of the Federal Republic and the Länder in the criminal police and in matters concerning the protection of the constitution, the establishment of a Federal Office of Criminal Police, as well as the combating of international crime; (11) federal statistics.

In the field of finance the Federal Republic has exclusive legislation on customs and financial monopolies and concurrent legislation on: (1) excise taxes and taxes on transactions, in particular, taxes on real-estate acquisition, incremented value and on fire protection; (2) taxes on income, property, inheritance and donations; (3) real estate, industrial and trade taxes, with the exception of the determining of the tax rates. The Federal Republic can claim part of the income and corporation taxes to cover its expenditures not covered by other revenues. Financial jurisdiction is uniformly regulated by federal legislation.

Federal laws are passed by the Bundestag and after their adoption submitted to the Bundesrat, which has a limited veto. The Basic Law may be amended only upon the approval of two-thirds of the members of the Bundestag and two-thirds of the votes of the Bundesrat.

FURTHER READING

Die Bundesrepublik Deutschland: Staatshandbuch. Cologne, annual
Hucko, E. M. (ed.) *The Democratic Tradition* [Texts of German constitutions].
Leamington Spa, 1987

Koch, J. W., *A Constitutional History of Germany in the Nineteenth and Twentieth Centuries.* London, 1984

König, K. et al. (eds.) Public Administration in the Federal Republic of Germany. Boston (MA), 1983

National Anthem

'Einigkeit und Recht und Freiheit' ('Unity and right and freedom'); words by H. Hoffmann, tune by J. Haydn.

RECENT ELECTIONS

On 23 May 1999 Johannes Rau was elected President by the Federal Convention against 2 opponents.

Bundestag elections were held on 27 Sept. 1998; the electorate was 60·5m. (31·75m. women; 28·75m. men) including 3·3m. first-time voters. There were a record 5,062 candidates competing for the 656 seats, 27·3% of them women. The age of the candidates ranged from 18 to 96. Turn-out was 80·2%. The Social Democratic Party (SPD) won 298 seats with 40·9% of votes cast (252 with 36·4% in 1994); the Christian Democratic Union/Christian Social Union (CDU/CSU; the CSU is a Bavarian party where the CDU does not stand) won 245 seats with 35·2% of votes cast (294 with 41·4% in 1994); the Greens, 47 with 6·6% (49 with 7·3%); the Free Democratic Party (FDP), 44 seats with 6·2% (47 with 6·9%); the Party for Democratic Socialism (PDS; former Communists), 35 with 5·2% (30 with 4·4%). With the SPD forming an alliance with the Green party, the new government had a 21-seat majority. This was the first time in the Federal Republic's 49 year history that a government changed through the ballot box rather than through a reshuffling of coalition partners between elections. However, in 6 out of 7 state elections during the 12 months that followed the SPD was defeated. As a result the government has lost its majority in the 69-seat Bundesrat (the upper house of parliament).

European Parliament. Germany has 99 representatives. At the June 1999 elections turn-out was 45·2%. The CDU won 43 seats with 39·3% of votes cast (group in European Parliament: Popular European Party); the SPD, 33 with 30·7% (European Socialist Party); the CSU, 10 with 9·4% (Popular European Party); the Greens, 7 with 6·4% (Greens); PDS, 6 with 5·8% (Confederal Group of the European United Left).

CURRENT ADMINISTRATION

Federal President: Johannes Rau, b. 1931 (SPD; sworn in 1 July 1999).

Speaker of the Bundestag: Rita Süssmuth (elected Nov. 1988; re-elected Nov. 1994).

In Oct. 1998 an SPD-Green party coalition was formed, the first time that the Green party had entered national government in Germany. The government comprised in Sept. 1999:

Chancellor: Gerhard Schröder (b. 1944; SPD).

Vice-Chancellor and Foreign Minister: Joschka Fischer (Greens). *Interior:* Otto Schily (SPD). *Justice:* Herta Däubler-Gmelin (SPD). *Finance:* Hans Eichel (SPD). *Economy:* Werner Müller (Ind.). *Food, Agriculture and Forestry:* Karl-Heinz Funke (SPD). *Labour and Social Affairs:* Walter Riester (SPD). *Defence:* Rudolf Scharping (SPD). *Family, Youth, Women and Senior Citizens:* Christine Bergmann (SPD). *Health:* Andrea Fischer (Greens). *Transport and Construction:* Franz Müntefering (SPD). *Environment, Nature Conservation and Reactor Safety:* Jürgen Trittin (Greens). *Education and Research:* Edelgard Bulmahn (SPD). *Economic Co-operation and Development:* Heidemarie Wieczorek-Zeul (SPD).

POLITICAL AND FINANCIAL PROFILES

Johannes Rau

President of the Federal Republic of Germany

On 23 May 1999, Johannes Rau succeeded Roman Herzog as the eighth Federal President. He was born in Wuppertal-Barmen in North Rhine-Westphalia in 1931 to parents whose strongly religious humanist views would later influence him to enter politics and earn him the nickname 'Bruder Johannes' (Father John). Between 1945 and 1951 he worked as a publishers' apprentice, a journalist and a bookseller. In 1952 he became a member of the All German People's Party (Gesamtdeutsche Volkspartei – GVP) and then in 1957 a member of the Social Democratic Party (SPD). He was a member of the North Rhine-Westphalia Landtag (state government) between 1958 and 1998 and served as the Minister President of the State from 1978 to 1998. He is also deputy chairman of the SDFP. Under his leadership, the North Rhine-Westphalian government transformed the Rhine and Ruhr districts from a narrow industrialized economy to a forward-looking region with high-tech and modern service industries.

Gerhard Schröder

Chancellor of the Federal Republic of Germany

Gerhard Schröder was born in 1944 in Mossenberg-Lippe. After his schooling, Schröder took an apprenticeship as a retail assistant and attended evening school. He went on to study law at Göttingen University, was admitted to practice as a lawyer in 1976 and worked as an independent lawyer in Hanover from 1978–90. Schröder joined the SPD in 1978 and acted as chairman of the young socialists from 1978–80. He entered the *Bundestag* in 1980. He was head of the SPD parliamentary group in the State Parliament of Lower Saxony from 1986 until 1990. When the people of Lower Saxony voted him into office with an absolute majority, Gerhard Schröder became minister-president of Lower Saxony four years later and served until 1998.

Gerhard Schröder was elected seventh chancellor of the Federal Republic of Germany with the votes of the SPD, Alliance 90 and the Greens on 27 Oct. 1998. He became leader of the SPD following an election after Oskar Lafontaine's resignation in March 1999.

Joschka Fischer

Federal Minster of Foreign Affairs, Vice-Chancellor of the Federal Republic of Germany and Leader of the Green Party (Die Grünen)
Fischer was born on 12 April 1948 in Gerabronn in Baden-Württemberg. He joined the Green party in 1982 and was elected one of German's first Green Party MPs in the elections of 1983, at the height of the protest movement against the US deployment of Pershing II and cruise missiles. In his election campaign he advocated the immediate shutdown of nuclear plants, a shorter working week, withdrawal from NATO and the dismantling of the German army. In the Bundestag, Fischer gained a reputation for being outspoken and humorous. He emerged as leader of the Greens after the failure of the party to win seats in the elections of 1990. His 'Realo' faction wanted to work within the political system pursuing environmental goals while the 'Fundi' (or fundamentalist) faction advocated a purist ideology and pushed for extraparliamentary roots and change at local level. Fischer's ideology elevated the Green Party above grassroots and began to appeal to young professionals and others whose parents would never have voted Green. Despite his former stance on the army, Fischer now saw Germany militarily bound to the West, if not through NATO then through a European Alliance. In 1994, the Greens were returned to Bonn with 7·3% of the vote. Between 1990 and 1995, the Green Party replaced the Free Democratic Party as the third force in German politics and after the elections of 1998, Joschka Fischer was appointed Federal Minister of Foreign Affairs in the coalition government under the Chancellorship of Gerhard Schröder.

Hans Eichel

Federal Minister of Finance

Hans Eichel was born on Christmas Eve 1941 in Kassel. He studied philosophy, political science and history at Marburg and Berlin and joined the Social Democratic Party of Germany (SPD) in 1964. Between 1969 and 1972, he served as Chairman of the Young Socialists (Jusos). He held a number of posts in Kassel (Hesse) including Chairman of the SPD group in Kassel City Council (1970–75), Lord Mayor of Kassel (1975–91) and Minister President of the State of Hesse (1991–99). He served as Chairman of the Hesse State SPD from 1989 until his appointment as Federal Minster of Finance in 1999. Eichel took over as Finance Minister after the surprise resignation of Oskar Lafontaine. Hans Eichel has worked closely with Ernst Welteke (the newly appointed head of the Bundesbank from Sept. 1999) and the two men are expected to work towards restoring business confidence and economic growth. His agenda includes corporate tax reform and a reassessment of some personal taxes.

Wolfgang Schäuble

Leader of the Christian Democratic Union (Christlich Demokratische Union) (CDU)

Born in 1943, Wolfgang Schäuble is a pro-European, agreeing with Helmut Kohl's view that Europe's fate and that of Germany are inextricably bound together. Losing the elections of 1998 traumatized the CDU and Schäuble, who was backed by Kohl for the leadership, has faced a formidable task in restoring party confidence. His reputation for dogged determination was tested in 1990 when an assassination attempt left him paralyzed from the chest down. Within a month of the attack Schäuble was working from his hospital bed. Wolfgang Schäuble's task is to rebuild party support around his policy of economic and structural reform combined with Christian values while keeping the extreme factions of the party united. The CDU invariably finds itself united with the CSU in opposing the SPD-led government.

Edmund Stoiber

Leader of the Christian Social Union (Christlich Soziale Union) in Bavaria (CSU)

Edmund Stoiber has been Prime Minister of Bavaria since 1993. He was born in 1941 and stands firmly on the political right of German politics with pro-business and pro-family ideals. He coined the slogan 'lap-top and Lederhosen', signifying the combination of tradition and innovation that has helped to attract inward investment to his region. At the last elections, the CSU attracted 53% of the vote in Bavaria, where its support is impregnable. Stoiber has a reputation for self-reliance and he is more sceptical than most other German politicians towards European integration and Brussels centralization.

Ernst Welteke

Head of the Bundesbank

Hans Welteke, who succeeded Hans Tietmeyer as head of the Bundesbank after his retirement in Aug. 1999, was born in 1943. He comes to the Bundesbank after serving as head of the central bank of Hesse. He has a close relationship with Hans Eichel, Federal Minster of Finance, which should stand him in good stead as he faces the challenge of implementing the Euro with the consequent shift of control of monetary policy to the European Central Bank.

Oskar Lafontaine

Born in Saarlouis and educated at Bonn University, Lafontaine was Chairman of the SPD from 1977 to 1996, having served as Mayor of Saarbrücken from 1976–85. His radicalism earned him various titles including 'Red Oskar' and the 'Ayatollah of the Saarland'. After his election as Prime Minister of the Saarland regional Parliament in 1985 he began to mellow. He was the SPD candidate as chancellor in the 1990 general election. He became leader of the SPD in 1995, was President of the SPD controlled Bundesrat (or upper chamber) and was made Finance Minister in Gerhard Schröder's government in Nov. 1998. Lafontaine resigned from all his political positions and posts in March 1999.

Helmut Kohl

In Nov. 1994 the 64-year-old Helmut Kohl was elected to serve his thirteenth year as Chancellor of Germany. Despite winning confirmation by the slimmest margin of his long political career, Kohl claimed that his fragile coalition government would hold together. He reflected that his mentor, former chancellor Konrad Adenauer, had won his first election by a narrow margin and went on to rule Germany for 14 years, a record that Kohl was eager to break. He remained as Chancellor until the elections of 1998, when he was defeated by Gerhard Schröder (SPD).

Kohl was born in Ludwigshafen am Rhein, on 3 April 1930. He studied at the University of Frankfurt and received a Ph.D. from the University of Heidelberg in 1958. Entering politics the next year, he was elected to the Rhineland-Palatinate state legislature. He became minister-president (Prime Minister) of that state in 1969 and served until 1976 when he was elected to the Bundestag (parliament), where he became Christian Democratic floor leader. After losing his bid for chancellor in the 1976 election, Kohl did not run again until 1982, when changes in the makeup of the coalition government resulted in his confirmation as chancellor. He was re-elected in 1987 and 1990.

German reunification, of which Kohl had long dreamed, was achieved in Oct. 1990 with the signing of the Two-plus-Four Treaty. But the resulting financial and social problems were formidable. Efforts to integrate the economically depressed former East Germany with the prosperous West took public debt to unprecedented levels. Unemployment hit record levels, and the recession was showing no signs of letting up. Unification was a continuing drain on funds, while Germany's allies urged that the government become a more active player in the European and international arena. However, as the economy began to recover, Kohl was viewed once again as a steadying influence. In the 1994 election he was elected for a fourth term by the narrowest of majorities. Helmut Kohl left office in Oct. 1998 when the office of Chancellor passed to Gerhard Schröder.

Konrad Adenauer (1876–1967)

Konrad Adenauer, born in Cologne, was the Federal Republic of Germany's first Chancellor. Adenauer, a graduate of law, was elected to the Cologne City Council in 1906. During World War I he was chosen as Oberbürgermeister (Lord Mayor) of Cologne. This was a job that he took to well and he remained in this post until 1933.

With the rise of Nazi power in Germany Adenauer was persecuted and lost his positions of political prominence in Cologne. In 1944 he was sent to a concentration camp. After World War II Adenauer was briefly restored to office in Cologne, only to be removed again, this time by British officials. Released from the shackles of political power in Cologne, Adenauer was now able to devote all his energy to the formation of the new Christian Democratic Union, a political party established by Catholics and Protestants to oppose Nazism and promote economic growth in a devastated Germany. In 1946 Adenauer became the CDU's chairman in the British zone of occupation and soon after became its President. When the Allies conceded a federal style government to West Germany Adenauer became its President. The Parliamentary Council produced a provisional constitution for the proposed republic. In 1949 the CDU formed a coalition with the CSU (Christian Social Union) and won the election to the first Bundestag. As Party President of the CDU for all of West Germany Adenauer became the Federal Republic's first Chancellor, a position he held until 1963. Adenauer was innately suspicious of communist intentions in the Eastern Block and sought to fortify West Germany against the threat of communist expansion. To do this he knew he would have to reconcile Germany with its recent enemies. In 1951 Adenauer established a German Foreign Office, he established West Germany as a member of the Council of Europe and he was a co-founder of the project for the European Defence Community. In 1955, four years after its founding, West Germany joined the North Atlantic Peace Treaty. Under Adenauer West Germany was a founding member of the European Economic Community, established in 1958. It was only after his success in signing a treaty of co-operation with France in 1963 and as a result of increasing pressure from within his coalition government that Konrad Adenauer resigned as West Germany's Chancellor.

Despite being attacked for doing little to promote the reunification of Germany, Adenauer was a very popular and well-respected statesman. When he died in 1967 at the age of 91, many politicians from around the world attended his funeral.

Willy Brandt (1913–92)

Willy Brandt, German Statesman and Nobel Laureate, was born Herbert Ernst Karl Frahm in Lübeck, Schleswig-Holstein.

At the outbreak of World War II Brandt was a Social Democrat. This brought him into direct conflict with the Gestapo and he fled Germany and changed his name to escape arrest. Whilst living in Norway he became a journalist. In response to the German invasion and occupation of Norway Brandt fled to Sweden where he remained for the duration of the war.

After the war, Brandt returned to Germany where he was urged to return to politics.

He was elected Berlin's representative on the Social Democratic Party Executive Committee. He was elected as a member of the federal parliament in 1949. In 1957 he became Governor Mayor of West Berlin. It was during this time that he sadly witnessed the erection of the Berlin Wall. In 1964 he became Chairman of the SPD.

After forming a coalition government with the Free Democratic Party he was elected as Chancellor in 1970. It was from this political vantagepoint that Brandt was able to promote peace within and towards Germany. He worked hard to relax the tension between East and West Germany, forming a policy he called 'Ostpolitik' (Eastern Policy).

He signed a nuclear non-proliferation treaty and non-aggression treaties with Poland and the Soviet Union. In his role as Chancellor and later, from 1987, as Chairman of the SDP he tirelessly sought the reunification of East and West Germany, a crusade that earned him the Nobel Prize for Peace in 1971. In 1974 Willy Brandt resigned as Chancellor of the Federal Republic of Germany after it was revealed that his colleague and aide, Günther Guillaume, was in fact an East German secret agent.

Helmut Schmidt

Helmut Schmidt, German statesman and publisher of the influential *Die Zeit*, was born in 1918 in Hamburg to a half Jewish teacher. During World War II Schmidt served in an armoured division on the eastern front and in the Ardennes. After the war he joined the Social Democratic party. In 1953 he was elected to the Bundestag, the Lower House of the legislative chambers of the Federal Republic. He served two terms in the Bundestag before being elected Vice Chairman of the Social Democratic Party in 1968.

Schmidt's term in office as Chancellor came with the resignation of Willy Brandt after a spy scandal. (See Willy Brandt profile above). Schmidt proved to be a popular Chancellor and he continued many of the popular policies of Willy Brandt. He continued to promote better ties with East Germany and the Soviet Union, and he attempted to heal the old wounds between France and Germany, and economic co-operation among western European nations. In response to his insistence to follow an unpopular social welfare policy the Free Democratic Party left the coalition that had given the SPD their mandate to govern. Schmidt resigned from his post in 1982 following a vote of no confidence from the Bundestag. Schmidt went on to serve in the Bundestag until 1987 and has been publisher of *Die Zeit* (The Times), a review and critique of politics, since 1983.

LOCAL GOVERNMENT

The 16 Länder are divided into a total of 29 administrative regions (*Regierungsbezirke*). Below Land level local government is carried on by elected councils to 426 rural districts (*Landkreise*) and 117 urban districts (*Kreisfreie Städte*), which form the electoral districts for the *Land* governments, and are subdivided into 16,043 communes (*Gemeinden*).

DEFENCE

Defence Budget

Defence expenditure, in Deutsche Marks (DM):

1995 expenditure	DM58,986m. (US$41,249m.)
1996 expenditure	DM58,671m. (US$41,908m.)
1997 expenditure	DM57,947m. (US$36,217m.)
1998 budget	DM46,700m. (US$25,944m.)
1999 budget	DM47,283m. (US$27,814m.)

Government expenditure plans approved in June 1999 forecast the defence budget as:

2000	DM45,333m.
2001	DM44,807m.
2002	DM44,493m.
2003	DM43,678m.

Up to DM2,000m. may be added to the annual defence outlay to cover peacekeeping deployments, such as to the Balkans in 1999. Peacekeeping funds may not be transferred to the defence budget.

Strength of Armed Forces

The active strength of the Armed Forces is:

Army	230,600	
Navy	26,700	(includes Naval Air)
Air Force	76,200	
Total	*333,500*	

The Armed Forces are organized into Reaction Forces and Main Defence Forces. Reaction Forces within the above totals are: Army, 37,000; Navy, 40% of assets on a rotating basis; and Air Force, 12,300. Main Defence Forces have responsibility for the defence of Germany; they also train conscripts and provide a backup for Reaction Forces. Officers and Non-Commissioned Officers are required to serve in the Reserve until they are 60; the remainder until they are 45. The total number of Reserves is about 315,000 (Army, 258,000; Navy, 10,200; Air Force, 46,800).

Paramilitary Forces

The 20,000-strong Border Police (BGS) is a paramilitary force, with its own procurement procedures.

Conscription

Compulsory male conscription, which is an emotive issue, is for
10 months. Of the Armed Forces' strength of 333,500, an estimated
137,500 (41%) are conscripts. Within the Services approximately 48%
of the Army, 18% of the Navy and 29% of the Air Force are conscripts.

Nuclear Capability

Germany has no nuclear weapons.

Policy

The legacy of German unification has been a massive debt load,
which is to be addressed from 2000 with severe expenditure cuts
throughout Government. While Germany sees itself as a good
European and as an accepted diplomatic force, it is acknowledged
as not being a totally 'normal' country and unlikely to be one in the
foreseeable future. Germany's history remains fresh in many of its
neighbours' minds.

On 3 May 1999 the Defence Minister appointed a Commission to
examine the future structure and tasks of the Bundeswehr (Armed
Forces). Chaired by a former President of Germany, the Commission
is due to report by 15 Sept. 2000. Issues to be examined by the
Commission include the size, structure and equipment of the
Bundeswehr and the future for conscription. The Commission is
working on the assumption that Germany will continue as a member of
NATO and that the Armed Forces will be committed to the Alliance
while the security capability of the European Union is strengthened.
At the inaugural meeting of the Bundeswehr Commission, the Defence
Minister presented a summary of his findings since taking office in
Oct. 1998. Points made by the Minister included:

a) The Armed Forces require an overhaul, since they are structured
   for the end of the Cold War and not for an increasing peacekeeping
   role.

b) With over 6,000 serving in the Balkans there was 'not much latitude left'. The limited size of Reaction Forces was exacerbated by a growing shortage of officers, shortage of material and a lack of funds.

c) All three Services were 'structurally distorted'.

The severe budget cuts announced by the Government in June 1999 appear to pre-empt any conclusions which the Bundeswehr Commission may reach. A despondent Defence Minister was quoted as saying that 'You can not permanently play in the world league of foreign affairs while sliding into the second league of security policy'.

INTERNATIONAL RELATIONS

A treaty of friendship with Poland signed on 17 June 1991 recognized the Oder-Neisse border and guaranteed minorities' rights in both countries.

Germany is a member of the UN, OECD, EU, WEU, NATO and the Council of Europe, and is a signatory to the Schengen Accord which abolishes border controls between Germany, Austria, Belgium, Denmark, Finland, France, Greece, Iceland, Italy, Luxembourg, the Netherlands, Norway, Portugal, Spain and Sweden.

ECONOMY

After more than a generation as the driving force of Europe, the German economy has shown recent signs of faltering. Industrial productivity is far higher than in neighbouring countries but so too are wages. Average unit costs of production in Germany are £16·40 an hour compared with £9·80 in Britain. Unemployment at 4·5m. is at its highest level since the war while the cost of reconstructing the east German economy has put a heavy burden on the public debt. But on the plus side, German workers are better trained than elsewhere, labour relations are excellent and there are growing export opportunities in the emerging countries of eastern and central Europe. 1999 has seen a modest upturn in industrial output. Much now depends on the government's ability to hold down public spending, particularly on social welfare (state pensions, for example, have been pegged at an incredible 20% of average earnings) while introducing more flexible working practices to stimulate entrepreneurial skills. The recent package of budget cuts and tax and pension reforms worth £2·6bn. a year is a pointer to the way forward.

Germany's GNP per capita in 1996 for purchasing power was $21,110.

Performance

Real GDP growth was 1·3% in 1996, 2·2% in 1997, and forecast to rise to 2·7% in 1998. Growth in the Länder of the former German Democratic Republic was estimated to be around 0·6% lower than the overall national average in both 1997 and 1998.

Budget

Tax reforms introduced by the Schröder government in 1998 mean the average working family will be 2,700 DM better off by 2002. The cost is to be borne by industry through the ending or tightening of tax reliefs. A tax reform package announced in June 1999 will mean pensions rising less quickly over the next couple of years than in the past, unemployment benefit being reduced and the civil service bureaucracy being shaved. The benchmark corporate tax rate is being cut from 40% to 25%.

Since 1 Jan. 1979 tax revenues have been distributed as follows:
Federal Government. Income tax, 42·5%; capital yield and corporation tax, 50%; turnover tax, 67·5%; trade tax, 15%; capital gains,
insurance and accounts taxes, 100%; excise duties (other than on
beer), 100%. Länder. Income tax, 42·5%; capital yield and corporation tax, 50%; turnover tax, 32·5%; trade tax, 15%; other taxes,
100%. Local authorities. Income tax, 15%; trade tax, 70%; local
taxes, 100%.

VAT is 16% (reduced rate, 7%).

Budget for 1998 (in 1m. DM):

Revenue	All public authorities	Federal portion
	Current	
Taxes	730,176	369,554
Economic activities	17,367	8,937
Interest	5,652	2,242
Current allocations and subsidies	134,354	5,477
Other receipts	31,787	11,209
minus equalising payments	113,740	. . .
	805,596	397,419
	Capital	
Sale of assets	47,156	36,405
Allocations for investment	27,633	5
Repayment of loans	12,274	4,277
Public sector borrowing	738	. . .
minus equalising payments	24,544	. . .
	63,257	40,688
Totals	871,291	438,107

Expenditure		Current
Staff	248,621	52,472
Materials	84,704	39,557
Interest	128,939	56,490
Allocations and subsidies	489,831	287,540
minus equalising payments	113,740	. . .
	838,355	436,059
		Capital
Construction	23,516	11,262
Acquisition of property	6,992	2,402
Allocations and subsidies	88,842	34,739
Loans	27,576	9,690
Acquisition of shares	3,071	1,367
Repayments in the public sector	910	. . .
minus equalising payments	24,544	. . .
	126,363	59,460
Totals	960,072	494,593

The current account balance for 1997 was a provisional deficit of 10·1bn. DM.

Currency

On 1 Jan. 1999 the euro (EUR) became the legal currency in Germany and the *deutsche Mark* became a subdivision of it, at an irrevocable conversion rate of 1·95583 DM to 1 euro. The euro, which consists of 100 cents, will not be in circulation until 1 Jan. 2002. There will be 7 euro notes in different colours and sizes denominated in 500, 200, 100, 50, 20, 10 and 5 euros, and 8 coins denominated in 2 and 1 euros, then 50, 20, 10, 5, 2 and 1 cents. The euro is already in use in banking for cheques, travellers' cheques, bank transfers, credit cards and electronic purses. Banking will be possible in both euros and deutsche Marks until the deutsche Mark is withdrawn from circulation – which must be by 1 July 2002.

The *deutsche Mark* (DEM) consists of 100 *pfennig* (pf.). In Feb. 1998 gold reserves were 95·18m. troy oz. (only the USA, with 261·7m. troy oz., had more), and foreign exchange reserves were US$69,257m. Inflation was at a record low of 0·9% in 1998, down from 1·8% in 1997. Total money supply in Feb. 1998 was 864bn. DM.

Banking and Finance

The Deutsche Bundesbank (German Federal Bank) is the central bank and bank of issue. Its duty is to protect the stability of the currency. It is independent of the government but obliged to support the government's general policy. Its Governor is appointed by the government for 8 years. The *Governor* is Ernst Welteke (b. 1943). Its assets were 369,463m. DM in 1997. There are 340 commercial private banks including the 'Big Three' – the Deutsche Bank, Dresdner Bank and Commerzbank. The former GDR central bank Staatsbank has become a public commercial bank. In 1997 there were 3,414 credit institutes, including 326 banks, 598 savings banks, 35 mortgage lenders and 2,420 credit societies. They are represented in the wholesale market by the 12 public sector Länder banks. (see each Land for details). Total assets, 1997, 9,109,858m. DM. Savings deposits were 1,204,999m. DM in 1997. A single stock exchange, the Deutsche Börse, was created in 1992, based on the former Frankfurt stock exchange in a union with the smaller exchanges in Berlin, Bremen, Düsseldorf, Hamburg, Hanover, Munich and Stuttgart (see Länder for details).

Deutsche Bundesbank: Wilhelm-Epstein Str. 14, 60431 Frankfurt am Main. Tel: (0)69 95661. Fax: (0)69 5601071.

Founded 1957. Issues bank notes and regulates note and coin circulation and supply of credit. Although an independent organization which advises the government on monetary policy, the Bank is required to support government policy. Government members may take part in deliberations but not vote.

Marsh, D., *The Bundesbank: the Bank that Rules Europe*. London, 1992

Private Commercial Banks

Deutsche Bank AG: Central Office: Taunusanlage 12, 60325 Frankfurt am Main.

Tel: (0)69 91000. Fax: (0)69 71504225.

Founded 1870. One of the 'Big Three' private banks in Germany.

Gull, L. *et al., The Deutsche Bank, 1870–1995.* London, 1996

Dresdner Bank AG: Central Office: Jürgen-Ponto-Platz 1, 60301 Frankfurt am Main. Postfach 110661.

Tel: (0)69 2630. Fax: (0)69 2634831.

Founded 1872. One of the 'Big Three' private banks in Germany.

Commerzbank AG: Neue Mainzer Str. 32–36, 60311 Frankfurt am Main; Postfach 100505, 60005 Frankfurt am Main. Tel: (0)69 13620. Fax: (0)69 285389.

Founded 1870. One of the 'Big Three' private banks in Germany.

Selected commercial banks

Bankhaus Max Flessa & Co: Luitpoldstr. 2–6, 97421 Schweinfurt.

Tel: (0)9721 5310. Fax: (0)9721 531231.

Bayerische Hypotheken- und Wechsel-Bank AG (Hypo-Bank): Arabellastr. 12, 81925 München.

Tel: (0)89 92440. Fax: (0)89 92442880.

Berliner Volksbank eG: Kaiserdamm 86, 14057 Berlin.
Tel: (0)30 30630. Fax: (0)30 30631550.

Landesgirokasse: Königstrasse 3–5, 70144 Stuttgart.
Tel: (0)711 1240. Fax: (0)711 1244144.

Weberbank Berliner Industriebank KgaA: Landecker Str. 2–3, 14199
Berlin.
Tel: (0)30 897980. Fax: (0)30 8243003.

Westfalenbank AG: Huestr. 21–25, 44787 Bochum.
Tel: (0)234 6160. Fax: (0)234 616400.

Central Bank of Co-operative Banking System

DG BANK Deutsche Genossenschaftsbank: Am Platz der Republik,
60325 Frankfurt am Main.
Tel: (0)69 744701. Fax: (0)69 74471685.

Founded 1949. A specialist wholesale bank and central institution
in the co-operative German banking sector (there are 3,184 local
cooperative banks, three regional central banks and a number of specialist financial institutions).

Public Law Credit Institutions

Deutsche Girozentrale-Deutsche Kommunalbank: Taunusanlage 10,
60329 Frankfurt am Main. Postfach 110542, 60040 Frankfurt am Main.
Tel: (0)69 2693-0. Fax: (0)69 26932490.

Founded 1918. Central clearing house.

Bayerische Landesbank Girozentrale: Brienner Str. 20, 80333
München.
Tel: (0)89 217101. Fax: (0)89 21713579.

L-Bank Landeskreditbank Baden-Württemberg: Schlossplatz 10–12,
76113 Karlsruhe.
Tel: (0)721 1500. Fax: (0)721 1501001.

Landesbank Berlin Girozentrale: Bundesallee 171, 10889 Berlin-Wilmersdorf.

Tel: (0)30 86901. Fax: (0)30 24557640.

Landesbank Schleswig-Holstein Girozentrale: Martensdamm 6, 24103 Kiel.

Tel: (0)431 90001. Fax: (0)431 9002446.

Norddeutsche Landesbank Girozentrale: Georgplatz 1, 30159 Hannover.

Tel: (0)511 3610. Fax: (0)511 3612502.

Bankers Organizations

Bundesverband deutscher Banken: Postfach 100555, 50455 Köln.

Tel: (0)221 16630. Fax: (0)221 1663280.

(Association of German Banks) – founded 1951.

Bundesverband der deutschen Volksbanken und Raiffeisenbanken eV: Heussallee 5, Postfach 120440, 53113 Bonn.

Tel: (0)228 5090. Fax: (0)228 509201.

Association of German Industrial and Agricultural Credit Co-operatives – founded 1971.

Bundesverband öffentlicher Banken Deutschlands eV: Godesberger Allee 88, 53175 Bonn. Tel: (0)228 81920.

Association of German Public-Sector Banks.

Deutscher Sparkassen- und Giroverband eV: Simrockstr. 4, Postfach 1429, 53113 Bonn.

Tel: (0)228 2040. Fax: (0)228 204250.

German Savings Bank Association.

Stock Exchange

Frankfurt am Main: Deutsche Börse AG, Börsenplatz 4, 60313 Frankfurt am Main. Tel: (0)69 29977-0. Fax: (0)69 29977580.

Founded in 1585 as the Frankfurter Wertpapierbörse (became the main German stock exchange in 1992). (See Länder for details of other stock exchanges).

Weights and Measures

The metric system is in force.

ENERGY AND NATURAL RESOURCES

Environmental Policy

Responsibility for environmental matters at Federal level lies with the Federal Ministry for the Environment, Nature Conservation and Nuclear Safety. Each of the federal states has a ministry for the environment.

The Federal policy is based on three main principles.

1. The Prevention Principle: New projects (industrial and others) are to be developed in such a way as to avoid pollution and/or damage to the environment.
2. The 'Polluter Pays' principle: The organization or person causing the pollution or environmental damage is the person who pays to put it right or repair the damage.
3. The Co-operation Principle: Government, the business community, citizens and groups in society join forces to solve environmental problems since the responsibility for safeguarding the environment lies with each individual.

A comprehensive clean air policy has been introduced dealing with emission from power plants, factories, car exhausts etc. by the use of filters and catalytic converters. Unleaded gasoline is widely used and all new cars throughout the EU (European Community) must be fitted with the new three-way catalytic converter that limits the emissions of nitrogen oxide, hydrocarbons and carbon monoxide.

Measures have been introduced to minimize the introduction of pollutants into the waterway systems and Germany is a signatory to international agreements designed to limit pollution across boundaries.

The Federal Government has introduced a waste management policy at both national and individual level, based on the principle of avoiding waste in the first place and then concentrating on recycling the rest.

Electricity

Installed capacity in 1994 was 109·73m. kW. In 1994 there were 21 nuclear reactors. Production was 529·1bn. kWh in 1995, of which about a third was nuclear. There is a moratorium on further nuclear plant construction. Consumption per capita was estimated to be 5,727 kWh in 1995.

Oil and Gas

The chief oilfields are in Emsland (Lower Saxony). In 1996, 2·85m. tonnes of crude oil were produced. Gas production was 899,208,000 MWh in 1994, of which 818,034,000 MWh were natural gas.

Minerals

The main production areas are: North Rhine-Westphalia (for coal, iron and metal smelting-works), Central Germany (for lignite), and Lower Saxony (Salzgitter for iron ore; the Harz for metal ore).

Production (in tonnes), 1997: Coal, 46,791,557; lignite, 177,159,708.

Agriculture

Land in agricultural use, 1997 (in 1,000 ha): 17,327·1, including arable, 11,831·6; pasture, 5,268·4. Sown areas included: Wheat, 2,719·7; rye,

843·4; barley, 2,208·4; oats, 312·4; maize, 368·3; potatoes, 303·6; sugar-beet, 507·7; rape, 914·0; fodder, 1,796·2. Crop production, 1997 (and 1994) (in 1,000 tonnes): Wheat, 19,826·8 (16,480·5); rye, 4,580·1 (3,450·6); barley, 13,398·9 (10,902·5); oats, 1,599·0 (1,663·0); maize, 3,188·4 (2,446·0); potatoes, 11,659·3 (9,668·6); sugar-beet, 25,768·9 (24,211·3); rape, 2,866·9 (2,895·5); fodder, 61,183·8 (52,187·9).

In 1997 there were 525,121 farms, of which 66,737 were under 2 ha and 22,312 over 100 ha. In 1995 there were 561,900 farmers assisted by 586,400 household members and 263,000 hired labourers (84,800 seasonal). In the former GDR in 1990 state farms were leased to farmers until 2004 and will then be sold. Collective farms have continued operating as co-operatives or been turned over to their former members.

In 1997 wine production was 9,249,000 hectolitres.

Livestock, 1997 (in 1,000): Cattle, 15,612·2 (including milch cows, 5,069·3); sheep, 2,884·4; pigs, 24,416·0; horses, 652·4 (1996); poultry, 102,731·3 (1996). Livestock products, 1997 (in 1,000 tonnes): Milk, 28,702; meat, 4,892·4; eggs, 536,931,000 units.

Forestry

Forest area in 1997 was 9,463,300 ha, of which about half was owned by the State. Timber production was 34·0m. cu metres in 1995.

In recent years depredation has occurred through pollution with acid rain.

Fisheries

In 1996 the yield of sea fishing was 113,992 tonnes live weight. The fishing fleet consisted of 49 ocean-going vessels and 2,307 coastal cutters.

INDUSTRY

Public limited companies are managed on the 'co-determination' principle, and have 3 statutory bodies: a board of directors, a works council elected by employees, and a supervisory council which includes employee representatives but which has an in-built management majority.

In 1994 there were 67,660 firms (with 20 and more employees) employing 8·9m. persons, made up of 363,000 in energy and water services, 174,000 in mining, 1·3m. in raw materials processing, 3·71m. in the manufacture of producers' goods, 1·28m. in the manufacture of consumer goods, 572,000 in food and tobacco production and 1·50m. in building.

Output of major industrial products, 1996 (in 1,000 tonnes): Cement, 35,845; pig-iron (1994), 29,923; crude steel (1994), 40,837; rolled steel (1994), 26,691; aluminium, 709; copper (1994), 1,926; nitrogenous fertilizers (1994), 1,199; plastics, 10,001; glassware (1994), 4,882; cotton yarn (1994), 108; synthetic fibre (1994), 85; flour, 3,851; paper, 10,636; passenger cars, 4,702,000 (units); refrigerators, 3,102,000; beer, 108·9m. hectolitres.

Top Ten Companies

Company name	Industry	Revenue ($m)	World Ranking
Daimler-Benz Group	Automobiles	71,536	11
Volkswagen Group	Automobiles	65,306	14
Siemens Group	Electrical and Electronics	63,731	16
Allianz Worldwide	Insurance	55,397	17
VEBA Group	Utilities – Electrical and Gas	43,866	27
Deutsche Bank Group	Banking	40,778	31
Deutsche Telekom	Telecommunications	38,956	35
RWE Group	Utilities – Electrical and Gas	38,243	37
BMW	Automobiles	34,679	41
Metro	Merchandising	32,778	43

Labour

Retirement age is 63 years. At April 1997 the workforce was 40·28m. (17·35m. females), of whom 33·40m. (13·50m. females) were working and 3·26m. (1·39m. females) were unemployed. In 1997 there were on average during the year 3·62m. self-employed or helping other family members, 2·48m. officials and 27·78m. employees. 2·69m. foreign workers were employed in 1997. Major categories (1997): Manufacturing industries, 11·52m.; services, 7·99m.; commerce and transport, 6·37m.; agriculture, forestry and fishing, 0·93m. In 1996 there were 327,278 unfilled vacancies. In June 1999 there were 3,938,000 unemployed, a rate of 10·1%. The rate in the Länder of the former West Germany was 8·4%, but in the former GDR it stood at 16·8%. In the Länder of the former West Germany unemployment was higher among men (9·5% compared to 9·4% among women), whereas in the former GDR the rate among women was 20·2% but only 16·0% among men. Among people under 20 years of age, the unemployment rate was higher in the former West Germany, at 6·9% compared to 6·5% in the former GDR.

Trade Unions

The majority of trade unions belong to the *Deutscher Gewerkschaftsbund* (DGB, German Trade Union Federation), which had 8·6m. (2·6m. women) members in 1997, including 5·21m. (1·03m.) manual workers, 2·46m. (1·33m.) white-collar workers and 642,595 (169,770) officials. DGB unions are organized in industrial branches such that only one union operates within each enterprise. Outside the DGB are several smaller unions: The *Deutscher Beamtenbund* (DBB) or public servants' union with 1,116,714 (330,414) members, the *Deutsche Angestellten-Gewerkschaft* (DAG) or union of salaried staff with 489,266 (269,100) members and the *Christlicher Gewerkschaftsbund Deutschlands* (CGD, Christian Trade Union Federation of Germany) with 302,874 (76,222) members. Strikes are not legal unless called by a union with the backing of 75% of members. Certain public service employees are contractually not permitted to strike. 98,135 working days were lost through strikes in 1996; 247,460 in 1995.

Trade Union Organization

Deutscher Gewerkschaftsbund (DGB): 40476 Düsseldorf, Hans-Böckler-Str. 39. Tel: (0)211 43010. Fax: (0)211 4301471.
    Founded 1949.

INTERNATIONAL TRADE

In 1997 Germany had its highest annual trade surplus since unification, at 130·9bn. DM for the year compared to 98·5bn. DM a year earlier.

Imports and Exports

Imports and exports in 1m. DM:

Imports				Exports			
1994	1995	1996	1997	1994	1995	1996	1997
616,955	634,271	669,060	755,865	690,573	727,732	771,913	886,766

Most important trading partners in 1997 (trade figures in 1m. DM). Imports: France, 79,273; Netherlands, 64,135; Italy, 58,905; USA, 58,551; UK, 52,596; Belgium with Luxembourg, 46,521; Japan, 36,839. Exports: France, 94,431; USA, 76,617; UK, 75,020; Italy, 65,332; Netherlands, 62,022; Belgium with Luxembourg, 51,605; Austria, 45,938; Switzerland, 39,848. Some 10% of Germany's trade is now with central and eastern Europe, roughly the same as that with France.

Distribution by commodities in 1997 (in 1m. DM). Imports and exports: Live animals, 592 and 985; foodstuffs, 59,031 and 33,703; drinks and tobacco, 11,910 and 7,251; raw materials, 38,065 and 6,857; semi-finished goods, 71,784 and 42,686; finished goods, 517,480 and 757,055.

Internationales Handelszentrum GmbH: 10117 Berlin, Friedrichstr. 95. Tel: (0)30 26431500. Fax: (0)30 26431515.

Founded 1978. International Trade Centre. Offices of foreign enterprises.

TRADE FAIRS

Trade Fair Organizers: (see each Land for details)

There are more than 200 international trade fairs in Germany – some of them annual events, some of them every two or three years. In 2000 there will be 130 events. Information regarding the German Trade Fairs can be obtained from individual state offices of trade fair organizers (see each state for details) or:

AUMA (Ausstellungs- und Messe-Ausschuss der deutschen Wirtschaft eV): (Association of the German Trade Fair Industry) Lindenstr. 8, D-50674 Köln. Tel: (0)221 2-09-07-0. Fax: (0)221 2-09-07-12. Email: info@auma.de Web: www.auma.de

FKM (Gesellschaft zur freiwilligen Kontrolle von Messe- und Ausstellungszahlen): (Society for Voluntary Control of Fair and Exhibition Statistics) Lindenstr. 8, D-50674 Köln. Tel: (0)221 2-09-07-0. Fax: (0)221 2-009-07-61.

For a selection of the most notable annual events see below:

Frankfurter Buchmesse (Frankfurt Book Fair)

Ausstellungs- und Messe-GmbH des Börsenvereins des Deutschen Buchhandels, Reineckstr. 3, 60313 Frankfurt am Main. Tel: (0)69 22-10-20. Fax: (0)69 22-10-22-27. Email: marketing@book-fair.com Web: www.frankfurt-book-fair.com

Art, Books, Electronic media, Magazines, Newspapers, Topographical maps.

Exhibitors: 6,800 Visitors: 289,000.

Usually held in Oct.

Automechanika (World's Meeting Place for the Automotive Industry)

Messe Frankfurt GmbH, Ludwig-Erhard-Anlage 1, 60327 Frankfurt am Main.

Tel: (0)69 75-75-0. Fax: (0)69 75-75-6433.

Web: www.messefrankfurt.com

Cars and related products.

Exhibitors: 3,400. Visitors: 151,000. Usually held in autumn every two years.

Spielwarenmesse (International Toy Fair Nürnberg)

Spielwarenmesse eG, Messezentrum, 90471 Nürnberg.

Tel: (0)911 99-13-0. Fax: (0)911 86-96-60.

Email: info@spielwarnmesse.de Web: www.spielwarenmesse.de

CeBIT (World Business Fair Office Automation-Information Technology-Telecommunications)

Deutsche Messe AG, Messegelände, 30521 Hannover.

Tel: (0)511 890. Fax: (0)511 89-32-62-6.

Email: webmaster@messe.de Web: www.messe.de

Bank, Technology, CIM, Card Technology, Computer Software, Data Protection, Information technology, Internet, Multimedia, Net Work,

Office Technology, Research and development, Security Systems, Services, Telecommunications.

Exhibitors: 7,000. Visitors: 600,000.

Usually held early spring.

COMMUNICATIONS

Roads

In 1996 the total length of classified roads was 231,076 km, including 11,246 km of motorway *(Autobahn)*, 41,487 km of federal highways, 86,789 km of first-class and 91,554 km of second-class country roads. The motorway network is the largest in Europe. On 1 Jan. 1998 there were 49·0m. motor vehicles, including: Passenger cars, 41,326,900 (approximately 1 car for every 2 persons); trucks, 2,344,600; buses, 83,700; motor cycles, 2,759,200. In 1997, 7,838m. passengers were transported by long-distance road traffic. The average distance travelled by a passenger car in the year 1994 was 12,700 km (1995 estimate, 12,400 km).

645,384 motorists were arrested at the scene of an accident for driving offences in 1996, of which 52,185 were alcohol related and 139,117 due to exceeding speed limits.

Road casualties in 1997 (and 1995) totalled 500,707 injured (512,141) and 8,516 killed (9,454).

Rules of the Road

Foreigners may drive for up to one year on a foreign driving licence. Third party insurance is a minimum requirement and seatbelts are compulsory for all passengers and the driver. Children under 12 years must sit in the back. Main roads have a yellow diamond indicating who has priority but generally vehicles coming from the right have priority. There are on the spot fines for speeding. In cities trams always have right of way. There are no enforced speed limits on the motorways (Autobahnen). Official speed limit of country roads is 80–100 km/h, and 50 km/h in built up areas.

Rail

Legislation of 1993 provides for the eventual privatization of the railways. On 1 Jan. 1994 West German Bundesbahn and the former GDR Reichsbahn were amalgamated as the Deutsche Bahn, a joint-stock company in which track, long-distance passenger traffic, regional passenger traffic and goods traffic are run as 4 separate administrative entities. These were intended after 3–5 years to become themselves companies, at first under a holding company, and ultimately independent. Initially the government will hold all the shares. Length of railway in 1996 was 46,300 km (1,435 mm gauge) of which 18,866 km were electrified. There were 5,640 stations. 1,735m. passengers were carried in 1997 and 316·0m. tonnes of freight.

There are metros in Berlin (136 km), Hamburg (95 km), Frankfurt am Main (51 km), Munich (63 km) and Nuremberg (23 km), and tram/light rail networks in 56 cities.

Deutsche Bahn AG: 60326 Frankfurt am Main, Stephensonstr. 1. Tel: (0)69 97330. Fax: (0)69 97337500. Web site: www.bahn.de

10365 Berlin, Ruschestr. 59. Tel: (0)30 2970. Fax: (0)30 29726130.

Founded 1994. German Railways, renamed following merger of the Deutsche Bundesbahn and Deutsche Reichsbahn. State owned.

Verband Deutscher Verkehrsunternehmen (VDV): 50672 Köln, Kamestr. 37–39. Tel: (0)221 579790. Fax: (0)221 514272.

Founded 1895 as Association of German Transport Authorities.

Civil Aviation

Lufthansa, the largest carrier, was set up in 1953 and is 36% state-owned. Other airlines include Condor, Deutsche-British Airways,

Eurowings and LTU International Airways. In 1997 civil aviation had 476 aircraft over 20 tonnes (441 jets). Lufthansa flew 516·5m. km in 1995, carrying 32,537,700 passengers (19,347,500 on international flights).

In 1997 there were 60·39m. passenger arrivals and 60·76m. departures. Main international airports: Bremen, Cologne-Bonn, Düsseldorf, Frankfurt am Main, Hamburg (Fuhlsbüttel), Hanover, Leipzig, Munich, Nuremberg, Stuttgart and 3 at Berlin (Tegel, Tempelhof and Schönefeld). Airports at Dortmund, Dresden, Mönchengladbach, Paderborn, Rostock and Saarbrücken are used for only a few scheduled international flights in addition to domestic flights. In 1997 Frankfurt am Main handled 39,612,000 passengers (30,918,720 on international flights) and 1,367,862 tonnes of freight. It was the busiest airport in Europe in 1996 in terms of freight handled. Munich was the second busiest German airport in terms of passenger traffic in 1997 (17,575,000 including 9,590,560 on international flights) but third for freight. Cologne-Bonn was the second busiest in 1997 for freight, with 375,051 tonnes, but only seventh for passenger traffic.

Shipping

At 31 Dec. 1996 the mercantile marine comprised 1,397 ocean-going vessels of 6,002,000 GRT. Sea-going ships in 1996 carried 206m. tonnes of cargo.

Navigable rivers have a total length of 4,842 km; canals, 2,087 km. The inland-waterways fleet on 31 Dec. 1995 included 1,477 motor freight vessels totalling 1·52m. tonnes and 355 tankers of 495,887 tonnes. 227m. tonnes of freight were transported in 1996.

Shipping Organizations

Verband Deutscher Küstenschiffseigner: Hamburg-Altona. Tel: (0)40 313435. Fax: (0)40 315925.

Founded: 1896. German Coastal Shipowners' Association.

Verband Deutscher Reeder eV: 20354 Hamburg, Esplanade 6.
20317 Hamburg, Postfach 305580. Tel: (0)40 350970.
Fax: (0)40 35097211.

German Shipowners' Association.

Zentralverband der Deutschen Seehafenbetriebe eV: Hamburg.
Tel: (0)40 311561.

Founded 1932. Federal Association of German Seaport Operators.

Abteilung Binnenschiffahrt und Wasserstrassen: 53175 Bonn, Robert-Schuman-Platz 1. Tel: (0)228 30000. Fax: (0)228 3003428.

Federal Ministry of Transport Inland Waterway department. Deals with construction, maintenance and administration of federal waterways and with national and international water transport.

Telecommunications

Telecommunications were deregulated in 1989. On 1 Jan. 1995, 3 state-owned joint-stock companies were set up: Deutsche Telekom, Postdienst and Postbank. The partial privatization of Deutsche Telekom began in Nov. 1996.

In 1997 there were 45·2m. telephone main lines, equivalent to 549·8 per 1,000 population. In 1996 there were 44·2m. private telephones and 164,100 public telephones. There were 1·45m. fax transmitters in 1995 and 13·5m. PCs (165 per 1,000 persons). 3·71m. mobile telephones were in use in 1996. There were approximately 7·3m. Internet users in Oct. 1998 (nearly 9% of the population).

Postal Services

In 1996 there were 16,600 post offices and 4,000 affiliated agents. A total of 19,963m. pieces of mail were processed during the year, or 244 items per person.

SOCIAL INSTITUTIONS

Justice

Justice is administered by the federal courts and by the courts of the Länder. In criminal procedures, civil cases and procedures of non-contentious jurisdiction the courts on the *Land* level are the local courts *(Amtsgerichte)*, the regional courts *(Landgerichte)* and the courts of appeal *(Oberlandesgerichte)*. Constitutional federal disputes are dealt with by the Federal Constitutional Court *(Bundesverfassungsgericht)* elected by the Bundestag and Bundesrat. The Länder also have constitutional courts. In labour law disputes the courts of the first and second instance are the labour courts and the *Land* labour courts and in the third instance, the Federal Labour Court *(Bundesarbeitsgericht)*. Disputes about public law in matters of social security, unemployment insurance, maintenance of war victims and similar cases are dealt with in the first and second instances by the social courts and the *Land* social courts and in the third instance by the Federal Social Court *(Bundessozialgericht)*. In most tax matters the finance courts of the Länder are competent and in the second instance, the Federal Finance Court *(Bundesfinanzhof)*. Other controversies of public law in non-constitutional matters are decided in the first and second instance by the administrative and the higher administrative courts *(Oberverwaltungsgerichte)* of the Länder, and in the third instance by the Federal Administrative Court *(Bundesverwaltungsgericht)*.

For the inquiry into maritime accidents the admiralty courts *(Seeämter)* are competent on the *Land* level and in the second instance the Federal Admiralty Court *(Bundesoberseeamt)* in Hamburg.

The death sentence has been abolished.

Religion

In 1996 there were 27,659,000 Protestants in 17,991 parishes, 27,533,000 Roman Catholics in 13,329 parishes, and in 1997, 67,471 Jews with 17 rabbis and 70 synagogues.

There are 5 Roman Catholic archbishoprics (Bamberg, Cologne, Freiburg, Munich and Freising, Paderborn) and 23 bishoprics. Chairman of the German Bishops' Conference is Cardinal Joseph Höffner, Archbishop of Cologne. A concordat between Germany and the Holy See dates from 10 Sept. 1933.

The Evangelical (Protestant) Church (EKD) consists of 24 member-churches including 7 Lutheran Churches, 8 United-Lutheran-Reformed, 2 Reformed Churches and 1 Confederation of United member Churches: 'Church of the Union'. Its organs are the Synod, the Church Conference and the Council under the chairmanship of Bishop Dr Eduard Lohse (Hanover). There are also some 12 Evangelical Free Churches.

Religious Organizations

Arbeitsgemeinschaft Christlicher Kirchen in Deutschland: 60487 Frankfurt am Main, Ludolfusstr. 2–4. 60446 Frankfurt am Main, Postfach 900617. Tel: (0)69 2470270. Fax: (0)69 24702730.

The Council of Christian Churches in Germany represents 18 affiliated Christian churches including the Roman Catholic Church and the Greek Orthodox Metropoly.

Bishops' Conference (Deutsche Bischofskonferenz): 53113 Bonn, Kaiserstr. 163. Tel: (0)228 1030. Fax: (0)228 103299.

Central Committee of German Catholics: 5317 Bonn, Hochkreuzallee 246. Tel: (0)228 382970. Fax: (0)228 3829744.

Evangelische Kirche in Deutschland (EKD): 301419 Hannover, Herrenhäuser Str. 12. Tel: (0)511 27960. Fax: (0)511 2796-707. (Berlin: 10117 Berlin, Auguststr. 80)

Council of the Evangelical Church in Germany.

Deutscher Evangelischer Kirchentag: 36037 Fulda, Magdeburgerstr. 59, 36004 Fulda, Postfach 480. Tel: (0)661 969500.

Fax: (0)661 9695090.

Council for the Protestant Churches in Germany.

Alt-Katholische Kirche: 53115 Bonn, Gregor-Mendel-Str. 28.

Tel: (0)228 232285. Fax: (0)228 238314.

Old Catholic Church of Germany. Seceded from the Roman
Catholic Church in 1870. Part of the Utrecht Union of Old Catholic
Churches.

Griechisch-Orthodoxe Metropolie von Deutschland: 53227 Bonn,
Dietrich-Bonhoeffer-Str. 2, 53185 Bonn, Postfach 300555.

Tel: (0)228 462041. Fax: (0)228 464989.

Greek Orthodox Metropoly of Germany.

Religiöse Gesellschaft der Freunde (Quäker): 1080 Berlin, Plankstr. 20.

Tel: (0)30 2082284.

Society of Friends (Quakers).

Russische Orthodoxe Kirche-Berliner Diözese: 10138 Berlin,
Wildensteiner Str. 10, 10267 Berlin, Postfach 17. Tel: (0)30 5082024.

Fax: (0)30 5098153.

Zentralrat der Juden in Deutschland: 10117 Berlin, Orienburger Str.
31. Tel: (0)30 2828714.

Fax: (0)30 2386607. (Bonn: Rügsdorfer Str. 6. Tel: (0)228 357023.
Fax: (0)228 361148).

Central Council of Jews in Germany.

Education

Education is compulsory for children aged 6 to 15. After the first 4 (or
6) years at primary school *(Grundschulen)* children attend post-primary *(Hauptschulen)*, secondary modern *(Realschulen)*, grammar
(Gymnasien), or comprehensive schools *(Integrierte
Gesamtschulen)*. Secondary modern school lasts 6 years and

grammar school 9. Entry to higher education is by the final Grammar School Certificate (*Abitur* – Higher School Certificate). There are special schools *(Sonderschulen)* for handicapped children and children with special needs.

In 1996–97 there were 4,217 kindergartens with 82,420 pupils and 5,364 teachers; 17,892 primary schools with 3,691,648 pupils and 200,427 teachers; and 8,396 post-primary schools with 1,500,471 pupils and 99,411 teachers. There were also 3,410 special schools with 398,366 pupils and 63,434 teachers; 3,485 secondary modern schools with 1,202,952 pupils and 73,664 teachers; 3,167 grammar schools with 2,181,562 pupils and 153,983 teachers; 965 comprehensive schools with 591,404 pupils and 46,233 teachers.

In the 1996–97 academic year there were 671,733 working teachers, of whom 430,746 were female.

The adult literacy rate is 99·0%.

In 1995 total expenditure on education came to 4·8% of GNP and represented 9·5% of total government expenditure.

Vocational education is provided in part-time, full-time and advanced vocational schools (*Berufs-, Berufsaufbau-, Berufsfach-* and *Fachschulen,* including *Fachschulen für Technik* and *Schulen des Gesundheitswesens)*. Occupation-related, part-time vocational training of 6 to 12 hours per week is compulsory for all (including unemployed) up to the age of 18 years or until the completion of the practical vocational training. Full-time vocational schools comprise courses of at least one year. They prepare for commercial and domestic occupations as well as specialized occupations in the field of handicrafts. Advanced full-time vocational schools are attended by pupils over 18. Courses vary from 6 months to 3 or more years.

In 1996–97 there were 9,300 full- and part-time vocational schools with 2,479,584 students and 108,083 teachers.

Higher Education. In the winter term of the 1997–98 academic year there were 337 institutes of higher education *(Hochschulen)* with

1,832,758 students, including 84 universities (1,199,125 students), 7 polytechnics *(Gesamthochschulen;* 144,976), 6 teacher training colleges (17,738), 16 theological seminaries (2,589), 46 schools of art (29,944), 147 technical colleges (399,817) and 31 management schools (38,569). Only 12·3% of students were in their first year.

Health
In 1997 there were 282,737 doctors (equivalent to 1 for every 290 persons), 62,024 dentists and 52,076 pharmacists. In 1996 there were 2,269 hospitals with 593,743 beds.

Welfare
Social Health Insurance (introduced in 1883). Wage-earners and apprentices, salaried employees with an income below a certain limit and social insurance pensioners are compulsorily insured. Voluntary insurance is also possible.

Benefits: Medical treatment, medicines, hospital and nursing care, maternity benefits, death benefits for the insured and their families, sickness payments and out-patients' allowances. Economy measures of Dec. 1992 introduced prescription charges related to recipients' income.

50·85m. persons were insured in 1997 (29·6m. compulsorily). Number of cases of incapacity for work (1996) totalled 35·99m., and the number of working days lost were 331·8m. (men) and 260·1m. (women). Total disbursements, 234,274m. DM.

Accident Insurance (introduced in 1884). Those insured are all persons in employment or service, apprentices and the majority of the self-employed and the unpaid family workers.

Benefits in the case of industrial injuries and occupational diseases: Medical treatment and nursing care, sickness payments, pensions and other payments in cash and in kind, surviving dependants' pensions.

Number of insured in 1996, 55·42m.; number of current pensions, 1,179,743; total disbursements, 25,734m. DM.

Workers' and Employees' Old-Age Insurance Scheme (introduced in 1889). All wage-earners and salaried employees, the members of certain liberal professions and – subject to certain conditions – self-employed craftsmen are compulsorily insured. The insured may voluntarily continue to insure when no longer liable to do so or increase the insurance.

Benefits: Measures designed to maintain, improve and restore the earning capacity; pensions paid to persons incapable of work, old age and surviving dependants' pensions.

Number of insured in April 1997, 43·75m. (20·46m. women); number of current pensions (in July 1996), 20·30m.; pensions to widows and widowers, 5·06m. Total disbursements in 1995, 398,081m. DM.

There are also special retirement and unemployment pension schemes for miners and farmers, assistance for war victims and compensation payments to members of German minorities in East European countries expelled after the Second World War and persons who suffered damage because of the war or in connection with the currency reform.

Family Allowances. 40,466m. DM were dispensed to 8·56m. recipients (0·95m. foreigners) in 1997 on behalf of 14·33m. children. Paid child care leave is available for 3 years to mothers or fathers.

Unemployment Allowances. In 1996, 1·99m. persons (0·87m. women) were receiving unemployment benefit and 1·10m. (0·47m. women) earnings-related benefit. Total expenditure on these and similar benefits (e.g. short-working supplement, job creation schemes) was 105·59m. DM in 1996.

Public Welfare (introduced in 1962). In 1993, 48·92m. DM were distributed to 5·02m. recipients (2·67m. women).

Public Youth Welfare. For supervision of foster children, official guardianship, assistance with adoptions and affiliations, social assistance in juvenile courts, educational assistance and correctional education under a court order. Total number of recipients in 1996 was 725,468 persons.

CULTURE

Broadcasting

Television

There are 2 public service broadcasting companies – ARD and ZDF plus many private and regional stations. Deutsche Welle Fernsehen (DW-tv) is the foreign service broadcaster. Most German households subscribe to cable television. In 1997 there were 33·5m. TV licences.

ARD (Arbeitsgemeinschaft der öffentlich-rechtlichen Rundfunkanstalten der Bundesrepublik Deutschland)

Bertramstr. 8. 60320 Frankfurt am Main. Tel: (0)69 590607. Fax: (0)69 1552075. Web: www.ard.de

The Association of Public Broadcasting Corporations in the Federal Republic of Germany is the co-ordinating body for television and radio. Represents public-right broadcasters and organizes co-operation between them, broadcasting as **Das Erste** (Arnulfstr. 42, 80335 Munich. Tel: (0) 89 590001. Fax: (0) 89 59003249. Web: www.das-erste.de).

ZDF (Zweites Deutsches Fernsehen)

Postfach 4040, 55100 Mainz. Tel: (0)6131 702050. Fax: (0)6131 702052. Web: www.zdf.de

Founded in 1963, ZDF is Germany's second public service broadcaster.

Verband Privater Rundfunk und Telekommunikation eV: Gurgstrasse 69, 53177 Bonn.

The association which represents private broadcasters and telecommunications companies.

Radio

Public service radio is provided by ARD and ZDF via DeutschlandRadio. Private radio stations also broadcast in the regions. Deutsche Welle (DW-radio) broadcasts overseas. In 1997 there were 37·5m. radio licences.

Foreign Radio Stations

American Forces Network: 60320 Frankfurt am Main, Bertramstr. 6. Tel: (0)69 15688240.

Founded in 1943; has 19 affiliated stations worldwide. Transmits 3 television channels via satellite.

British Forces Broadcasting Service, Germany: 32049 Herford, Wentworth Barracks, Liststr. Tel: (0)5221 98340.

Since 1982 a division of Services Sound and Vision Corp.

Radio Free Europe/Radio Liberty Inc.: Oettingenstr. 67, 80538 München. Tel: (0)89 21020. Fax: (0)89 21023322.

A non-profit private corporation operating under US management with grants from the Board for International Broadcasting. Broadcasts all over Europe.

Voice of America (VOA Europe): 80539 München, Ludwigstr. 2. Tel: (0)89 286-91. Fax: (0)89 289210.

Broadcasts 24 hours a day in English to parts of Europe and Asia in 46 languages. Music, news, features of US life and culture.

Theatre

There were 154 theatre companies in 1995–96, performing on 655 stages. Audiences totalled 20·6m.

Press

The daily press is mainly regional. In 1996 the largest dailies with a national circulation were *Das Bild* (Hamburg, 4·5m. copies per day); *Süddeutsche Zeitung* (Munich, 0·4m.); *Frankfurter Allgemeine Zeitung* (0·4m.); *Die Welt* (Berlin, 0·22m.); *Frankfurter Rundschau* (0·2m.). In 1994, 381 newspapers and 9,093 periodicals were published with respective circulations of 30·6m. and 387·8m. Newspapers are widely read and many of the principal dailies have national as well as local readerships. In western Germany, political parties have no direct ownership of newspapers. In the eastern Länder most newspapers were transferred from party to private control in 1990. The total circulation of daily newspapers in Germany is the highest in Europe.

Daily Newspapers

Bild-Zeitung: 20355 Hamburg, Axel-Springer-Platz 1.
Tel: (0)40 34700. Fax: (0)40 345811. Web site: www.bild.de
Founded 1952. Published by Axel Springer. Tabloid daily has the largest (4·5m.) daily circulation in Germany.

Süddeutsche Zeitung: 80331 München, Sendlingerstr. 8, 80019 München, Postfach 201902.
Tel: (0)89 21830. Fax: (0)89 2183795.
Founded 1945. Published in Munich but second largest (0·4m.) daily circulation Germany wide.

Frankfurter Allgemeine Zeitung: 60327 Frankfurt am Main, Hellerhofstr. 2–4.
Tel: (0)69 75910. Fax: (0)69 75911743.
Founded 1949. Local daily newspaper. Widely read nationally and has considerable influence on political and business leaders.

Die Welt: 10888 Berlin, Axel-Springer-Str. 65. Tel: (0)30 25910.
Fax: (0)30 25911929. Web site: www.welt.de

(Also in Hamburg – Axel-Springer-Platz, 1. Tel: (0)40 34700.
Fax: (0)40 345811).

Founded 1946. Published seven days a week by the Axel Springer
Group. Strongly influential in political and business worlds.

Frankfurter Rundschau: 60313 Frankfurt am Main, Grosse
Eschenheimer Str. 16–18.

Tel: (0)69 21991. Fax: (0)69 2199521. Web site: www.fr-aktuell.de

A regional daily newspaper whose influence reaches all over
Germany.

Der Tagesspiegel: 10785 Berlin, Potsdamer Str. 87, 10723 Berlin,
Postfach 304330.

Tel: (0)30 260090. Fax: (0)30 26009332.

Web site: www.tagesspiegel.de

Founded 1945. Published in Berlin as a regional daily newspaper
with national influence.

Sunday and Weekly Newspapers

Bild am Sonntag: 20350 Hamburg, Axel-Springer-Platz 1.
Tel: (0)40 3470. Fax: (0)40 345811.

Founded 1956. Published by the Axel Springer Group, it has a
circulation of over 2m.

Welt am Sonntag: 20355 Hamburg, Axel-Springer-Platz 1.
Tel: (0)40 34700. Fax: (0)40 34724912.

Frankfurter Allgemeine Sonntagszeitung: 60327 Frankfurt am Main,
Hellerhofstr. 2–4. Tel: (0)69 75910. Fax: (0)69 75911773.

Periodicals

Capital: Gruner und Jahr AG, 20444 Hamburg, Postfach 110011.
Tel: (0)40 3703-2480. Fax: (0)40 3703-5607.

Founded 1962. Monthly business magazine.

Focus: 81925 München, Arabellstr. 23. Tel: (0)89 92500.
Fax: (0)89 92502026.

Founded 1993. Weekly political and general magazine.

Der Spiegel: 20457 Hamburg, Brandestweite 19/Ost-West-Str,
Postfach 110420. Tel: (0)40 3007. Fax: (0)40 30072247.

Founded 1947. Weekly political and general magazine.

Stern: Gruner und Jahr AG, 20444 Hamburg, Postfach 11011.
Tel: (0)40 41181.

Illustrated weekly magazine.

Bunte: 81925 München, Arabellstr. 23. Tel: (0)89 92500.
Fax: (0)89 92503427.

Founded 1948. Illustrated family weekly magazine.

News Agencies

There are two principal facilities. The German Press Agency (DPA)
supplies newspapers and broadcasters throughout the Federal
Republic. It also broadcasts services in foreign languages. The
General German News Service (ADN) was launched in 1946
as the official East German Agency and was reorganized in
1990.

dpa Deutsche Presse-Agentur GmbH (DPA): 20148 Hamburg,
Mittelweg 38. Tel: (0)40 41130. Fax: (0)40 4113357.

Supplies all German daily newspapers, broadcasting stations and
1,000 other subscribers, transmits foreign language news bulletins
and transmits German language news to press agencies, newspapers, radio and television stations and ministries of information in
about 100 countries.

Allgemeiner Deutscher Nachrichtendienst GmbH (ADN): 1026 Berlin,
Mollstr. 1. Tel: (0)30 231220. Fax: (0)30 23122119.

Formerly News Agency of the GDR, it became independent in 1990. Has eight offices in Germany and foreign corespondents abroad. Provides a daily German news and features service.

Foreign Bureaux

Associated Press GmbH (AP) (USA): Frankfurt am Main, Moselstr. 27. Tel: (0)69 2713-0. Fax: (0)69 251289.

Web: www.ap.org

US news service with offices in Hanover, Hamburg, Stuttgart, Wiesbaden, Saarbrücken, Bonn, Berlin, Munich, Düsseldorf, Dresden, Leipzig, Magdeburg, Schwerin and Erfurt.

Reuters (UK): 53113 Bonn, Bonn-Center, Bundeskanzlerplatz 2–10, Postfach 1209725.

Tel: (0)228 260970. Fax: (0)228 2609725. Web: www.reuters.de

United Press (UPI) (USA): 53113, Bonn, Heussallee 2–10, Pressehaus II/224. Tel: (0)228 263787.

Press and Journalists Associations

Bundesverband Deutscher Zeitungsverleger eV. 53175 Bonn, Reimenschneiderstr. 10, 53170 Bonn, Postfach 205002. Tel: (0)228 810040. Fax: (0)228 8100415.

German Newspaper Publishers' Association with 11 affiliated Land Associations.

Deutscher Journalisten-Verband: 53115 Bonn, Bennauerstr. 60. Tel: (0)228 22971-80. Fax: (0)228 214917.

German Journalists' Association.

Verband Deutscher Zeitschriftenverleger eV: 53177 Bonn, Winterstr. 50. Tel: (0)228 382030. Fax: (0)228 3820345.

Association of Publishers of Periodicals with seven affiliated Land Associations.

GERMANY

National boundary

Railway

0   100 km

Map © Rough Guides Ltd, 1999

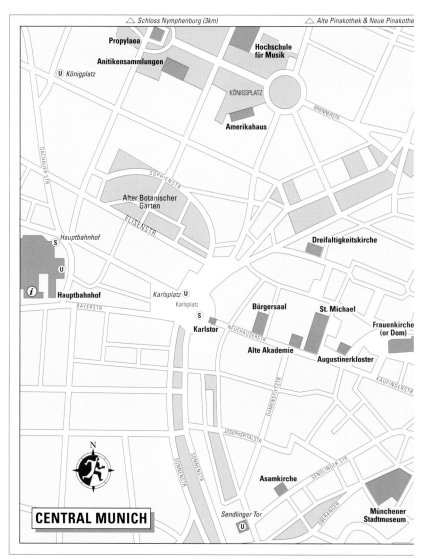

Schloss Nymphenburg (3km)

Alte Pinakothek & Neue Pinakothe

Propylaea

Hochschule
für Musik

Anitikensammlungen

U Königplatz

KÖNIGSPLATZ

BRIENNERSTR

Amerikahaus

SOPHIENSTR

DACHAUER STR

Alter Botanischer
Garten

ELISENSTR

S Hauptbahnhof

Dreifaltigkeitskirche

U

i Hauptbahnhof

Karlsplatz **U**

Karlsplatz

BAYERSTR

S

Karlstor

NEUEHAUSERSTR

Bürgersaal

St. Michael

Frauenkirche
(or Dom)

Alte Akademie

Augustinerkloster

KAUFINGERSTR

DAMENSTIFTSTR

JOSEPHSPITALSTR

N

SONNENSTR

Asamkirche

SENDLINGER STR

CENTRAL MUNICH

Sendlinger Tor

U

OBERANGER

Münchener
Stadtmuseum

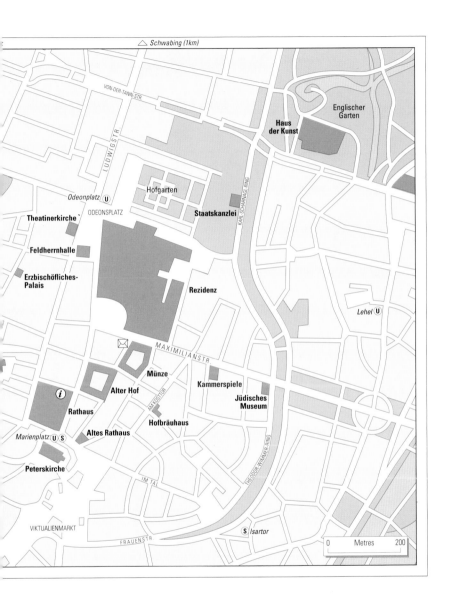

Schwabing (1km)

VON-DER-TANN-STR

LUDWIGSTR

Englischer
Garten

Haus
der Kunst

Hofgarten

KARL-SCHARNAGL-RING

Odeonplatz Ⓤ

ODEONSPLATZ

Staatskanzlei

Theatinerkirche

Feldherrnhalle

Erzbischöfliches-
Palais

Rezidenz

Lehel Ⓤ

MAXIMILIANSTR

Münze

Kammerspiele

Alter Hof

Jüdisches
Museum

MAXTORSTR

ⓘ

Rathaus

Hofbräuhaus

THEODOR-WIMMER-RING

Marienplatz Ⓤ Ⓢ

Altes Rathaus

Peterskirche

IM TAL

VIKTUALIENMARKT

FRAUENSTR

Ⓢ Isartor

0   Metres   200

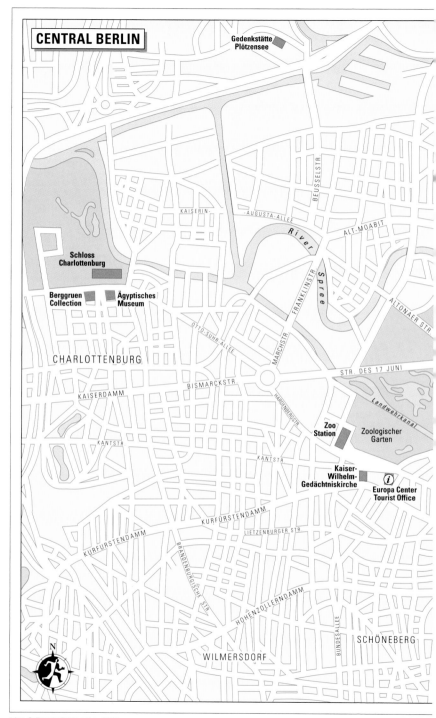

CENTRAL BERLIN

Gedenkstätte
Plötzensee

BEUSSELSTR

KAISERIN-

AUGUSTA-ALLEE

River

ALT-MOABIT

Spree

ALTONAER STR

FRANKLINSTR

**Schloss
Charlottenburg**

**Berggruen
Collection**

**Ägyptisches
Museum**

OTTO-SUHR-ALLEE

MARCHSTR

CHARLOTTENBURG

STR. DES 17 JUNI

BISMARCKSTR.

KAISERDAMM

HARDENBERGSTR

Landwehrkanal

KANTSTR.

**Zoo
Station**

Zoologischer
Garten

KANTSTR.

**Kaiser-
Wilhelm-
Gedächtniskirche**

(i)

**Europa Center
Tourist Office**

KURFÜRSTENDAMM

LIETZENBURGER STR.

KURFÜRSTENDAMM

BRANDENBURGISCHE STR.

HOHENZOLLERNDAMM

BUNDESALLEE

SCHÖNEBERG

N

WILMERSDORF

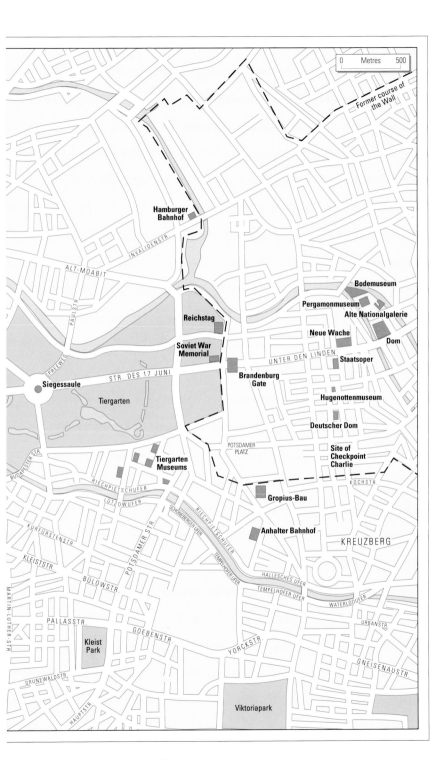

0   Metres   500

Former course of
the Wall

Hamburger
Bahnhof

INVALIDENSTR.

ALT-MOABIT

PAULSTR.

SPREEWEG

Bodemuseum

Pergamonmuseum

Alte Nationalgalerie

Reichstag

Neue Wache

Dom

Soviet War
Memorial

UNTER DEN LINDEN

Staatsoper

Siegessaule

STR. DES 17 JUNI

Brandenburg
Gate

Tiergarten

Hugenottenmuseum

Deutscher Dom

BUDAPSTR STR.

Tiergarten
Museums

POTSDAMER
PLATZ

Site of
Checkpoint
Charlie

KOCHSTR.

RIECHPIETSCHUFER

LUTZOWUFER

Gropius-Bau

RIECHPIETSCHUFER

SCHÖNEBERGER UFER

TEMPELHOFER UFER

KURFURSTENSTR.

POTSDAMER STR.

Anhalter Bahnhof

KREUZBERG

KLEISTSTR.

BÜLOWSTR.

HALLESCHES UFER

TEMPELHOFER UFER

WATERLOOUFER

MARTIN-LUTHER-STR.

PALLASSTR.

GOEBENSTR.

URBANSTR.

Kleist
Park

YORCKSTR.

GNEISENAUSTR.

GRUNEWALDSTR.

HAUPTSTR.

Viktoriapark

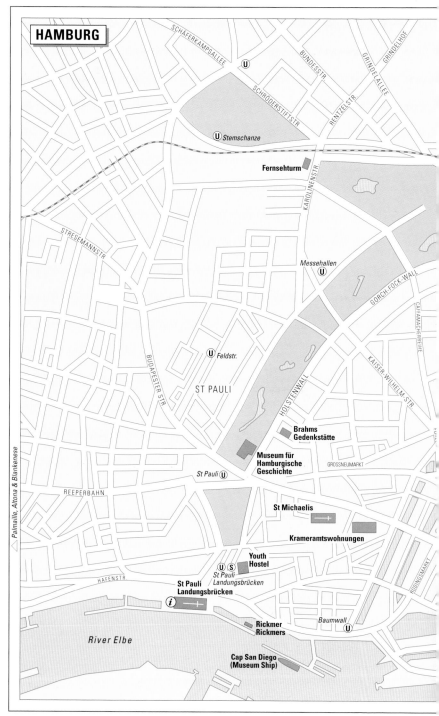

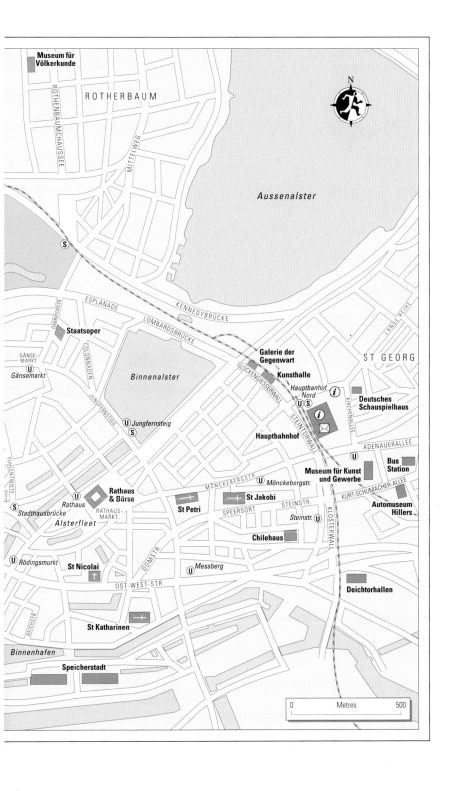

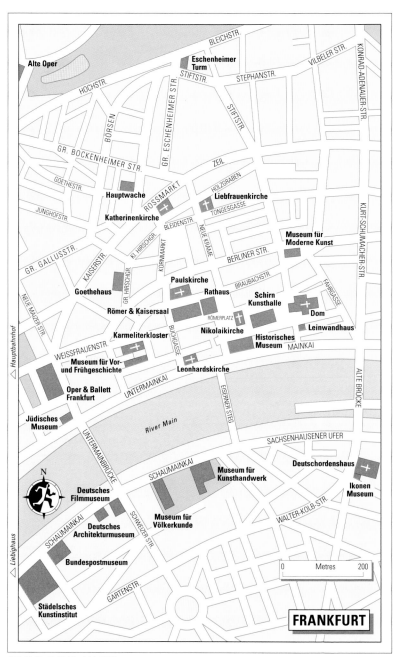

Alte Oper

Eschenheimer
Turm

BLEICHSTR.

STIFTSTR.

STEPHANSTR.

VILBELER STR.

KONRAD-ADENAUER-STR.

HOCHSTR.

BÖRSEN

GR. ESCHENHEIMER STR.

STIFTSTR.

GR. BOCKENHEIMER STR.

GOETHESTR.

ZEIL

JUNGHOFSTR.

HOLZGRABEN

Hauptwache

ROSSMARKT

Liebfrauenkirche

TONGESGASSE

Katherinenkirche

BLEIDENSTR.

NEUE KRÄME

Museum für
Moderne Kunst

KURT-SCHUMACHER-STR.

GR. GALLUSSTR.

KAISERSTR.

KL. HIRSCHGR.

KORNMARKT

BERLINER STR.

NEUE MAINZER STR.

GR. HIRSCHGR.

Paulskirche

BRAUBACHSTR.

Goethehaus

Rathaus

Schirn
Kunsthalle

FAHRGASSE

Römer & Kaisersaal

RÖMERPLATZ

Dom

Nikolaikirche

Leinwandhaus

Karmeliterkloster

BUCHGASSE

Historisches
Museum

MAINKAI

Hauptbahnhof

WEISSFRAUENSTR.

Museum für Vor-
und Frühgeschichte

Leonhardskirche

Oper & Ballett
Frankfurt

UNTERMAINKAI

EISERNER STEG

ALTE BRÜCKE

Jüdisches
Museum

UNTERMAINBRÜCKE

River Main

SACHSENHAUSENER UFER

N

Deutsches
Filmmuseum

SCHAUMAINKAI

Museum für
Kunsthandwerk

Deutschordenshaus

Ikonen
Museum

SCHWEIZER STR.

Deutsches
Architekturmuseum

Museum für
Völkerkunde

WALTER-KOLB-STR.

SCHAUMAINKAI

Liebighaus

Bundespostmuseum

0   Metres   200

GARTENSTR.

Städelsches
Kunstinstitut

FRANKFURT

Map © Rough Guides Ltd, 1999

Verein der Ausländischen Presse in der BRD (VAP): 53113 Bonn,
Heussallee 2–10, Pressehaus I/35. Tel: (0)228 210885.
Fax: (0)228 219672.
Foreign Press Association.

Publishing in Germany

It is generally accepted that the publishing industry as we know it
originated in Germany during the 14th century with the invention of
typographic printing. Although there is some dispute, most accept
that Johannes Gutenberg's use of movable type and a printing press
that has been used without important change until the 20th century is
the basis of the publishing industry.

Certainly Germany has a very strong tradition of publishing and
there would be no room to publish an exhaustive list of German
publishers here.

71,515 book titles were published in 1996, of which 53,793 were
new works.

Publishers

Verlag C. H. Beck (OHG)

Wilhelmstr. 9, 80801 München. Tel: (0)89 381890.
Fax: (0)89 38189398.

Founded in 1763. Publishes general non-fiction, anthropology,
archaeology, art, dance, economics, essays, history, language, law,
linguistics, literature, literary criticism, music, philosophy, social
sciences, sociology and theology.

Bertelsmann AG

Carl-Bertelsmann-Strasse 270, Postfach 111, 33311 Gütersloh.
Tel: (0)52 41800. Fax: (0)52 4175166.

Bertelsmann AG is the third largest media company in the
world. The company has significant interests in all areas of media

including book, magazine and newspaper publishing, music, television, online, film and radio. Books published include fiction and non-fiction titles, anthropology, art, biography, business, career development, economics, film, history, how-to, law, management, marketing, medicine, dentistry, nursing, radio, television, video, technology and travel. Bertelsmann owns Gruner und Jahr (see below).

Carlsen Verlag GmbH

Postfach 500380, 22703 Hamburg. Tel: (0)40 39110090.
Fax: (0)40 39100962.

Founded in 1953. Publishes humour and general non-fiction.

Deutscher Taschenbuch Verlag GmbH & Co. KG (dtv)

Postfach 400422, 80704 München. Tel: (0)89 38167-0.
Fax: (0)89 346428.

Founded in 1961. Publishes fiction and general non-fiction, art, astronomy, biography, child care and development, cookery, computer science, dance, education, government, history, how-to, music, poetry, psychiatry, psychology, philosophy, political science, religion, medicine, dentistry, nursing, social sciences, literature, literary criticism, essays, humour and travel.

Droemersche Verlagsanstalt Th. Knaur Nachfolger

Rauchstr. 9–11, 81679 München. Tel: (0)89 92710.
Fax: (0)89 9271168.

Founded in 1901. Publishes fiction, general non-fiction, cookery, how-to, self-help, travel and general science.

Econ-Verlag GmbH

Postfach 300321, 40403 Düsseldorf. Tel: (0)211 43596.
Fax: (0)211 4359768.

Founded in 1950. Publishes general non-fiction and fiction, economics and general science.

Falken-Verlag GmbH

Postfach 1120, 65521 Niederhausen. Tel: (0)6127 7020.
Fax: (0)6127 702133.

Founded in 1923. Publishes crafts, cookery, education, games,
gardening, health, history, hobbies, how-to, humour, nutrition, photography and sport.

S. Fischer Verlag GmbH

Postfach 700355, 60553 Frankfurt am Main. Tel: (0)69 60620.
Fax: (0)69 6062319.

Founded in 1886. Publishes fiction, general non-fiction, essays,
literature and literary criticism.

Gruner und Jahr AG & Co., Druck- und Verlagshaus

25524 Itzehoe, Am Vossbarg. Tel: (0)4821 7771.
Fax: (0)4821 777449.

Publishes, among others, Stern, Brigitte, Geo, Online Today and
Hamburger Morgenpost. Gruner und Jahr is owned by Bertelsmann
AG (see above).

Carl Hanser Verlag

Postfach 860420, 81631 München. Tel: (0)89 998300.
Fax: (0)89 984809.

Founded in 1928. Publishes general non-fiction, poetry, computer
science, economics, electronics, electrical, mechanical and general
engineering, environmental studies, management, mathematics,
medicine, nursing dentistry, philosophy and physics.

Wilhelm Heyne Verlag

Türkenstr. 5–7, 80333 München. Tel: (0)89 286350.
Fax: (0)89 2800934.

Founded in 1934. Publishes fiction, mystery, romance, humour,
science fiction, fantasy, astrology, biography, cookery, film, history,
how-to, occult, psychology, psychiatry and video.

Hoffmann und Campe Verlag

Postfach 130444, 20139 Hamburg. Tel: (0)40 441880.

Fax: (0)40 44188 290.

   Founded in 1781. Publishes fiction and general non-fiction, art, biography, dance, history, music, poetry, philosophy, psychiatry, general science, social sciences and sociology.

Verlagsgruppe Georg von Holtzbrinck GmbH

Gansheidestrasse 26, 70184 Stuttgart. Tel: (0)711 215-00.

Fax: (0)711 215-0269.

   Founded in 1948. Holtzbrinck is one of the world's largest publishing groups with 12 book publishing houses and 40 imprints, including the 112-year-old S. Fischer Verlag, publisher of Sigmund Freud and Franz Kafka. It also owns the country's largest business daily, Handelsblatt, and the highbrow general-interest weekly, Die Zeit.

Ernst Klett Verlag GmbH

Postfach 106016, 70049 Stuttgart. Tel: (0)711 66720.

Fax: (0)711 628053.

   Founded in 1897. Publishes education, career development, geography and geology.

Langenscheidt-Verlag

Neusser Strasse 3, 80807 München. Tel: (0)89 360960.

Fax (0)89 36096258.

   Founded in 1856. Publishes dictionaries, foreign languages, German for foreigners, textbooks and language guides.

Gustav Lübbe Verlag GmbH

Postfach 200127, 51431 Bergisch Gladbach. Tel: (0)2202 1210.

Fax: (0)2202 121708.

   Founded in 1963. Publishes fiction and general non-fiction, archaeology, biography, history and how-to.

Mosaik Verlag GmbH

Postfach 800360, 81673 München 80. Tel: (0)89 431890.
Fax: (0)89 43189743.

Publishes animals, antiques, architecture and interior design, child care and development, cookery, crafts, economics, finance, career development, film, gardening, games, hobbies, health, house and home, human relations, nutrition, pets, self-help, sport, video, wine and spirits and women's studies.

Pestalozzi Verlag Graphische Gesellschaft mbH

Am Pestalozziring 14, 91058 Erlangen. Tel: (0)9131 60600.
Fax: (0)9131 773090.

Founded in 1844. Publishes crafts, games and hobbies.

Rowohlt Taschenbuch Verlag GmbH

Postfach 1349, 21465 Reinbeck. Tel: (0)40 72720.
Fax: (0)40 7272319.

Founded in 1953. Publishes fiction and general non-fiction, archaeology, art, computer science, crafts, education, essays, games and hobbies, gay and lesbian, government, history, literature, literary criticism, philosophy, psychology, psychiatry, religion, general science, social sciences and sociology.

Axel Springer Verlag AG

10888 Berlin, Axel-Springer-Strasse 65. Tel: (0)30 25910.
Fax (0)30 2516071.

20350 Hamburg: Axel-Springer-Platz 1. Tel: (0)40 34700.
Fax: (0)40 343180).

Founded in 1946. The largest newspaper publishing group in Europe includes 5 major daily newspapers (Die Welt, Hamburger Abendblatt, Bild-Zeitung, Berliner Morgenpost, Berliner Zeitung), 2 Sunday newspapers (Welt am Sonntag, Bild am Sonntag), as well as radio, television, women's and family magazines. In addition to

publishing newspapers, magazines, specialist titles and free adver-
tisers (both in Germany and abroad), Axel Springer Verlag owns a
number of book publishers and operates its own printing plants and
distribution organizations.

Suhrkamp Verlag

Postfach 101945, 60019 Frankfurt am Main. Tel: (0)69 756010.
Fax: (0)69 75601522.

Founded in 1950. Publishes biography, fiction, philosophy, poetry,
psychology, psychiatry and general science.

SV-Hüthig Fachinformation GmbH

Sendlingstr. 8, 80331 München. Tel: (0)89 2183620.
Fax: (0)89 21838490.

Founded in 1998 by the merger of Süddeutscher Verlag and
Hüthig. This is Germany's fourth largest professional publisher.

Libraries

In 1996 there were 1,250 academic and special libraries,
and 12,727 public libraries, the latter with 10·26m. active users who
borrowed 316·6m. books.

SPORT

Sports occupy a central position in German life. Gymnastics were
introduced into the school curriculum as early as the Napoleonic
Wars as a form of pre-military training. Germany has continued to
place considerable emphasis on the importance of sporting activities, investing large amounts of public money in providing facilities
for a wide variety of sports as well as supporting sport in a variety of
ways including training, competitions and medical treatment for the

athletes, training and employment of coaches, and scientific research into sport related subjects. Football (soccer) is virtually a national sport, and Germany has won the World Cup three times (only Brazil has more wins). Other popular sports include tennis, athletics (gymnastics in particular), motor racing and winter sports.

The top ten sports

(Figures based on membership of Sporting Associations)

German Football Federation	5,675,783
German Gymnastics Federation	4,604,485
German Tennis Federation	2,333,326
German Shooting Federation	1,540,929
German Athletics Association	831,618
Deutscher Handball-Bund (handball)	826,618
Deutscher Tischtennis-Bund (table tennis)	750,049
German Equestrian Association	680,960
German Ski Federation	680,782
German Swimming Federation	631,744

TOURISM

In 1997 there were 53,830 places of accommodation with 2,360,037 beds (including 13,052 hotels with 859,367 beds). 14,891,200 foreign visitors and 77,732,800 tourists resident in Germany spent a total of 287,169,700 nights in holiday accommodation. Berlin is the most visited city with 3,448,996 visitors in 1997, and Bavaria the most visited Land with 19,556,800. More foreign visitors were from the Netherlands (1,806,800) than any other country. In 1996 foreign visitors spent US$16·5bn. in Germany.

Tourist Headquarters

Deutsche Zentrale für Tourismus eV (DZT). Beethovenstr. 69, 60325
Frankfurt am Main. Tel: (0)69 974640. Fax: (0)69 751903.

Web: www.germany-tourism.de www.germany-info.org
www.goethe.de/

Central Hotel Reservations

Central reservation numbers of hotels chains/booking services represented in the UK and Hotel Chains and Reservation Agency Numbers

Most of the hotels or hotel chains represented below offer a high
standard of accommodation for the business traveller as well as
meeting, conference and fitness facilities.

Hilton International: 0345 581 595. Web: www.hilton.com
Holiday Inn: 0800 897 121. Web: www.basshotels.com
ITT Sheraton: 0800 353535. Web: www.starwood.com

Airco Hotels: Tel: (0)69 92-31-99-28. Fax: (0)69 92-31-99-32.
Email: uiaz@ibm.net

(Family owned independent hotels in more than 65 cities all over
Germany)

ArabellaSheraton: Tel: (0)89 92-00-32-00.
Fax: (0)89 92-00-32-01, or 0080-03-25-35-35-35.

(in the top ten of hotel companies operating in Germany)

Best Western: Tel: 0800 39 31 30. (0)6196 47-240.
Fax: (0)6196 47-24-12. Web: www.bestwestern.com

(American owned chain of hotels with conference and meetings
facilities)

Maritim Hotels: Tel: (0)6151 90-57-10. Fax: (0)6151 90-57-17.
Email: 101657.652@compuserve.com

(Germany's largest hotel group with hotels in cities all over Germany)

Minotel: Tel: (0)89 53-29-590. Fax: (0)89 18-44-16.
Email: minotel@compuserve.com. Web: www.minotel.com

(An alliance of more than 700 privately owned 3 star hotels with 64 in Germany)

TOP International Hotels: (0)211 55-98-55-55.

Fax: (0)211 55-98-55-54. Email: Top@top-hotel.de

Web: www.top-hotels.com

Many good hotels can be booked through central German Tourist Offices and related web sites.

Hotel Reservation Service: www.hrs.de www.hrs.com

Tourist Board central reservations: www.germany-tourism.de www.bookings.org/de

Central Car Hire Reservations

Avis: http://www.avis.com Tel: (0)6171 681800.

Hertz: http://www.hertz.com Tel: 01805 333535.

Budget: http://www.budgetrentacar.com Tel: (0)805 244388

Thrifty: http://www.thrifty.com Tel: 0990 168238 (UK number)

Europcar: http://www.europcar.com Tel: (0)40 520 18211.

ETIQUETTE

Social

The public face of German etiquette – formal and rather cold – is in sharp contrast to the warmth and informality of the private face. In Germany, formal manners are seen as a sign of respect and should not be interpreted as 'standoffishness'. When addressing a German, it is customary to use Herr, Frau or the highest title the person possesses. An invitation to a German home is a big compliment and it is usual to bring a small gift for the hostess. Punctuality (especially for meals) is expected and being late is seen as an insult.

Older people still use the formal third person 'Sie' (you) when addressing strangers and the informal 'du' should only be used if invited to do so (except to children or young people). It is safer to address all women as 'Frau' (followed by a name if you know it) – these days, only waitresses in traditional restaurants are addressed as 'Fräulein'. German society places such importance on good manners that if you speak insultingly or rudely to a policeman you can be liable for a hefty on-the-spot fine. Germany is a law-abiding country and if you break the law in public e.g. park illegally, jay walk, etc., passers-by will probably comment quite forcefully.

Business

In business, even though German society is democratic with workers and management sharing canteens, car parks and washrooms, working relationships tend to be formal, with the emphasis on careful thought and planning. Making an effort to speak the language creates a positive impression, especially if you want to sell to a German company. Many German company officials will insist on speaking their own language. In Germany only the written word is legally binding. The 'gentleman's agreement' should only be seen as the first step in ongoing negotiations. The working day is long and early morning meetings are common. Punctuality is considered extremely important in both business and social life. Business contacts and prospective clients will be formally dressed and will expect the same from a visitor. It is customary to shake hands with everyone present when arriving for a meeting. Business and pleasure do not mix easily in Germany until the relationships are well progressed, and invitations to private homes are a rare compliment.

On a few occasions, birthdays, the feast of St. Nikolaus on 6 Dec., and around Christmas and New Year, the barriers break down and close colleagues give each other small gifts and bosses do likewise for their employees.

FESTIVALS AND MILLENNIUM EVENTS

Web Site:- www.deutschland2000.de

The first of its kind to be held in Germany, Expo 2000 will take place at the refurbished Hanover Exhibition Grounds and a new development next to it. Even by 1998 the exhibition had broken all records by attracting the support of the largest number of countries and international organizations at the highest level ever. The theme of Expo 2000 is 'Mankind, Nature, Technology' and it runs from 1 June to 31 Oct. 2000.

Web sites: www.expo2000.de/ or www.expo20000.de/index-e.html (English page)

New Year's Eve 'Millennium' Parties will be held in Düsseldorf (which is attempting a world record for the longest New Year's Eve Party, to run from 31 Dec. 1999 through to 2 Jan. 2000), Bremen, Cologne, Dresden, Hamburg, Munich, Nuremberg, Potsdam and Wiesbaden. Up to date information will be available from the German Tourist Board or web sites (see above). Other festivals planned for 2000 include:

250th anniversary of Johann Sebastian Bach's death, to be celebrated in Leipzig, principally in July 2000.

Information from: Leipzig Tourist Service, Richard-Wagner-Strasse 1, 04109 Leipzig. Tel: (0)341 7104-260. Fax: (0)341 7104-260. Email: lipsia@aol.com

600 year anniversary of Gutenberg in Mainz with an exhibition 'Gutenberg's Time' (April–Oct. 2000).

Information from: Tel: (0)6131 286210.

Bremen is building a Space Park, which they say will feature 'huge numbers of extraterrestrials'.

For the Passion Play cycle in Oberammergau (May–Oct.), a special millennium production is planned.

Information from: Verkehrs- und Reisebüro, Gemeinde Oberammergau OHG, Eugen-Pabst-Strassse 9a, 82487

Oberammergau. Tel: (0)8822 92310. Fax: (0)8822 923144.
Email: H.Rettelbach@gap.baynet.de Web: www.oberammergau.de/
Wagner Festspiele (the Wagner Festival) in Bayreuth. Every summer between 25 July and 28 Aug.

Information from: Festpielhaus Bayreuther Festpiele, Kongress-Tourismuscentrale.

Tel: (0)921 88588. Fax: (0)921 88555.
Email: tourismus@bayreuth.btl.de

Annual Festivals

Jan.–Feb.	Fasching (Carnival)	Munich
Late Feb.–Early March	Film Festival	Berlin
Mid-Feb.	Karneval	Cologne
May	Hafensgeburtstag	Hamburg
Late June	International Film Festival	Munich
26 June	Christopher Street Day	Berlin
July–Aug.	Bach Festival	Leipzig
Mid-July	Love Parade	Berlin
Late July	Das Fest	Karlsruhe
July–Aug.	Wagner Festspiele	Bayreuth
7–17 Aug.	Gäubodenvolksfest	Straubing
25 Aug.–5 Sept.	Wine Festival	Stuttgart
18 Sept.–3 Oct.	Oktoberfest	Munich
24–27 Dec.	Christmas Market	Nuremberg

Information on other festivals can be obtained from German Tourist offices throughout the country and on the Tourist Board web site: www.germany-tourism.de

Public Holidays

1 Jan.	New Year's Day
6 Jan.	Epiphany (Bavaria, Baden-Württemberg and Saxony-Anhalt only)

Good Friday	
Easter Monday	
1 May	May Day
Ascension Day	
Whit Monday	
Early or mid-June	Corpus Christi (Baden-Württemberg, Bavaria, Hesse, Rhineland-Palatinate, North Rhine-Westphalia and Saarland only)
15 Aug.	The Assumption (Bavaria and Saarland only)
3 Oct.	Day of German Unity
31 Oct.	Reformation Day (Brandenburg, Mecklenburg-Vorpommern, Saxony and Saxony-Anhalt only)
1 Nov.	All Saints Day (Baden-Württemberg, Bavaria, North Rhine-Westphalia, Rhineland Palatinate, Saarland and Thuringia)
1st Wednesday after 8 Nov.	Repentance Day, in Saxony only
25 Dec.	Christmas Day
26 Dec.	Boxing Day

DIPLOMATIC REPRESENTATIVES

Of Germany in Great Britain (23 Belgrave Sq., 1 Chesham Place, London, SW1X 8PZ)

Ambassador: Gebhardt von Moltke.

Of Great Britain in Germany (Friedrich-Ebert-Allee 77, 53113 Bonn)

Ambassador: Sir Paul Lever.

Of Germany in the USA (4645 Reservoir Rd, NW, Washington, D.C., 20007)

Ambassador: Jürgen Chrobog.

Of the USA in Germany (Deichmanns Aue, 53170 Bonn)

Ambassador: John Kornblum.

Of Germany to the United Nations

Ambassador: Dr Dieter Kastrup.

Other German Embassies in the EU

Austria

Metternichgasse 3, A-1030 Wien.

Ambassador: Ursula Seiler-Albring.

Belgium

Avenue de Tervueren 190, B-1150 Brussel.

Ambassador: Dr Rolf Hofstetter.

Denmark

Stockholmsgade 57, DK-2100 Copenhagen Ø.

Ambassador: Johann Georg Dreher.

Finland

Krogiuksentie 4b, FIN-00340 Helsinki.

Ambassador: Henning von Wistinghausen.

France

13/15 Avenue Franklin D. Roosevelt, F-75008 Paris.

Ambassador: Dr Peter Hartmann.

Greece

Karaoli and Dimitriou 3, GR101, 10 Athens.

Ambassador: Dr Karl Heinz Kuhna.

Ireland

31 Trimleston Avenue, Booterstown, Blackrock, Co. Dublin.

Ambassador: Dr Hartmut Hillgenberg.

Italy

Via San Martino della Battaglia 4, I–00185 Roma.
Ambassador: Fritjof von Nordenskjold.

Luxembourg

20–22 Avenue Emile Reuter, L-2420 Luxembourg.
Ambassador: Horst Pakowski.

Netherlands

Groot Hertoginnelaan 18–20, 2517 EG Den Haag.
Ambassador: Eberhard von Puttkamer.

Portugal

Campo dos Matires da Patria 38, P-1169–043 Lisboa.
Ambassador: Wilfried Richter.

Spain

Calle de Fortuny 8, E-28010 Madrid.
Ambassador: Dr Henning Wegener.

Sweden

Skarpogatan 9, S-11527 Stockholm.
Ambassador: Klaus-Hellmuth Ackermann.

Major German Embassies Worldwide

Russia

Mosfilmowskaja 56, 119285 Moscow.
Ambassador: Dr Ernst-Jorg von Studnitz.

Australia

119 Empire Circuit, Yarralumla, ACT 2600.
Ambassador: Dr Horst Bachmann.

New Zealand

90–92 Hobson Street, Thorndon, Wellington, PO Box 1687.
Ambassador: Eberhard Noldeke.

South Africa
180 Blackwood Street, Arcadia, Pretoria 0083.
Ambassador: Harald Ganns.

Canada
1 Waverley Street, Ottawa, Ontario, K2P 0T8.
Ambassador: Dr Jürgen Pohlmann.

Japan
4–5–10 Minami-Azabu, Minato-ku, Tokyo 106.
Ambassador: Frank Elbe.

EU Embassies in Germany
Austria
Johannitestr. 2, 53113 Bonn.
Ambassador: Dr Markus Lutterotti.

Belgium
Kaiser-Friedrich-Str. 7, 53113 Bonn.
Ambassador: Dominicus Struye de Swielande.

Denmark
Pfalzer Str. 14, 53111 Bonn.
Ambassador: Bent Haakonsen.

Finland
Friesdorfer Str. 1, 53173 Bonn.
Ambassador: Arto Mansala.

France
An der Marienkapelle 3, 53179 Bonn.
Ambassador: François Scheer.

Greece
An der Marienkapelle 10, 53179 Bonn.
Ambassador: Dr Ioannis Bourloyannis-Tsangaridis.

Ireland
Godesberger Allee 119, 53175 Bonn.
Ambassador: Noel Fahey.

Italy
Karl Finkelnburg-Str. 51, 53173 Bonn.
Ambassador: Enzo Perlot.

Luxembourg
Adenauerallee 108, 53113 Bonn.
Ambassador: Julian Alex.

Netherlands
Sträßchensweg 10, 53113 Bonn.
Ambassador: Dr Nikolaos van Dam.

Portugal
Ubierstr. 78, 53173 Bonn.
Ambassador: João Diogo Correia Saraiva Nuntes Barata.

Spain
Schloßstr. 4, 53115 Bonn.
Ambassador: José Pedro Sebastian de Erice y Gomez-Acebo.

Sweden
Konsularabteilung der Botschaft, Heussallee 2–10, 53113 Bonn.
Ambassador: Mats Hellstrom.

Major non-EU Embassies in Germany
Russia
Waldstr. 42, 53177 Bonn.
Ambassador: Sergej Borissovich Krylov.

Australia
Godesberger Allee 105–107, 53175 Bonn.
Ambassador: Paul O'Sullivan.

New Zealand

Bundeskanzlerplatz 2–10, Bonn Center, 53113 Bonn.
Ambassador: Winston A. Cochrane.

Canada

Friedrich-Wilhelm-Str. 18, 53113 Bonn.
Ambassador: Gaetan Lavertu.

South Africa

Auf der Hostert 3, 53173 Bonn.
Ambassador: None at present.

Japan

Godesberger Allee 102–104, 53175 Bonn.
Ambassador: S.E. Kunisada Kume.

EMBASSY ADDRESSES

The relocation to Berlin of the Federal Government and Parliament means that foreign missions are also moving from Bonn. Although most of the foreign missions will have established a presence by the year 2000, it will be several years before the move (which will involve at least 17,000 people from 154 accredited missions) will be completed. In the past, foreign embassies in Berlin have been associated with the Tiergarten Quarter of the city where most foreign missions set up representation from the turn of this century. Although some countries will return to their historical locations, others will have to find new properties.

To find new addresses for Foreign Embassies in Berlin, please consult either the address below or one of the following web sites:–

Auswärtiges Amt Dienststelle Berlin, 10992 Berlin, Postfach 610187 (or visit them at Wedersches Markt). Tel: (0)30 20-18-60. Fax: (0) 30 20-18-62-52.

www.bau.berlin.de (the 'Embassy Exchange' page is devoted to Embassy and Consulate moves.)

www.embassyweb.com

www.embassyworld.com

FURTHER READING

Statistisches Bundesamt. *Statistisches Jahrbuch für die Bundesrepublik Deutschland; Wirtschaft und Statistik* (monthly, from 1949); *Das Arbeitsgebiet der Bundesstatistik* (latest issue 1988; Abridged English version: *Survey of German Federal Statistics*).

Ardagh, J., *Germany and the Germans.* 3rd ed. Penguin, London, 1996

Balfour, M., *Germany: the Tides of Power.* Routledge, London, 1992

Bark, D. L. and Gress, D. R., *A History of West Germany, 1945–1991.* 2nd ed. 2 vols. Oxford, 1993

Betz, H. G., *Postmodern Politics in Germany.* St. Martin's Press, London, 1991

Blackbourn, D., *The Long Nineteenth Century: A History of Germany, 1780–1918.* Oxford University Press, 1997

Blackbourn, D. and Eley, G., *The Peculiarities of German History.* Oxford University Press, 1985

Carr, W., *A History of Germany, 1815–1990.* 4th ed. Edward Arnold, London, 1995

Childs, D., *Germany in the 20th Century.* London, 1991 – *The Stasi: The East German Intelligence and Security Service.* Macmillan, London, 1999

Dennis, M., *The German Democratic Republic: Politics, Economics and Society.* Pinter, London, 1987

Detwiler, D. S. and Detwiler, I. E., *West Germany* [Bibliography]. ABC-Clio, Oxford and Santa Barbara (CA), 1988

Edinger, L. J., *West German Politics.* Columbia University Press, New York, 1986

Eley, G., *From Unification to Nazism: Reinterpreting the German Past.* London, 1986

Frowen, Stephen F. *The German Currency Union of 1990: A Critical Assessment.* Macmillan, London, 1999

Fulbrook, M., *A Concise History of Germany.* CUP, 1991. – *The Divided Nation: a History of Germany, 1918–1990.* Cambridge University Press, 1992 – Interpretation of the Two Germanies, 1945–1997. Macmillan, London, 1999

Glees, A., *Reinventing Germany: German political development since 1945.* Berg, Oxford, 1996

Huelshoff, M. G. *et al.* (eds.) *From Bundesrepublik to Deutschland: German Politics after Reunification.* Michigan Univ. Press, 1993

Kielinger, T., *Crossroads and Roundabouts, Junctions in German-British Relations.* Bonn, 1997

Langewiesche, Dieter, *Liberalism in Germany.* Macmillan, London, 1999

Loth, W., *Stalin's Unwanted Child – The Soviet Union, the German Question and the Founding of the GDR.* St. Martin's Press, New York, 1998

Maier, C. S., *Dissolution: The Crisis of Communism and the End of East Germany.* Princeton University Press, N.J., 1997

Marsh, D., *The New Germany: at the Crossroads.* London, 1990

Marshall, B., *The Origins of Post-War German Politics.* London, 1988

Merkl, Peter H., (ed.) *The Federal Republic of Germany at Fifty: The End of a Century of Turmoil.* Macmillan, London, 1999

Neville, P. *Appeasing Hitler: The Diplomacy of Sir Neville Henderson.* Macmillan, London, 1999

Nicholls, A. J., *The Bonn Republic: West German Democracy, 1945–1990.* Addison-Wesley, Harlow, 1998

Orlow, D., *A History of Modern Germany, 1871 to the Present.* 4th ed. Prentice Hall, New York, 1994

Parkes, K. S., *Understanding Contemporary Germany.* Routledge, London, 1996

Pulzer, P., *German Politics, 1945–1995.* Oxford University Press, 1995

Schmidt, H., *Handeln für Deutschland.* Berlin, 1993

Schweitzer, C.-C., (ed.) *Politics and Government in Germany: Basic Documents.* 2nd ed. Berghahn Books, Oxford, 1995

Sinn, G. and Sinn, H.-W., *Jumpstart: the Economic Reunification of Germany.* MIT Press, Boston (MA), 1993

Smyser, W.R., *The Economy of United Germany: Colossus at the Crossroads.* New York, 1992 – *The Cold War Struggle Over Germany.* Macmillan, London, 1999

Stürmer, M., *Die Grenzen der Macht.* Berlin, 1992

Taylor, R., *Berlin and its Culture.* Yale University Press, 1997

Thompson, W. C. *et al., Historical Dictionary of Germany.* Scarecrow Press, Metuchen (NJ), 1995

Turner, H. A., *Germany from Partition to Reunification.* 2nd ed. [of *Two Germanies since 1945*]. Yale Univ. Press, 1993

Tusa, A., *The Last Division – A History of Berlin, 1945–1989.* Perseus Books, Reading, Mass., 1997

Wallace, I., *East Germany: the German Democratic Republic* [Bibliography]. ABC-Clio, Oxford and Santa Barbara (CA), 1987

Watson, A., *The Germans: Who Are They Now?* 2nd ed. London, 1994

TOURIST AND HOTEL GUIDES

Baedeker Guide: Germany. AA Publishing, 1996, ISBN: 0–749–51398–5

Coles, W., and Koreik, U., *The Simple Guide to Germany, Customs and Etiquette.* Global Books, 1998, ISBN: 1–860–34031–8

Fallon, S. *et al, Lonely Planet: Germany.* Lonely Planet Publications, 1998, ISBN: 0–864–42487–6

Fodor's 99 Germany (Fodor's Gold Guides). Fodor's Travel Publications, 1998 ISBN: 0–679–00137–9

Frommer's 99 Germany. Macmillan, 1998, ISBN: 0–028–62275–8

Johansens Recommended Hotels: Europe and the Mediterranean 2000. Johansens, 1999, ISBN: 1–860–17711–5

Kraus, A., *Essential Germany*. AA Publishing, 1998,
ISBN: 0–749–51656–9

Let's Go: Germany. Macmillan, 1999, ISBN: 0–333–74739–9

McLachlan, G., *Germany: the Rough Guide*. Rough Guides, 1998,
ISBN: 1–858–28309–4

Michelin Green Tourist Guide: Germany. Michelin, 1999,
ISBN: 2–061–50402–7

Michelin Guide Europe 1999: Hotels – Restaurants. Michelin, 1999,
ISBN: 2–069–70999–X

Other more specialized titles are listed under CONSTITUTION AND
GOVERNMENT *and* BANKING AND FINANCE, *above*.

National statistical office: Statistiches Bundesamt, D-65189
Wiesbaden, Gustav Stresemann Ring 11. *President:* Johann Hahlen.
Website: www.statistik-bund.de

National libraries: Deutsche Bibliothek, Zeppelinallee 4–8;
Frankfurt am Main. *Director:* K.-D. Lehmann; (Berliner)
Staatsbibliothek Preussischer Kulturbesitz, Potsdamer Str. 33,
Postfach 1407, D-10785 Berlin. *Director:* Dr. Richard Landwehrmeyer.

THE LÄNDER

BADEN-WÜRTTEMBERG

KEY HISTORICAL EVENTS

The *Land* is a combination of former states. Baden (the western part
of the present *Land*) became a united margravate in 1771, after being
divided as Baden-Baden and Baden-Durlach since 1535; Baden-
Baden was predominantly Catholic and Baden-Durlach, Protestant.

The margrave became an ally of Napoleon, ceding land west of the Rhine and receiving northern and southern territory as compensation. In 1805 Baden became a grand duchy and in 1806 a member state of the Confederation of the Rhine, extending from the Main to Lake Constance. In 1815 it was a founder-state of the German Confederation. A constitution was granted by the grand duke in 1818, but later rulers were less liberal and there was revolution in 1848, put down with Prussian help. The grand Duchy was abolished and replaced by a *Land* in 1919.

In 1949 Baden was combined with Württemberg to form three states; the three were brought together as 1 in 1952.

Württemberg, having been a duchy since 1495, became a kingdom in 1805 and joined the Confederations as did Baden. A constitution was granted in 1819 and the state remained liberal. In 1866 the king allied himself with Austria against Prussia, but in 1870 joined Prussia in war against France. The liberal monarchy came to an end with the abdication of William II in 1918, and Württemberg became a state of the German Republic. In 1945 the state was divided between different Allied occupation authorities but the divisions ended in 1952.

Baden-Württemberg combines some of Germany's most scenic countryside with large-scale industry, medium and small-sized companies and agriculture. The Black Forest is a world famous beauty and recreation spot generating a thriving tourist industry and the hilly region of Kaiserstuhl in the Upper Rhine is famous for its wine. Global companies such as Bosch and Porsche have their headquarters in Baden-Württemberg and the region exports more than Switzerland. The smaller businesses manufacture a wide variety of highly special-ized products that are exported all over the world. The region enjoys a mild climate and produces fruit, ornamental plants, vegetables, hops and tobacco. Baden-Württemberg ploughs back much of the profit from exports into research with the emphasis on motor vehicle engi-neering as well as communications and environmental technologies.

Biotechnology and genetic engineering are also strongly supported. The State has 9 universities, 39 Fachochschulen (technical colleges) and approximately 130 research institutes (including the Research Centre in Karlsruhe, the German Cancer Research Centre in Heidelberg and several Max Planck and Frauhofer institutes) all linked by a high speed data transmission link. Marbach holds the German Literary Archive where the literary legacy of most German writers is conserved. The region also has the headquarters of most of the main publishing companies – 40% of all German books are published here. The University of Heidelberg (founded in 1386) is the oldest in Germany and Karlsruhe Technical College was the first to be established.

The region has more than a thousand museums, two State theatres, ten city theatres, festivals and film festivals.

TERRITORY AND POPULATION

Baden-Württemberg comprises 35,751 sq. km, with a population (at 31 Dec. 1997) of 10,396,610 (5,307,977 females, 5,088,633 males).

The *Land* is divided into 4 administrative regions, 9 urban and 35 rural districts, and numbers 1,111 communes. The capital is Stuttgart.

SOCIAL STATISTICS

Calendar years	Live births	Marriages	Divorces	Deaths
1994	113,398	59,591	19,910	96,638
1995	112,459	58,198	19,921	97,733
1996	114,657	57,898	20,759	98,908
1997	116,419	57,094	21,572	97,167

CONSTITUTION AND GOVERNMENT

The *Land* Baden-Württemberg is a merger of the 3 *Länder*, Baden, Württemberg-Baden and Württemberg-Hohenzollern, which were formed in 1952. The merger was approved by a plebiscite held on 9 Dec. 1951, when 70% of the population voted in its favour. It has 6 votes in the Bundesrat.

RECENT ELECTIONS

At the elections to the 155-member Diet of March 1996, turn-out was 67·6%. The Christian Democrats won 69 seats with 41·3% of the vote, the Social Democrats 39 with 25·1%, the Greens 19 with 12·1%, the Free Democrats 14 with 9·6% and the Republicans 14 with 9·1%.

CURRENT ADMINISTRATION

Erwin Teufel (CDU) is *Prime Minister* (Minister President).

Local Government

Since the creation of the Land in 1952, the CDU has always been the largest party.

ECONOMY

Performance

GDP in 1997 was 523,136m. DM which amounted to 16·2% of Germany's total GDP.

BANKING

Central Bank

Landeszentralbank in Baden-Württemberg: 70173 Stuttgart, Marstallstr. 14. Tel: (0)711 9440. Fax: (0)711 9941903.

Stock Exchange

Baden-Württembergische Wertpapierbörse zu Stuttgart: 70173 Stuttgart, Königstr. 28. Tel: (0)711 290183. Fax: (0)711 2268119.

ENERGY AND NATURAL RESOURCES

Electricity

Hydroelectric power is a significant source of electricity in the Land.

Oil and Gas

A small quantity of oil and gas was produced in Baden-Württemberg but production ceased in Sept. 1997.

Agriculture

Area and yield of the most important crops:

	Area (in 1,000 ha)			Yield (in 1,000 tonnes)		
	1995	*1996*	*1997*	*1995*	*1996*	*1997*
Rye	15·5	12·7	11·2	73·0	71·9	60·4
Wheat	214·9	214·7	217·7	1,185·4	1,576·6	1,444·7
Barley	191·1	202·9	211·8	885·7	1,170·0	1,174·1
Oats	55·6	54·8	54·8	254·3	324·5	294·9
Potatoes	9·7	9·7	8·3	274·7	391·7	270·2
Sugar-beet	22·5	22·5	22·0	1,289·8	1,336·2	1,249·1

Livestock in 1,000 (Dec. 1997): Cattle, 1,327·1 (including 465·7 milch cows); pigs, 2,275·8; sheep, 285·3; poultry, 5,490·5 (1996).

INDUSTRY

In 1997, 8,890 establishments (with 20 and more employees) employed 1,225,886 persons; of these, 266,655 were employed in machine construction (excluding office machines, data processing equipment and facilities); 27,486 in the textile industry; 200,813 in electrical engineering; 201,451 in car manufacture.

Labour

Economically active persons totalled 4,769,400 at the 1%-EU-sample survey of April 1997. Of the total 545,700 were self-employed (including family workers). Of 4·22m. employees: 122,600 were engaged in agriculture and forestry; 1,958,600 in power supply, mining, manufacturing and building; 951,700 in commerce and transport; 1,736,600 in other industries and services.

INTERNATIONAL TRADE

Imports and Exports

Total imports (1997): 98,759m. DM. Total exports: 149,664m. DM, of which 70,970m. DM went to the EU.

Trade Fair Organizers

Stuttgarter Messe und Kongress-GmbH: 70028 Stuttgart, Postfach 103252. Tel: (0)711 25890. Fax: (0)711 2589440.

COMMUNICATIONS

Roads

On 1 Jan. 1998 there were 28,101 km of 'classified' roads, including 1,023 km of Autobahn, 4,972 km of federal roads, 10,030 km of first-class and 12,076 km of second-class highways. Motor vehicles, at 1 Jan. 1998, numbered 6,562,874, including 5,487,322 passenger cars, 9,425 buses, 263,742 trucks, 326,961 tractors and 381,560 motor cycles.

Rail

Railway track operated by Deutsche Bahn AG covered 3,987 km in 1996. In addition, 488 km of track was operated by private railway companies.

Civil Aviation

The largest airport in Baden-Württemberg is at Stuttgart which in 1998 had 6·7m. users. This is expected to rise to over 8m. by 2010. There are another 2 regional airports and 20 airstrips in use in the Land.

Shipping

The harbour in Karlsruhe is the largest in Baden-Württemberg. In 1997 it handled 8·3m. tonnes of freight, compared to 7·9m. tonnes in Mannheim.

SOCIAL INSTITUTIONS

Justice

There are a constitutional court *(Staatsgerichtshof)*, 2 courts of appeal, 17 regional courts, 108 local courts, a *Land* labour court,

9 labour courts, a *Land* social court, 8 social courts, a finance court, a higher administrative court *(Verwaltungsgerichtshof)* and 4 administrative courts.

Religion

On 1 Jan. 1998, 39·0% of the population were Protestants and 43·6% were Roman Catholics.

Education

In 1997–98 there were 2,695 primary schools *(Grund- und Hauptschulen)* with 34,717 teachers and 693,322 pupils; 552 special schools with 9,337 teachers and 50,068 pupils; 452 intermediate schools with 11,512 teachers and 210,949 pupils; 415 high schools with 18,506 teachers and 271,236 pupils; 42 *Freie Waldorf* schools with 1,347 teachers and 19,224 pupils. Other general schools had 584 teachers and 8,507 pupils in total; there were also 739 vocational schools with 364,870 pupils. There were 39 *Fachhochschulen* (colleges of engineering and others) with 57,404 students in winter term 1997–98.

In the winter term 1997–98 there were 9 universities (Freiburg, 20,182 students; Heidelberg, 24,767; Konstanz, 7,953; Tübingen, 21,432; Karlsruhe, 15,868; Stuttgart, 16,770; Hohenheim, 4,745; Mannheim, 10,728; Ulm, 4,802); 6 teacher-training colleges with 17,739 students; 5 colleges of music with 2,680 students and 3 colleges of fine arts with 1,315 students.

CULTURE

Cinema

In 1996 there were 544 cinema screens and 95,354 seats.

Tourism

There were 6,874 places of accommodation in 1997 with 283,371 beds. There were a total of 11,747,000 visitors during the year.

Libraries

Baden-Württemberg had 1,424 libraries and 15,056,000 books in 1996.

Theatre and Opera

In 1998 the Baden-Baden Festival Hall opened with seating for 2,500 persons.

Museums

In 1996 there were 742 museums putting on 1,024 exhibitions for 13,052,000 visitors.

FURTHER READING

Statistical Information: Statistisches Landesamt Baden-Württemberg (P.O.B. 10 60 33, 70049 Stuttgart) (*President:* Dr Eberhard Leibing), publishes: *'Baden-Württemberg in Wort und Zahl'* (monthly); *Jahrbücher für Statistik und Landeskunde von Baden-Württemberg; Statistik von Baden-Württemberg* (series); *Statistisch-prognostischer Bericht* (latest issue 1998); *Statistisches Taschenbuch* (latest issue 1998).

State libraries: Württembergische Landesbibliothek, Konrad-Adenauer-Str. 8, 70173 Stuttgart. Badische Landesbibliothek Karlsruhe, Lamm-Str. 16, 76133 Karlsruhe.

BAVARIA

KEY HISTORICAL EVENTS

Bavaria was ruled by the Wittelsbach family from 1180. The duchy remained Catholic after the Reformation, which made it a natural ally of Austria and the Hapsburg Emperors.

The present boundaries were reached during the Napoleonic wars, and Bavaria became a kingdom in 1805. Despite the granting of a constitution and parliament, radical feeling forced the abdication of King Ludwig I in 1848. Maximilian II was followed by Ludwig II who allied himself with Austria against Prussia in 1866, but was reconciled with Prussia and entered the German Empire in 1871.

In 1918 the King Ludwig III abdicated. The first years of republican government were filled with unrest, attempts at the overthrow of the state by both communist and right-wing groups culminating in an unsuccessful coup by Adolf Hitler in 1923.

The state of Bavaria included the Palatinate from 1214 until 1945, when it was taken from Bavaria and added to the Rhineland. The present *Land* of Bavaria was formed in 1948.

Munich became capital of Bavaria in the reign of Albert IV (1467–1508) and remains capital of the *Land*.

Bavaria is the largest Federal State with nearly 12m. inhabitants. The region has its own anthem and dialect, and the population often wear colorful traditional dress (not only during folk festivals). With its Alpine scenery and forests (Bavaria has Germany's highest mountain, at 2,962 metres), the region is a favourite recreation and vacation spot and a wealth of palaces and parks (especially the fairy-tale palaces of King Ludwig II) attract a large quantity of tourists each year. Until the 1950s, Bavaria's main industry was agriculture and in the Alpine regions, farming and forestry still play a large part in the region's economy. Bavarian beer that is still brewed to the purity regulations of 1516 is made from hops grown in the region. The cities of Nuremberg and Fürth were linked by Germany's first railway line in 1835 and they form the centre of an industrial area which focuses on the manufacture of electrical goods, plastics, toys and food, mechanical and vehicle engineering and printing. Other industries include textiles, wood products, oil refining, electronics and wine making. In the eastern part of Bavaria, the traditional manufacture of glass and porcelain is much in evidence. Munich – the capital – is a mix of 'high tech' and folk traditions. Bavaria spends DM 100 million on preserving its cultural heritage. Munich is home to the Deutsches Museum, which houses the world's largest exhibitions devoted to the history of science and technology. Nuremberg is particularly rich in medieval treasures and churches and also houses the National Museum of German Culture. Bayreuth, the birthplace of Richard Wagner, holds a world famous annual festival of Wagner operas. Folk dancing is popular in Bavaria and there are many local folk festivals. Once every ten years, the inhabitants of Oberammergau perform a Passion Play, which attracts visitors from all over the world. The next performance will be in the year 2000.

TERRITORY AND POPULATION

Bavaria has an area of 70,548 sq. km. The capital is Munich. There are 7 administrative regions, 25 urban districts, 71 rural districts, 251 unadopted areas and 2,056 communes, 1,004 of which are members of 319 administrative associations. The population (31 Dec. 1997) numbered 12,066,375 (5,884,415 males, 6,181,960 females).

SOCIAL STATISTICS

Calendar years	Live births	Marriages	Divorces	Deaths
1994	127,828	69,401	23,087	121,581
1995	125,995	67,075	23,434	121,992
1996	129,376	66,767	24,259	123,329
1997	130,517	65,419	26,046	121,441

CONSTITUTION AND GOVERNMENT

The Constituent Assembly, elected on 30 June 1946, passed a constitution on the lines of the democratic constitution of 1919, but with greater emphasis on state rights; this was agreed upon by the Christian Social Union (CSU) and the Social Democrats (SPD). Bavaria has 6 seats in the Bundesrat. The CSU replaces the Christian Democratic Party in Bavaria.

RECENT ELECTIONS

At the Diet elections on 13 Sept. 1998 the CSU won 123 seats with 52·9% of votes cast; the SPD, 67 with 28·7%, and Alliance '90/The Greens, 14 with 5·7%. Turnout was 70%.

CURRENT ADMINISTRATION

The *Prime Minister* is Dr Edmund Stoiber (CSU).

Local Government

At the *local government* elections of March 1996 the CSU won 43·1% of votes cast and the SPD 25·7%.

BANKING

Central Bank

Landeszentralbank im Freistaat Bayern: 80539 München, Ludwigstr. 13. Tel: (0)89 71128895. Fax: (0)89 2889-3890.

Stock Exchange

Bayerische Börse: 80333 München, Lenbachplatz, 2a/1. Tel: (0)89 5490450. Fax: (0)89 54904532.

ENERGY AND NATURAL RESOURCES

Agriculture

Area and yield of the most important products:

	Area (in 1,000 ha)			Yield (in 1,000 tonnes)		
	1996	1997	1998	1996	1997	1998
Wheat	446·6	469·1	469·4	3,162·4	3,077·8	3,241·0
Rye	54·0	50·6	58·0	285·4	244·3	319·3
Barley	473·4	483·7	460·2	2,511·9	2,575·5	2,574·2
Oats	75·0	76·1	63·6	388·9	385·5	291·6
Potatoes	62·5	55·7	55·1	2,727·2	2,156·4	2,184·7
Sugar-beet	79·0	78·2	79·7	4,804·2	4,601·7	5,024·3

Livestock, 1997: 4,126,000 cattle (including 1,513,000 milch cows); 109,000 horses; 382,000 sheep; 3,651,000 pigs; 9,968,000 poultry.

INDUSTRY

In 1997, 8,013 establishments (with 20 or more employees) employed 1,168,301 persons; of these, 145,483 were employed in the manufacture of motor vehicles, 188,388 in the manufacture of machinery and equipment and 51,970 in the manufacture of textiles and textile products.

Labour

The economically active persons totalled 5,701,000 at the 1% sample survey of the microcensus of 1997. Of the total, 670,000 were self-employed, 119,000 unpaid family workers, 4,913,000 employees; 2,069,000 in power supply, mining, manufacturing and building; 1,277,000 in commerce and transport; 2,134,000 in other industries and services.

Trade Fair Organizers

Messe München GmbH: 80325 München, Messegelände. Tel: (0)89 51070. Fax: (0)89 5107506.

COMMUNICATIONS

Metropolitan Railways

Stadtwerke München, Werkbereich Verkehr: 80287 München, Einsteinstr. 28. Tel: (0)89 21911. Fax: (0)89 21912155.

Roads

There were, on 1 Jan. 1998, 41,671 km of 'classified' roads, including
2,202 km of Autobahn, 6,842 km of federal roads, 13,963 km of first-
class and 18,664 km of second-class highways. Number of motor
vehicles on 1 Jan. 1998 was 8,177,157, including 6,543,935
passenger cars, 337,384 trucks, 13,935 buses, 588,698 tractors,
577,388 motor cycles.

SOCIAL INSTITUTIONS

Justice

There are a constitutional court *(Verfassungsgerichtshof)*, a supreme
Land court *(Oberstes Landesgericht)*, 3 courts of appeal, 22 regional
courts, 72 local courts, 2 *Land* labour courts, 11 labour courts, a *Land*
social court, 7 social courts, 2 finance courts, a higher administrative
court *(Verwaltungsgerichtshof)* and 6 administrative courts.

Religion

At the census of 25 May 1987 there were 67·2% Roman Catholics and
23·9% Protestants.

Education

In 1997–98 there were 2,844 primary schools with 47,306 teachers
and 858,884 pupils; 374 special schools with 7,322 teachers and
59,680 pupils; 330 intermediate schools with 9,400 teachers and
146,532 pupils; 397 high schools with 21,181 teachers and 305,587
pupils; 236 part-time vocational schools with 7,988 teachers and
283,154 pupils, including 47 special part-time vocational schools
with 905 teachers and 12,577 pupils; 604 full-time vocational
schools with 4,653 teachers and 61,153 pupils including 268 schools

for public health occupations with 1,434 teachers and 18,656 pupils; 373 advanced full-time vocational schools with 2,075 teachers and 24,987 pupils; 118 vocational high schools *(Berufsoberschulen, Fachoberschulen)* with 1,981 teachers and 30,731 pupils.

In 1997–98 there were 11 universities with 177,852 students (Augsburg, 13,154; Bamberg, 7,794; Bayreuth, 7,535; Eichstätt, 4,005; Erlangen-Nürnberg, 22,895; München, 59,804; Passau, 7,532; Regensburg, 15,961; Würzburg, 19,313; the Technical University of München, 17,701; München, University of the Federal Armed Forces *(Universität der Bundeswehr)*, 2,158; plus the college of politics, München, 577; the college of philosophy, München, 383, and 2 philo-sophical-theological colleges with 268 students in total (Benediktbeuern, 120; Neuendettelsau, 148). There were also 2 colleges of music, 2 colleges of fine arts and 1 college of television and film, with 2,599 students in total; 18 vocational colleges *(Fachhochschulen)* with 56,575 students including one for the civil service *(Bayerische Beamtenfachhochschule)* with 4,003 students.

Welfare

At Dec. 1997 there were 253,000 persons receiving benefits of all kinds.

CULTURE

Cinema

Bavaria had 655 cinema screens with 117,791 seats in 1996.

Tourism

At the end of June 1997 there were 14,152 hotels and guest houses (with 9 beds or more) providing beds for 549,339 people.

In 1997 they received 19,556,751 guests of whom 3,691,548 were foreigners. They stayed an average of 3·4 nights each, totalling 66,752,537 nights (7,551,424 nights stayed by foreign visitors).

Festivals

Oktoberfest, Munich's famous beer festival, takes place each year in late Sept. and early Oct.

Libraries

In 1996 there were 2,247 libraries holding 20,286,000 books.

Theatre and Opera

There are 33 theatre companies and opera houses with their own ensembles in Bavaria.

Museums

Bavaria had 688 museums in 1996. During that year 16,907,000 people visited 983 exhibitions.

FURTHER READING

Statistical Information: Bayerisches Landesamt für Statistik und Datenverarbeitung, Neuhauser Str. 8, 80331 Munich, was founded in 1833. *President:* Wolfgang Kupfahl. It publishes: *Statistisches Jahrbuch für Bayern.* 1894 ff. – *Bayern in Zahlen.* Monthly (from Jan. 1947). – *Zeitschrift des Bayerischen Statistischen Landesamts.* July 1869–1943; 1948 ff. – *Beiträge zur Statistik Bayerns.* 1850 ff. – *Statistische Berichte.* 1951 ff. – *Kreisdaten.* 1972 ff. – *Gemeindedaten.* 1973 ff.

Nawiasky, H. and Luesser, C., *Die Verfassung des Freistaates Bayern vom 2. Dez. 1946.* Munich, 1948; supplement, by H. Nawiasky and H. Lechner, Munich, 1953

State Library: Bayerische Staatsbibliothek, Munich. *Director:* Dr Hermann Leskin.

BERLIN

KEY HISTORICAL EVENTS

After the end of World War II, Berlin was divided into 4 occupied sectors, each with a military governor from one of the victorious Allied Powers (the USA, the Soviet Union, Britain and France). On 30 Nov. 1948 a seperate municipal government was set up in the Soviet sector which led to the political division of the city. In contravention of the special Allied status agreed for the entire city, East Berlin became 'Capital of the GDR' in 1949 and thus increasingly integrated into the GDR as a whole. In West Berlin, the formal supreme authority of the Western Allies endured until 1990.

On 17 June 1953 the protest by workers in East Berlin against political oppression and economic hardship was supressed by Soviet military forces. To stop refugees, the east German government erected the Berlin Wall to seal off West Berlin's borders on 13 Aug. 1961.

The Berlin Wall unexpectedly collapsed on 9 Nov. 1989 as the regime in the GDR bowed to the internal pressure which had been building for months. East and West Berlin were amalgamated on the re-unification of Germany in Oct. 1990, and Berlin was declared the national capital. With the move of the national government, the parliament (Bundestag), and the federal organ of the Länder (Budesrat) in 1999, Berlin once again fulfils the functions of a capital city.

Berlin has always been a cultural centre and a magnet for foreign artists and intellectuals. Today, while that role continues to grow, Berlin is once again a capital city rich in cultural activities and also a major centre for science and industry. Berlin has long been the largest industrial centre in Europe and today is home to some of Germany's largest corporations – Siemens and AEG both have their headquarters in Berlin. The University community contributes to the combined knowledge of more than 250 non-university research institutes (including the Berlin Electron Storage Ring for Synchrotron Radiation (BESSY), the Max Delbrück Centre for Molecular Medicine and the Konrad Zuse centre for Information Technology). The transfer to Berlin of government offices, embassies and other government-related businesses and services has meant a boom in building and some of Europe's most innovative building designs are to be found here. The Reichstag building has been drastically renovated by the British architect Norman Foster (whose design was chosen over entries by 800 architects from 44 countries) and was formally opened in 1999 in preparation for the first session of the unified German parliament in Berlin in 2000.

Most of the leading German newspapers are published in Berlin, including Die Welt, Berliner Morgenpost, Berliner Zeitung and Der Tagesspiegel. Berlin boasts three opera houses, several major orchestras (including the Berlin Philharmonic) and dozens of theatres. For details of museums and galleries see page 55.

TERRITORY AND POPULATION

The area is 890·77 sq. km. Population, 31 Dec. 1997, 3,425,759 (51·6% female), including 432,990 foreign nationals; density, 3,846 per sq. km.

SOCIAL STATISTICS

Calendar years	Live births	Marriages	Divorces	Deaths
1994	28,503	17,269	8,108	40,738
1995	28,648	16,383	9,184	39,245
1996	29,905	15,813	9,182	38,099
1997	30,369	15,399	9,782	36,447

CONSTITUTION AND GOVERNMENT

According to the constitutions of Sept. 1950 and Oct. 1995, Berlin
is simultaneously a *Land* of the Federal Republic and a city. It is
governed by a House of Representatives (of at least 150 members);
executive power is vested in a Senate, consisting of the Governing
Mayor, the Mayor and not more than 16 senators.

After a proposed merger was rejected by Brandenburg in the 1996
referendum, a Joint Berlin-Brandenburg Co-operation Council was
set up.

Berlin has 5 seats in the Bundesrat.

RECENT ELECTIONS

At the elections of 10 Oct. 1999 the Christian Democrats (CDU) won
76 seats in the House of Representatives with 40·8% of votes cast; the
Social Democrats (SPD), 42, with 22·4%; the Party of Democratic
Socialism (former Communists), 33, with 17·6%; and the Greens, 18,
with 9·9%. The SPD thus suffered a sixth defeat in state elections
since the general election of Sept. 1998.

CURRENT ADMINISTRATION

Governing Mayor: Eberhard Diepgen (CDU).

In Jan. 1996 a CPU-SPD coalition government was formed.

BANKING

Central Bank

Landeszentralbank in Berlin und Brandenburg: 10831 Berlin, Postfach 110160. Tel: (0)30 2387-0. Fax: (0)30 2387-2500.

Stock Exchange

Berliner Wertpapierbörse: 10623 Berlin, Fasanenstr. 85. Tel: (0)30 311091-0. Fax: (0)30 311091-78.

INDUSTRY

In 1997 the main industries in terms of percentage of the labour force employed were: Electronics, 28·2%; food and tobacco, 14·0%; machine-building, 11·1%; chemicals, 9·2%; vehicle production, 6·1%; metallurgy, 9·5%; printing, 12·8%.

Labour

In 1997 the workforce was 1,531,300, including 0·24m. craft workers. There were 265,665 persons registered unemployed in 1997 and 5,340 on short time in 1997. 6,714 jobs were available in 1997.

Trade Fair Organizers

Messe Berlin GmbH: Messedamm 22, 14055 Berlin. Tel: (0)30 30380. Fax: (0)30 30382325.

COMMUNICATIONS

Metropolitan Railways

Berliner Verkehrs-Betriebe (Berlin Transport Authority): 10773 Berlin, Potsdamer Str. 188. Tel: (0)30 2561. Fax: (0)30 2164186.

Roads

In 1997 there were 252·8 km of roads, made up of 63·6 km
of Autobahn and 189·2 km of federal roads. At June 1997, 1,398,734
motor vehicles were registered, including 1,211,348 passenger
cars, 86,850 trucks, 2,741 buses, and 72,206 motor cycles. There
were 151,588 road accidents in 1997 of which 19,102 involved
badly damaged vehicles or injured persons, of whom there were
20,336.

Civil Aviation

223,880 flights were made from Berlin's 3 airports (Tegel, Tempelhof
and Schönefeld) in 1997, carrying a total of 11,564,952 passengers.

SOCIAL INSTITUTIONS

Justice

There are a court of appeal *(Kammergericht)*, a regional court, 9 local
courts, a *Land* Labour court, a labour court, a *Land* social court, a
social court, a higher administrative court, an administrative court
and a finance court.

Religion

In 1997, membership and number of places of worship for major reli-
gions was as follows:

Religion	Members	Places of Worship
Protestant	896,353	393
Roman Catholic	344,826	171
Jewish	11,676	6
Moslem	199,259	104

Education

In 1995–96 there were 413,449 pupils attending schools. There were 497 primary schools with 146,622 pupils, 551 post-primary schools with 83,098 pupils, 98 special schools with 13,297 pupils, 87 secondary modern schools with 31,346 pupils, 129 grammar schools with 84,726 pupils and 81 comprehensive schools with 54,360 pupils. In 1994–95 there were 2 universities and 1 technical university, 4 art colleges and 9 technical colleges. There was a total of some 147,000 students in higher education.

CULTURE

Cinema

In 1996 there were 182 cinema screens with 39,399 seats.

Tourism

In 1997 Berlin had 444 places of accommodation providing 49,744 beds for 3,449,000 visitors.

Libraries

In 1996 there were 235 libraries holding 7,440,000 volumes.

Theatre and Opera

In 1996 Berlin had 27 theatres and concert halls putting on 4,403 productions for audiences numbering 2,041,000.

Museums

There were 117 museums in 1996. A total of 6,510,000 people visited the 276 exhibitions.

FURTHER READING

Statistical Information: The Statistisches Landesamt Berlin was founded in 1862 (Alt-Friedrichsfelde 60, 10315 Berlin (Lichtenberg)). *Director:* Prof. Günther Appel. It publishes: *Statistisches Jahrbuch* (from 1867): *Berliner Statistik* (monthly, from 1947). – *100 Jahre Berliner Statistik* (1962). *State Library:* Amerika-Gedenkbibliothek-Berliner Zentralbibliothek, Blücherplatz 1, D-10961 Berlin. *Director:* Dr Klaus Bock.

Read, A., and Fisher, D., *Berlin, Biography of a City.* London, 1994

Taylor, R., *Berlin and its Culture.* London, 1997

Wallace, Ian, *Berlin* [Bibliography]. Oxford and Santa Barbara (CA), 1993

BRANDENBURG

KEY HISTORICAL EVENTS

Brandenburg surrounds the new capital city of Germany, Berlin, but the people of the state voted against the recommendations of the Berlin House of Representatives and the Brandenburg State Parliament that the two states should merge around the year 2000. The state capital, Potsdam, is the ancient city of the Emperor Frederic II 'The Great' who transformed the garrison town of his father Frederic I 'The Soldier' into a beautiful and elegant city. Brandenburg is the most sparsely populated of the German States. Two major rivers, the Havel and the Spree, flow through the hilly countryside with numerous nature reserves, landscape reserves and biosphere reserves. The Havel-Oder Canal boasts the world's largest ship elevator. Built in 1934, it allows ships travelling along the canal to rise (or drop) 36 metres. The traditional backbone of the state's economy, agriculture (with crops of rye and oilseed), is gradually giving way to industries such as vehicle construction, mechanical engineering, electronics, the optical industry, and the energy, food and chemical industries. Frankfurt an der Oder on the border with Poland acts as a valuable trade link with the countries of Eastern Europe. The 16th century University of Viadrina has been recently reopened as a European University emphasising Polish/German co-operation in teaching and research. GFZ Potsdam is engaged in research into subjects of global interest and the geo-sciences. Other areas of interest to research institutes in Brandenburg include environmental engineering, materials salvage, recycling, medicine and climate change.

Potsdam-Babelsberg has the oldest cinema studio in Germany – directors Fritz Lang and Ernst Lubitsch and actors worked here as did Marlene Dietrich. Brandenburg has approximately 350 palaces and manor houses, 150 museums and a variety of cultural annual festivals.

TERRITORY AND POPULATION

The area is 29,476 sq. km. Population on 31 Dec. 1997 was 2,573,291 (1,306,095 females). There are 4 urban districts, 14 rural districts and 1,696 communes. The capital is Potsdam.

SOCIAL STATISTICS

Calendar years	Live births	Marriages	Divorces	Deaths
1994	12,443	8,502	3,851	28,490
1995	13,494	8,775	3,949	27,401
1996	15,140	8,756	4,016	27,622
1997	16,370	8,709	5,231	26,756

CONSTITUTION AND GOVERNMENT

The *Land* was reconstituted on former GDR territory on 14 Oct. 1990.
Brandenburg has 4 seats in the Bundesrat.

After a proposed merger was rejected by Brandenburg in the 1996
referendum, a Joint Berlin-Brandenburg Co-operation Council was
set up.

At a referendum on 14 June 1992, 93·5% of votes cast were in
favour of a new constitution guaranteeing direct democracy and the
right to work and housing.

RECENT ELECTIONS

At the Diet elections on 5 Sept. 1999 the Social Democrats (SPD) won
37 seats with 39·3% of the vote; the Christian Democrats (CDU),
25, with 26·6%; the Party of Democratic Socialism (PDS, former
Communists), 22, with 23·3%; and the far-right German People's
Union (DVU), 5, with 5·2%.

CURRENT ADMINISTRATION

The *Prime Minister* is Dr Manfred Stolpe (SPD).

Local Government

At the *local government* elections of Sept. 1998 the SPD won 38·97%
of votes cast, the PDS 21·62%, the CDU 21·42%, the FDP 4·14% and
the Greens, 4·13%.

ECONOMY

Performance

GDP in 1997 was 74,107m. DM.

ENERGY AND NATURAL RESOURCES

Electricity

Power stations in Brandenburg produced 23,851m. kWh in 1997. A minimal amount was produced from hydroelectric power.

Agriculture

Livestock in Dec. 1996: Cattle, 716,436 (including 229,582 milch cows); pigs, 718,415; sheep, 120,617; horses, 21,541; poultry, 6,193,040.

Area and yield of the most important crops:

	Area (in 1,000 ha)			Yield (in 1,000 tonnes)		
	1995	*1996*	*1997*	*1995*	*1996*	*1997*
Rye	214·7	220·5	233·4	950·4	883·7	990·0
Wheat	108·0	101·7	109·6	647·5	551·2	578·7
Barley	108·4	90·2	102·5	596·4	332·2	484·0
Oats	13·8	18·2	20·0	59·8	76·9	81·6
Potatoes	16·7	17·8	15·4	320·1	542·3	437·9
Sugar-beet	14·7	14·2	12·5	565·3	663·0	515·3

INDUSTRY

In 1997, 1,098 establishments (20 and more employees) employed 95,249 persons; of these, 10,500 were employed in mining and quarrying; 6,815 in machine construction; 12,914 in vehicle construction; 5,202 in chemical industries.

Labour
In April 1997 at the 1%-sample of the microcensus, 1,115,300 persons were economically active, including 88,100 self-employed and family assistants, 456,000 manual and 523,400 white-collar workers, and 47,700 civil servants. In Dec. 1997 there were 456,000 unemployed persons.

INTERNATIONAL TRADE
Imports and Exports
Total imports (1997): 7,723m. DM. Total exports: 5,663m. DM.

COMMUNICATIONS
Roads
In Jan. 1998 there were 1,480,755 registered vehicles including 1,271,356 passenger cars.

SOCIAL INSTITUTIONS
Education
In 1997–98 there were 1,168 schools providing general education (including special schools) with 397,983 pupils, and 43 vocational schools with 74,902 pupils.

In the winter term 1997–98 there were 3 universities and 8 colleges with 25,351 students.

CULTURE

Cinema

In 1996 Brandenburg had 109 screens with 24,350 seats.

Tourism

In 1997 there were 1,282 places of accommodation (with 9 or more beds), including 449 hotels, providing a total of 67,373 beds. 2,415,306 visitors spent a total of 7,312,522 nights in Brandenburg in 1997.

Libraries

In 1997 there were 279 public libraries with 322,244 active users who borrowed 11,179,020 items.

Theatre and Opera

There were 34 theatres in 1996 which put on 2,377 performances for audiences totalling 432,418 persons.

Museums

Brandenburg had 153 museums putting on 428 exhibitions in 1996. There were 2,829,000 visitors in that year.

BREMEN

KEY HISTORICAL EVENTS

Bremen was first mentioned 1,200 years ago. It has been a bishopric since 787 and was endowed with the rights of a free city by Emperor Frederick 'Barbarossa' in 1186. Bremen joined the Hanseatic League in 1358 and has been known as the 'Free Hanseatic City of Bremen' since 1806, having been elevated to the status of a free Imperial City in 1646.

The state is dominated by the Free City of Bremen and its port, Bremerhaven. In 1815, when it joined the German Confederation, Bremen was an autonomous city and Hanse port with important Baltic trade. In 1827 the expansion of trade inspired the founding of Bremerhaven on land ceded by Hanover at the confluence of the Geest and Weser rivers. Further expansion followed the founding of the Nord-deutscher Lloyd Shipping Company in 1857. Merchant shipping, associated trade and fishing were dominant until 1940 but there was diversification in the post-war years. In 1939 Bremerhaven was absorbed by the Hanoverian town of Wesermünde. The combined port was returned to the jurisdiction of Bremen in 1947.

Each year more than 10,000 ships link Bremen's ports with over 1,000 ports all over the world. Bremerhaven ships more than 830,000 vehicles overseas each year. The Free Hanseatic shipyards build ships of all sizes. Bremen is also known as a centre for the German food and beverage industry with coffee, chocolate, flour, milk products, spices, fish products and beer among the best known products. The aerospace industry in Bremen produces parts for rockets, satellites and the Airbus and high-tech electrical and electronics industries also play a prominent part in the state's economy. Experiments under conditions of weightlessness are conducted in the 148-metre high tower at the centre for Applied Space Technology and Microgravity.

Bremen has its own stock exchange that handles commodities trading for all of north-western Germany. Bremen's university contributes research on marine ecology, shipping economics and logistics, polar and marine research and other areas of engineering and natural sciences.

TERRITORY AND POPULATION

The area of the *Land*, consisting of the 2 urban districts and ports of Bremen and Bremerhaven, is 404 sq. km. Population, 31 Dec. 1996, 677,800 (326,600 males, 351,100 females).

SOCIAL STATISTICS

Calendar years	Live births	Marriages	Divorces	Deaths
1993	6,656	3,969	1,736	8,643
1994	6,288	3,859	1,614	8,123
1995	6,429	3,561	1,799	8,378
1996	6,623	3,509	1,870	8,080

CONSTITUTION AND GOVERNMENT

Political power is vested in the 100-member House of Burgesses *(Bürgerschaft)* which appoints the executive, called the Senate. Bremen has 3 seats in the Bundesrat.

RECENT ELECTIONS

At the elections of 6 June 1999 the Social Democratic Party won 47 seats with 42·6% of votes cast (37 with 33·4% in 1995); the Christian Democrats, 42 with 37·1% (37 with 32·6%); the Greens, 10 with 9·0%

(14 with 13·1%) and the nationalist DVU, 1 with 3·0%. The PDS gained no seats with 2·9% and the FDP none with 2·4%. The Senate president is Dr Henning Scherf (Social Democrat).

BANKING

Central Bank

Landeszentralbank in der Freien- und Hansestadt Bremen, in Niedersachsen und Sachsen-Anhalt
28203 Bremen, Kohlhökerstr. 29. Tel: (0)421 3291-0.

Stock Exchange

Bremer Wertpapierbörse: 28195 Bremen, Obernstr. 2–12, 28007 Bremen, Postfach 100726. Tel: (0)421 321282. Fax: (0)421 323123.

ENERGY AND NATURAL RESOURCES

Agriculture

Agricultural area comprised (1995) 9,400 ha. Livestock (2 Dec. 1996): 12,758 cattle (including 3,746 milch cows); 2,026 pigs; 253 sheep; 1,208 horses; 17,481 poultry.

INDUSTRY

In 1996, 338 establishments (with 20 and more employees) employed 67,164 persons; of these, 4,241 were employed in shipbuilding (except naval engineering); 5,528 in machine construction; 8,351 in electrical engineering; 1,591 in coffee and tea processing.

Labour

The economically active persons totalled 279,700 at the microcensus of April 1996. Of the total, 25,800 were self-employed, 253,900 employees; 83,200 in production industries, 77,100 in commerce, trade and communications, 117,100 in other industries and services.

COMMUNICATIONS

Roads

On 1 Jan. 1996 there were 112 km of 'classified' roads, including 48 km of Autobahn and 64 km of federal roads. Registered motor vehicles on 1 July 1997 numbered 331,139, including 290,940 passenger cars, 15,800 trucks, 2,766 tractors, 603 buses and 16,074 motor cycles.

Shipping

Vessels entered in 1996, 8,330 of 43,638,905 net tons; cleared, 8,365 of 43,931,175 net tons. Sea traffic, 1996, incoming 19,140,000 tonnes; outgoing, 12,360,000 tonnes.

SOCIAL INSTITUTIONS

Justice

There are a constitutional court *(Staatsgerichtshof)*, a court of appeal, a regional court, 3 local courts, a *Land* labour court, 2 labour courts, a *Land* social court, a finance court, a higher administrative court and an administrative court.

Religion

The census of 25 May 1987 showed 61% Protestants and 10% Roman Catholics.

Education

In 1996 there were 390 secondary schools with 5,026 teachers and 70,521 pupils; 27 special schools with 591 teachers and 2,698 pupils; 26 part-time vocational schools with 17,792 pupils; 25 full-time vocational schools with 4,638 pupils; 8 advanced vocational schools (including institutions for the training of technicians) with 890 pupils; 10 schools for public health occupations with 856 pupils.

In the winter term 1996–97, 17,078 students were enrolled at the university. In addition to the university there were 4 other colleges in 1996–97 with 8,817 students.

CULTURE

Cinema

In 1996 there were 43 cinema screens with 7,601 seats.

Tourism

Bremen had 83 places of accommodation providing 8,806 beds for 577,000 visitors in 1997.

Libraries

In 1996 there were 42 libraries with 1,043,000 volumes.

Theatre and Opera

Bremen had 11 concert halls and theatres in 1996. There were 1,011 productions and audiences numbered 338,000.

Museums

In 1996 there were 1,100,000 visitors to 79 exhibitions in 20 museums.

FURTHER READING

Statistical Information: Statistisches Landesamt Bremen (An der Weide 14–16, P.B. 101309, D-28195 Bremen), founded in 1850. *Director:* Reg. Dir. Jürgen Dinse. Its current publications include: *Statistisches Jahrbuch Bremen* (from 1992). – *Statistische Mitteilungen* (from 1948). – *Statistische Monatsberichte* (from 1954). – *Statistische Berichte* (from 1956). – *Statistisches Handbuch Bremen (1950–60,* 1961; *1960–64,* 1967; *1965–69,* 1971; *1970–74,* 1975; *1975–80,* 1982; *1981–85,* 1987). – *Bremen im statistischen Zeitvergleich 1950–1976.* 1977. – *Bremen in Zahlen.* 1997.
State and University Library: Bibliotheksstr., D-28359 Bremen. *Director:* Annette Rath-Beckmann.

HAMBURG

KEY HISTORICAL EVENTS

Hamburg was a free Hanse town owing nominal allegiance to the Holy Roman Emperor until 1806. In 1815 it became part of the German Confederation, sharing a seat in the Federal Diet with Lübeck, Bremen and Frankfurt. During the Empire it retained its autonomy. By 1938 it had become the third largest port in the world and its territory was extended by the cession of land (3 urban and 27 rural districts) from Prussia. In 1945 Hamburg became a *Land* of the Federal Republic with its 1938 boundaries.

Hamburg is the second largest city in Germany and largest overseas trade centre and port. Among the 3,000 firms engaged in import/export business, Far Eastern companies are well represented here. 150 companies from China as well as 25 from Hong Kong, 135 from Japan and 65 from Taiwan all have offices here. Hamburg also has a thriving service industry – the city is the banking and insurance centre for the whole of northern Germany. Hamburg is also famous for shipbuilding and has attendant port industries of refining and processing of raw materials. The city is also a publishing centre – 15 of Germany's best selling magazines are published here and 50% of German press circulation is based here (although some of these may move to Berlin after 2000). In the mid-eighties, Hamburg established strong links with Scandinavia to make up for the loss of trade movement through northern Germany. However, with reunification, the city has regained its traditional hinterland and now also profits from goods travelling from all over Germany for export through the port of Hamburg. Hamburg's effective Business Development Corporation has created 20,000 jobs in five years. Although Germany's second largest industrial centre, Hamburg is also one of the 'greenest' cities in the country. Nearly half the region's land is taken up with the farming of arable crops, and nature reserves and landscape accounts for 28% of the city's area. Hamburg has a long tradition of freedom and tolerance and a rich cultural heritage. The opera house was Germany's first (Händel staged his first opera here), and today there are four state, and more than forty, private theatres. The Beatles launched their international career here in the 1960s and The Guinness Book of Records claims that Hamburg has more bridges than any other European city.

TERRITORY AND POPULATION

Total area, 755·3 sq. km (1997), including the islands Neuwerk and Scharhörn (7·6 sq. km). Population (1 Jan. 1998), 1,704,700 (823,200 males, 881,500 females). The *Land* forms a single urban district (*kreisfreie Stadt*) with 7 administrative subdivisions.

SOCIAL STATISTICS

Calendar years	Live births	Marriages	Divorces	Deaths
1994	16,201	8,537	4,545	20,241
1995	15,872	8,242	4,652	20,276
1996	16,594	7,886	4,306	20,196
1997	16,970	7,800	5,092	19,328

CONSTITUTION AND GOVERNMENT

The constitution of 6 June 1952 vests the supreme power in the House of Burgesses *(Bürgerschaft)* of 121 members. The executive is in the hands of the Senate, whose members are elected by the Bürgerschaft. Hamburg has 3 seats in the Bundesrat.

RECENT ELECTIONS

The elections of 21 Sept. 1997 had the following results: Social Democrats, 54 seats with 36·2% of votes cast; Christian Democrats, 46 with 30·7%; Green Alternatives 21, with 13·9%. The First Burgomaster is Ortwin Runde (Social Democrat).

BANKING

Central Bank

Landeszentralbank in der Freien- und Hansestadt Hamburg, in Mecklenburg-Vorpommern und Schleswig-Holstein: 20459 Hamburg, Ost-West-Str. 73. Tel: (0)40 37070. Fax: (0)40 37072205.

Stock Exchange

Hanseatische Wertpapierbörse Hamburg: 20095 Hamburg, Schauenburgerstr. 49. Tel: (0)40 3613020. Fax: (0)40 36130223.

ENERGY AND NATURAL RESOURCES

Agriculture

The agricultural area comprised 13,390 ha in 1997. Yield, 1997, in tonnes, of cereals, 16,700; potatoes, 700.

Livestock (3 Dec. 1996): Cattle, 8,715 (including 1,537 milch cows); pigs, 3,289; horses, 2,847; sheep, 1,634; poultry, 11,764.

INDUSTRY

In June 1997, 624 establishments (with 20 and more employees) employed 107,509 persons; of these, 20,766 were employed in manufacturing transport equipment (including motor vehicles, aircraft and ships), 17,136 in manufacturing machinery, 15,218 in manufacturing electrical and optical equipment, 7,889 in manufacturing chemical products and 6,763 in mineral oil industry.

Labour

The economically active persons totalled 766,300 at the 1%-sample survey of the microcensus of April 1997. Of the total, 92,800 were self-employed or unpaid family workers, and 673,500 were employees; 7,800 were engaged in agriculture and forestry, 169,100 in power supply, mining, manufacturing and building, 224,000 in commerce and transport, 365,400 in other industries and services.

Trade Fair Organizers

Hamburg Messe und Congress GmbH: 20355 Hamburg, Jungiusstr. 13; 20303 Hamburg, Postfach 302480. Tel: (0)40 35690. Fax: (0)40 35692180.

COMMUNICATIONS

Roads

In April 1997 there were 4,369 km of roads, including 82 km of Autobahn, 149 km of federal roads. Number of motor vehicles (1 July 1997), 812,652, including 714,446 passenger cars, 42,687 trucks, 1,446 buses, 5,598 tractors, 34,771 motor cycles and 13,704 other motor vehicles.

Shipping

Hamburg is the largest sea port in Germany.

Vessels		1995	1996	1997
Entered:	Number	11,679	11,489	11,749
	Tonnage	58,640,110	61,181,978	62,806,340
Cleared:	Number	11,798	11,635	11,895
	Tonnage	58,898,385	61,045,871	62,617,624

SOCIAL INSTITUTIONS

Justice

There is a constitutional court (*Verfassungsgericht*), a court of appeal (*Oberlandesgericht*), a regional court (*Landgericht*), 6 local courts (*Amtsgerichte*), a *Land* labour court, a labour court, a *Land* social

court, a social court, a finance court, a higher administrative court
and an administrative court.

Religion

In 1997, 37·3% of the population went to the Evangelical Church and
Free Churches, whilst 10·3% were Roman Catholic.

Education

In 1997 there were 433 schools for general education (not including
Internationale Schule) with 13,662 teachers and 175,687 pupils; 54
special schools with 7,536 pupils; 43 part-time vocational schools
with 33,484 pupils; 42 schools with 3,776 pupils in manual instruction
classes; 42 full-time vocational schools with 9,101 pupils; 10 economic secondary schools with 1,842 pupils; 2 technical *Gymnasien* with
357 pupils; 19 advanced vocational schools with 4,235 pupils; 36
schools for public health occupations with 2,508 pupils; 1 vocational
introducing school with 54 pupils and 18 technical superior schools
with 1,478 pupils; all these vocational and technical schools had a
total number of 3,218 teachers.

In the winter term 1997–98 there was 1 university with 41,228 students; 1 technical university with 3,939 students; 1 college of music
and 1 college of fine arts with 2,105 students in total; 1 university of
the *Bundeswehr* with 1,690 students; 1 university of economics and
political sciences with 2,563 students; 3 professional colleges with a
total of 14,737 students.

CULTURE

Broadcasting

In the autumn of 1997 there was 1 public broadcasting service as well
as 9 private broadcasters.

Cinema

In Dec. 1997 there were 81 cinemas (including 1 drive-in) with a total of 19,327 seats. There were 5,024,360 tickets sold in 1997.

Tourism

At Dec. 1997 there were 249 places of accommodation with 26,067 beds. Of the 2,431,047 visitors in 1997, 20·8% were foreigners.

Libraries

In 1997 there were 123 branches of the Hamburg Public Library which held 1,740,605 books and other forms of media. 9,369,491 items were borrowed in 1997. The city and university library held 2,859,397 books, and lent 939,467 items.

Theatre and Opera

In the 1996–97 season the 3 national theatre and opera houses put on 1,154 performances, attracting 878,467 visitors. The 2 largest stages in Hamburg, the Neue Flora and Operettenhaus, are both private. The former put on 830 performances during 1996–97 for a total audience of 720,000, whilst Operettenhaus had 412 performances for 440,000 persons.

Museums and Galleries

The 7 national museums were visited by 1,496,199 people in 1997. There are a further 40 or so private and public museums and about 100 art galleries in Hamburg as well as a Planetarium, which received 127,338 visits in 1997.

FURTHER READING

Statistical Information: The Statistisches Landesamt der Freien und Hansestadt Hamburg (Steckelhörn 12, D-20457 Hamburg) publishes: *Hamburg in Zahlen, Statistische Berichte, Statistisches Taschenbuch, Statistik des Hamburgischen Staates, Hamburger Statistische Porträts.*

Hamburgische Gesellschaft für Wirtschaftsförderung mbH, *Hamburg.* Oldenburg, 1993

Klessmann, E., *Geschichte der Stadt Hamburg.* 7th ed. Hamburg, 1994

Kopitzsch, F./ Tilgner, D., *Hamburg Lexicon.* Hamburg, 1998

Möller, I., *Hamburg-Länderprofile.* Hamburg, 1985

Schubert, D. and Harms, H., *Wohnen am Hafen.* Hamburg, 1993

Schütt, E. C., *Die Chronik Hamburgs.* Hamburg, 1991

State Library: Staats- und Universitätsbibliothek, Carl von Ossietzky, Von-Melle-Park 3, D-20146 Hamburg. *Director:* Prof. Dr Horst Gronemeyer.

HESSEN

KEY HISTORICAL EVENTS

The *Land* consists of the former states of Hesse-Darmstadt and Hesse-Kassel, and Nassau. Hesse-Darmstadt was ruled by the Landgrave Louis X from 1790. He became grand duke in 1806 with absolute power, having dismissed the parliament in 1803. However, he granted a constitution and bicameral parliament in 1820. Hesse-Darmstadt lost land to Prussia in the Seven Weeks' War of 1866, but retained its independence, both then and as a state of the German Empire after 1871. In 1918 the grand duke abdicated and the territory became a state of the German Republic. In 1945 areas west of the Rhine were incorporated into the new *Land* of Rhineland-Palatinate, areas east of the Rhine became part of the *Land* of Greater Hesse.

Hesse-Kassel was ruled by the Landgrave William IX from 1785 until he became Elector in 1805. In 1807 the Electorate was absorbed into the Kingdom of Westphalia (a Napoleonic creation), becoming independent again in 1815 as a state of the German Confederation. In

1831 a constitution and parliament were granted but the Electors remained strongly conservative.

In 1866 the Diet approved alliance with Prussia against Austria; the Elector nevertheless supported Austria. He was defeated by the Prussians and exiled and Hesse-Kassel was annexed to Prussia. In 1867 it was combined with Frankfurt and some areas taken from Nassau and Hesse-Darmstadt to form a Prussian province (Hesse-Nassau). In 1801 Nassau west of the Rhine passed to France; Napoleon also took the northern state in 1806. The remnant of the southern states allied in 1803 and three years later they became a duchy. In 1866 the duke supported Austria against Prussia and the duchy was annexed by Prussia as a result. In 1944 the Prussian province of Hesse-Nassau was split in two: Nassau and Electoral Hesse, also called Kurhessen. The following year these were combined with Hesse-Darmstadt as the *Land* of Greater Hesse which became known as Hessen.

Hesse is Germany's fifth largest state and one of the major centres of business and industry. Although the capital city is Wiesbaden, the region's prosperity focuses on Frankfurt am Main, which is an international financial centre with more than 400 banks including the headquarters of the Deutsche Bundesbank. The German Stock Exchange and the European Monetary Exchange are both located in Frankfurt. Frankfurt's airport is home to Lufthansa, Germany's national carrier, and as one of Europe's busiest airports, employs over 60,000 people. Hesse is home to major industry, including Hoechst, Rütgers, Merck, Degussa, Volkswagen and Opel (representing the chemical, motor vehicle, mechanical and electrical engineering branches of industry) and this high level of industrial investment in the region is a major factor in the region's gross domestic product of DM 50,000 per capita. Frankfurt is a centre for trade fairs – the Frankfurt Book Fair (the world's biggest) each autumn alone attracts nearly 7,000 exhibitors and some 290,000 visitors each year.

Hesse also has a tradition of scientific discovery – research scientists and inventors laid the foundation for many branches of industry and technology including early work on agro-chemical fertilizers and the development of the electronic telephone (both in the 19th century).

The main cities of Hesse, Wiesbaden (the capital), Frankfurt and Darmstadt, are in the southern corner of the state and the land produces some of Germany's best wine (Riesling and Rheinwein both come from this area) and fruit. The north of the region is more sparsely populated and barren with typical volcanic landscapes.

TERRITORY AND POPULATION

Area, 21,115 sq. km. The capital is Wiesbaden. There are 3 administrative regions with 5 urban and 21 rural districts and 426 communes. Population, 31 Dec 1997, was 6,031,705 (2,951,639 males, 3,080,066 females).

SOCIAL STATISTICS

Calendar years	Live births	Marriages	Divorces	Deaths
1994	60,565	35,215	13,697	63,385
1995	59,858	34,517	13,387	63,346
1996	62,391	33,251	13,677	63,387
1997	63,124	32,877	14,830,	61,361

CONSTITUTION AND GOVERNMENT

The constitution was endorsed by popular referendum on 1 Dec. 1946. Hessen has 5 seats in the Bundesrat.

RECENT ELECTIONS

At the Diet elections on 7 Feb. 1999 the Christian Democrats gained 43·4% of votes cast, the Social Democrats 39·4%, the Greens 7·2% and the Free Democrats 5·1%.

CURRENT ADMINISTRATION

The cabinet is headed by *Prime Minister* Roland Koch (CDU).

ECONOMY

Performance

The gross domestic product at market prices (GDP) increased by 2·8% at constant prices of 1991 in comparison with the previous year. The total amount was 313·8bn. DM in 1997. The GDP per person engaged in labour productivity was 122,902 DM in 1997 (117,101 DM in 1996).

BANKING

Central Bank

Landeszentralbank in Hessen: 60329 Frankfurt am Main, Taunusanlage 5. Tel: (0)69 2388-0. Fax: (0)69 2388-2130.

ENERGY AND NATURAL RESOURCES

Electricity

Electricity production in 1997 was 27,813m. kWh (gross) and 25,156m. kWh (net). Total electricity consumption in 1997 was 31,832m. kWh.

Oil and Gas

Gas consumption in 1997 was 66,270m. kWh. All gas was imported from other parts of Germany.

Water

Public water production in 1995 totalled 600,050,000 cu. metres.

Agriculture

Area and yield of the most important crops:

	Area (in 1,000 ha)			Yield (in 1,000 tonnes)		
	1996	*1997*	*1998*	*1996*	*1997*	*1998*
Wheat	140·2	144·9	145·6	1,055·9	1,051·9	1,058·7
Rye	23·7	21·8	25·0	138·7	132·4	146·0
Barley	110·4	116·8	110·1	653·7	684·4	627·4
Oats	25·8	26·1	22·6	150·8	128·1	105·6
Potatoes	6·1	5·7	5·5	245·1	207·9	187·4
Sugar-beet	20·7	20·5	20·7	1,117·4	1,023·7	1,135·8
Rape	48·5	46·6	49·0	96·2	129·7	154·9

Livestock, Dec. 1997: Cattle, 575,153 (including 176,591 milch cows); pigs, 883,541; sheep, 157,799; horses, 46,018 (Dec. 1996); poultry, 2·19m (Dec. 1996).

INDUSTRY

In Sept. 1998, 3,242 establishments (with 20 and more employees) employed 472,469 persons; of these, 67,045 were employed in chemical industry; 64,705 in machine construction; 61,264 in car building; 41,186 in production of metal products.

Labour

The economically active persons totalled 2·7m. at the 1% sample survey of the microcensus of April 1996. Of the total, 276,200 were self-employed, 29,600 unpaid family workers, 2,383,400 employees; 52,900 were engaged in agriculture and forestry, 864,600 in power supply, mining, manufacturing and building, 651,300 in commerce, transport, hotels and restaurants, 1,120,300 in other services.

Trade Fair Organizers

Blenheim Heckmann GmbH, Wiesbaden. Tel: (0)611 58040. Fax: (0)611 580417.

COMMUNICATIONS

Roads

On 1 Jan. 1998 there were 16,312 km of 'classified' roads, comprising 950 km of Autobahn, 3,111 km of federal highways, 7,181 km of first-class highways and 5,070 km of second-class highways. Motor vehicles licensed on 1 July 1998 totalled 3,894,154, including 3,307,901 passenger cars, 5,975 buses, 160,674 trucks, 135,410 tractors and 203,475 motor cycles.

Civil Aviation

Frankfurt/Main Airport is one of the most important freight airports in the world. In 1997, 392,141 aeroplanes took off and landed, carrying

40,721,919 passengers, 1,400,978 tonnes of air freight and 144,328 tonnes of air mail.

Shipping
Frankfurt/Main Harbour and Hanau Harbour are the two most important harbours. In 1997, 12·8m. tonnes of goods were imported into the Land and 2·6m. tonnes were exported.

SOCIAL INSTITUTIONS

Justice
There is a constitutional court *(Staatsgerichtshof)*, a court of appeal, 9 regional courts, 58 local courts, a *Land* labour court, 12 labour courts, a *Land* social court, 7 social courts, a finance court, a higher administrative court *(Verwaltungsgerichtshof)* and 5 administrative courts.

Religion
In 1987 (census) there were 52·7% Protestants and 30·4% Roman Catholics.

Education
In 1997 there were 1,237 primary schools with 298,859 pupils (including *Förderstufen*); 155 intermediate schools with 49,984 pupils; 18,856 teachers in primary and intermediate schools; 228 special schools with 3,202 teachers and 20,505 pupils; 160 high schools with 8,892 teachers and 131,330 pupils; 216 *Gesamtschulen* (comprehensive schools) with 11,578 teachers and 182,490 pupils; 118 part-time vocational schools with 127,491 pupils; 259 full-time vocational schools with 40,913 pupils; 108 advanced vocational schools with 10,257 pupils; 7,771 teachers in the vocational schools.

In the winter term 1997–98 there were 3 universities (Frankfurt/Main, 35,366 students; Giessen, 20,939; Marburg/Lahn, 17,351); 1 technical university in Darmstadt (15,458); 1 private *Wissenschaftliche Hochschule,* (779); 1 *Gesamthochschule* (17,708); 16 *Fachhochschulen* (41,400); 2 Roman Catholic theological colleges and 1 Protestant theological college with a total of 375; 1 college of music and 2 colleges of fine arts with 1,276 students in total.

CULTURE

Cinema

In 1996 there were 263 cinemas with 48,433 seats in total.

Press

In 1996 there were 86 newspapers published in Hessen with a combined circulation of 2,120,500.

Tourism

In 1997, 8·5m. visitors stayed 22·8m. nights in Hessen. 3,408 places of accommodation provided 176,986 beds.

Libraries

In 1995 there were 1,018 public libraries which lent out 11,267,611 books. There were also 9 academic and scientific libraries.

Theatre and Opera

In 1996 there were 3,440 productions put on in 37 theatres and concert halls for audiences totalling 1,275,000.

Museums

Hessen had 333 museums in 1996. A total of 4,604,000 visitors came to 625 exhibitions.

FURTHER READING

Statistical Information: The Hessisches Statistisches Landesamt (Rheinstr. 35–37, D-65175 Wiesbaden). *President:* Eckart Hohmann. Main publications: *Statistisches Handbuch für das Land Hessen* (zweijährlich). – *Staat und Wirtschaft in Hessen* (monthly). – *Beiträge zur Statistik Hessens.* – *Statistische Berichte.* – *Hessische Gemeindestatistik* (annual, 1980 ff.).

State Library: Hessische Landesbibliothek, Rheinstr. 55–57, D-65185 Wiesbaden. *Director:* Dr Dieter Wolf.

LOWER SAXONY

KEY HISTORICAL EVENTS

The *Land* consists of the former state of Hanover with Oldenburg, Schaumburg-Lippe and Brunswick. It does not include the cities of Bremen or Bremerhaven.

Oldenburg, Danish from 1667, passed to the bishopric of Lübeck in 1773; the Holy Roman Emperor made it a duchy in 1777. As a small state of the Confederation after 1815 it supported Prussia, becoming a member of the Prussian Zollverein (1853) and North German Confederation (1867). The grand duke abdicated in 1918 and was replaced by an elected government.

Schaumburg-Lippe was a small sovereign principality. As such it became a member of the Confederation of the Rhine in 1807 and of the German Confederation in 1815. Surrounded by Prussian territory, it joined the Prussian-led North German Confederation in 1866. Part of the Empire until 1918, it then became a state of the new republic.

Brunswick, a small duchy, was taken into the Kingdom of Westphalia by Napoleon in 1806 but restored to independence in 1814. In 1830 the duke, Charles II, was forced into exile and replaced in 1831 by his more liberal brother, William. The succession passed to a Hanoverian claimant in 1913 but the duchy ended with the Empire in 1918.

As a state of the republican Germany, Brunswick was greatly reduced under the Third Reich. Its boundaries were restored by the British occupation forces in 1945.

Hanover was an autonomous Electorate of the Holy Roman Empire whose rulers were also kings of Great Britain from 1714 to 1837. From 1762 they ruled almost entirely from England. After Napoleonic invasions Hanover was restored in 1815. A constitution of 1819 made no radical change and had to be followed by more liberal versions in 1833 and 1848. Prussia annexed Hanover, despite its proclaimed neutrality, in 1866; it remained a Prussian province until 1946. On 1 Nov. 1946 all four states were combined by the British military administration to form the *Land* of Lower Saxony.

Lower Saxony is the second largest state in Germany, stretching from the North Sea island of Borkum to the Harz Mountains. Hanover is the capital of this region with just over 1m. of the state's 7·8m. inhabitants and is an industrial and service centre. Each year the city hosts the world's largest industrial fair and CeBIT – the international fair for communications technology. In the year 2000, Hanover will be the venue for Expo 2000, which will have the theme 'Mankind, Nature, Technology'. Wolfsburg is home to Volkswagen's 'beetle' factory that has manufactured over 50m. cars to date. The levitating train to link Berlin with Hamburg was built and is being tested in Emsland, and the port of Wilhelmshaven, once home to the German Imperial navy, is now Germany's deepwater super-tanker port. Brunswick (Braunschweig) is home to the Federal Institute of Physics and Meteorology that determines the exact Central European Time (CET). Schimmel Pianos and Rollei cameras are also made in Brunswick. Göttingen University was the alma mater of the Brothers Grimm who not only wrote their folk tales there, but also began work on compiling the Deutsches Wörterbuch (a comprehensive German dictionary, the last volume of which was completed in 1961). Lower Saxony produces one fifth of Germany's natural gas, and at the Lower Saxony Energy Agency research is being conducted into alternative sources of electrical power such as wind-power, solar-power, landfill gas and animal excrement.

The Friesian Islands in the North Sea and the Harz Mountains and Teutoborg Forest (Germany's oldest nature park) provide recreation grounds for millions of visitors each year. Europe's largest fruit growing area (two thirds of the state's economy is agricultural), the Altes Land, is a popular tourist spot when the millions of apple trees are in bloom. Lower Saxony also has the most extensive network of bicycle paths in Germany.

TERRITORY AND POPULATION

Lower Saxony has an area of 47,613 sq. km, and is divided into 4 administrative regions, 9 urban districts, 38 rural districts and 1,030 communes; capital, Hanover.

Estimated population, on 31 Dec. 1997, was 7,845,398 (3,831,467 males, 4,013,931 females).

SOCIAL STATISTICS

Calendar years	Live births	Marriages	Divorces	Deaths
1994	81,520	47,349	15,342	85,700
1995	80,994	46,267	15,588	86,827
1996	83,655	46,669	16,761	85,574
1997	85,907	46,490	17,334	83,958

CONSTITUTION AND GOVERNMENT

The *Land* Niedersachsen was formed on 1 Nov. 1946 by merging the former Prussian province of Hanover and the *Länder* Brunswick, Oldenburg and Schaumburg-Lippe. Lower Saxony has 7 seats in the Bundesrat.

RECENT ELECTIONS

At the Diet elections on 1 March 1998 the Social Democratic Party received 47·9% of the votes cast to secure an absolute majority, gaining 83 seats, the Christian Democratic Union 35·9% and the Greens 7·0%.

CURRENT ADMINISTRATION

The cabinet of the Social Democratic Party is headed by *Prime Minister* Gerhard Glogowski (SPD).

BANKING

361 credit institutions were operating in 1997. Deposits totalled 99,611m. DM.

Stock Exchange

Niedersächsische Börse zu Hannover: 30159 Hannover, Rathenaustr. 2. Tel: (0)511 327661. Fax: (0)511 324915.

ENERGY AND NATURAL RESOURCES

Electricity

Electricity production in 1995 was 54,570m. kWh. Consumption in 1997 was 44,983·7m. kWh.

Agriculture

Area and yield of the most important crops:

	Area (in 1,000 ha)			Yield (in 1,000 tonnes)		
	1995	*1996*	*1997*	*1995*	*1996*	*1997*
Wheat	318	336	368	2,537	2,678	3,067
Rye	160	157	168	923	936	1,028
Barley	302	326	330	1,779	1,794	1,985
Oats	38	34	34	174	185	166
Potatoes	125	136	130	4,386	5,230	5,334
Sugar-beet	132	134	130	6,523	6,576	6,575

Livestock, 3 Nov. 1998: Cattle, 2,880,375 (including 802,245 milch cows); pigs, 7,529,489; sheep, 226,237 (1996); horses, 113,479 (1996); poultry, 47,717,770 (1996).

Fisheries

In 1997 the yield of sea and coastal fishing was 31,433·9 tonnes valued at 71·5m. DM.

INDUSTRY

In Sept. 1997, 3,824 establishments employed 545,344 persons; of these 51,544 were employed in machine construction; 55,285 in electrical engineering.

Labour

The economically active persons totalled 3,358,400 in April 1997. Of the total, 330,900 were self-employed, 38,800 unpaid family workers, 2,988,600 employees; 146,300 were engaged in agriculture and forestry, 1,067,100 in power supply, mining, manufacturing and building, 806,700 in commerce and transport, 1,338,300 in other industries and services.

Trade Fair Organizers

Deutsche Messe AG: Messegelände, 30521 Hannover.
Tel: (0)511 890. Fax: (0)511 8932626.

COMMUNICATIONS

Roads

At 1 Jan. 1997 there were 28,278 km of 'classified' roads, including 1,334 km of Autobahn, 4,862 km of federal roads, 8,353 km of first-class and 13,729 km of second-class highways. Number of motor vehicles, 1 Jan. 1998, was 4,906,363 including 4,105,802 passenger cars, 214,630 trucks, 8,286 buses, 233,250 tractors, 277,375 motor cycles.

Rail

In 1997, 25·2m. tonnes of freight came into the Land by rail and 20·3m. tonnes left by rail.

Civil Aviation

76,500 planes landed at Hanover Airport in 1997, which saw 2,292,853 passenger arrivals and 1,804,374 departures. 4,419 tonnes of freight left by air and 4,781 tonnes came in.

SOCIAL INSTITUTIONS

Justice

There are a constitutional court *(Staatsgerichtshof)*, 3 courts of appeal, 11 regional courts, 79 local courts, a *Land* labour court, 15 labour courts, a *Land* social court, 8 social courts, a finance court, a higher administrative court and 4 administrative courts.

Religion

The census on 25 May 1987 showed 66·12% Protestants and 19·6% Roman Catholics.

Education

In 1997–98 there were 1,875 primary schools with 362,397 pupils; 964 post-primary schools with 224,743 pupils; 289 special schools with 33,307 pupils; 409 secondary modern schools with 106,992 pupils; 234 grammar schools with 144,619 pupils; 30 comprehensive schools with 23,378 pupils. In 1993 there were 1,801 vocational training institutes (full and part-time) with 256,917 pupils and 213 public health schools with 11,952 pupils.

In the winter term 1997–98 there were 6 universities (Göttingen, 27,193 students; Hanover, 31,281; Oldenburg, 11,843; Osnabrück, 12,269; Hildesheim, 3,524; Lüneburg, 6,678); 2 technical universities (Braunschweig, 14,453; Clausthal, 2,810); the medical college of Hanover (3,423); the veterinary college in Hanover (1,822).

Health

At Dec. 1996 there were 23,334 doctors and 211 hospitals with 6·6 beds per 1,000 population.

CULTURE

Broadcasting
Norddeutscher Rundfunk is the public broadcasting service for Lower Saxony.

Cinema
In 1996 there were 367 screens with 66,493 seats.

Tourism
In 1997, 8,832,000 guests spent 31,960,000 nights in Lower Saxony. 6,324 places of accommodation provided 258,577 beds.

Libraries
In 1996 there were 1,269 public libraries and 98 academic libraries.

Theatre and Opera
45 theatres and concert halls hosted 4,013 productions for audiences of 1,422,000 in 1996.

Museums and Galleries
6,859,000 people visited 431 museums in 1996.

FURTHER READING

Statistical Information: The Niedersächsisches Landesamt für Statistik, Postfach 4460, D-30044 Hanover. *Head of Division:* President Karl-Ludwig Strelen. Main publications are: *Statistisches Jahrbuch Niedersachsen* (from 1950). – *Statistische Monatshefte Niedersachsen* (from 1947). – *Statistiche Berichte Niedersachsen.* – *Statistisches Taschenbuch Niedersachsen 1998* Biennial.

State Libraries: Niedersächsische Staats- und Universitäts-bibliothek, Prinzenstr. 1, D-37073 Göttingen. *Director:* Helmut Vogt; Niedersächsische Landesbibliothek, Waterloostr. 8, D-30169 Hanover. *Director:* Dr W. Dittrich.

MECKLENBURG-WEST POMERANIA

KEY HISTORICAL EVENTS

Known as the 'Land of a Thousand Lakes', Mecklenburg-West Pomerania is a state historically divided in two. Pomerania was formerly under Swedish control while Mecklenburg was an independent part of the German Empire. The two states were not united until after the Second World War, and after a short period when it was subdivided into three districts under the GDR it became a state of the Federal Republic of Germany in 1990. The people of the region speak a dialect known as Plattdeutsch (Low German). The four main cities of this state are Hanseatic towns from the period when the area dominated trade with Scandinavia. This meant that the port of Rostock on the North Sea coast became the home of the GDR's biggest shipyards. Although shipbuilding is still a major industry in the region, luxury foods and beverages, engineering and construction are beginning to take more of a share of the state's economy. 80% of the region's land is tilled to produce grain, potatoes and oilseed. Tourism is a major industry, with over 2m. visitors enjoying the state's lakes, cliffs, nature reserves and three national parks every year.

TERRITORY AND POPULATION

The area is 23,170 sq. km. It is divided into 6 urban districts, 12 rural districts and 1,073 communes. Population on 31 Dec. 1997 was 1,807,799 (916,702 females). The capital is Schwerin.

SOCIAL STATISTICS

Calendar years	Live births	Marriages	Divorces	Deaths
1994	8,934	5,626	2,540	19,835
1995	9,878	6,113	3,128	19,290
1996	11,088	6,490	3,595	18,642
1997	12,046	6,299	3,815	17,940

CONSTITUTION AND GOVERNMENT

The *Land* was reconstituted on former GDR territory in 1990. It has 3 seats in the Bundesrat.

RECENT ELECTIONS

At the Diet elections of Sept. 1998, the Christian Democrats (CDU) won 24 seats with 30·2% of the vote; the Social Democrats (SPD), 27, with 34·3%; and the Party of Democratic Socialism (PDS, former Communists), 20, with 24·4%.

CURRENT ADMINISTRATION

The *Prime Minister* is Dr. Harald Ringstorff (SPD).

ENERGY AND NATURAL RESOURCES

Agriculture

Area and yield of the most important crops:

	Area (in 1,000 ha)			Yield (in 1,000 tonnes)		
	1995	*1996*	*1997*	*1995*	*1996*	*1997*
Wheat	238·3	236·2	243·2	1,619·1	1,487·5	1,798·2
Rye	100·5	93·8	104·8	544·5	491·8	593·6
Barley	147·8	156·0	158·5	964·6	730·3	1,091·7
Oats	15·5	14·7	16·1	74·8	75·6	85·4
Potatoes	18·3	19·3	16·8	520·9	599·5	507·4
Sugar-beet	34·4	34·7	33·7	1,428·1	1,510·5	1,515·0

Livestock in 1997: Cattle, 611,473 (including 226,013 milch cows); pigs, 601,104; sheep, 70,442; horses, 19,030 (1996); poultry, 7,304,150 (1996).

Fisheries

Sea catch, 1997: 17,891 tonnes (768 tonnes frozen, 17,123 tonnes fresh). Freshwater catch, 1997: 839·5 tonnes (mainly carp, trout and eels). Fish farming, 1997: 457·0 tonnes.

INDUSTRY

In 1997 there were 529 enterprises (with 20 or more employees) employing 45,107 persons.

Labour

776,600 persons (342,600 females) were employed at the 1%-sample survey of the microcensus of April 1997, including 57,100 self-employed and family assistants, 324,200 manual and 362,500 white-collar workers. 32,900 persons were employed as officials. Employment by sector: Manufacturing and mining, 79,900; agriculture, forestry and fisheries, 49,900; trade and guest business, 134,400; transport and communications, 44,900; construction, 141,100; energy and water resources, 7,600; public administration, 106,000; other services, 212,900.

COMMUNICATIONS

Roads
There were (March 1998) 9,732 km of 'classified' roads, including 262 km of Autobahn, 2,073 km of federal roads, 3,226 km of first-class and 4,171 km of second-class highways. Number of motor vehicles, 1 Jan. 1998, 969,757, including 833,968 passenger cars, 68,888 trucks, 2,019 buses and 28,373 motor cycles.

Shipping
There is a lake district of some 660 lakes. The ports of Rostock, Stralsund and Wismar are important for ship-building and repairs. In 1997 the cargo fleet consisted of 75 vessels (including 2 tankers) of 625,000 GT. Sea traffic, 1997, incoming 13,322,938 tonnes; outgoing 10,280,269 tonnes.

SOCIAL INSTITUTIONS

Justice
There is a court of appeal (*Oberlandesgericht*), 4 regional courts (*Landgerichte*), 31 local courts (*Amtsgerichte*), a *Land* labour court,

4 labour courts, a *Land* social court, 4 social courts, a finance court, a higher administrative court and 2 administrative courts.

Religion

In 1997 the Evangelical Lutheran Church of Mecklenburg had 244,000 adherents, 278 pastors and 342 parishes. Roman Catholics numbered 72,100, with 68 priests and 74 parishes. The Pomeranian Evangelical Church had 138,200 adherents, 167 pastors and 250 parishes in 1997.

Education

In 1997 there were 330 primary schools, 22 comprehensives, 477 secondary schools and 99 special needs schools. There are universities at Rostock and Greifswald with (in 1997–98) 15,492 students and 4,252 academic staff, and 5 institutions of equivalent status with 7,171 students and 1,601 academic staff.

CULTURE

Cinema

3·4m. cinema goers visited 88 cinemas in 1997.

Tourism

In July 1997 there were 1,868 places of accommodation (with 9 or more beds) providing a total of 107,501 beds. 3,078,170 guests stayed an average of 3·8 nights each.

Libraries

In 1996 there were 237 public libraries with 261,244 active users, who borrowed around 8m. items.

Theatre and Opera

In 1996 there were 32 theatres and concert halls. 464,000 people attended 2,716 productions during the year.

Museums and Galleries

More than 2·5m. visitors saw 283 exhibitions in 114 museums in 1996.

FURTHER READING

Statistical Office: Statistisches Landesamt Mecklenburg-Vorpommern, Postfach 020135, D-19018 Schwerin. Main publications are: *Statistische Monatshefte Mecklenburg-Vorpommern* (since 1991); *Statistische Berichte* (since 1991; various); *Statistisches Jahrbuch Mecklenburg-Vorpommern* (since 1991); *Statistische Sonderhefte* (since 1992; various).

NORTH RHINE-WESTPHALIA

KEY HISTORICAL EVENTS

Historical Westphalia consisted of many small political units, most of them absorbed by Prussia and Hanover before 1800. In 1807 Napoleon created a Kingdom of Westphalia for his brother Joseph. This included Hesse-Kassel, but was formed mainly from the Prussian and Hanoverian lands between the rivers Elbe and Weser.

In 1815 the kingdom ended with Napoleon's defeat. Most of the area was given to Prussia, with the small principalities of Lippe and Waldeck surviving as independent states. Both joined the North German Confederation in 1867. Lippe remained autonomous after the end of the Empire in 1918; Waldeck was absorbed into Prussia in 1929.

In 1946 the occupying forces combined Lippe with most of the Prussian province of Westphalia to form the *Land* of North Rhine-Westphalia. On 1 March 1947 the allied Control Council formally abolished Prussia.

North Rhine-Westphalia is half the size of Bavaria but has twice the population. The region produces more than one fifth of Germany's exports and consumes nearly one fourth of its imports. The Rhine-Ruhr conurbation is Germany's industrial heartland with more than fifteen cities – four of which, Dortmund, Essen, Bochum and Duisburg – have merged into one urban strip more than 60 kilometres long and 25 kilometres wide. The Ruhr has 30 power stations and is Germany's main source of energy, although since the 1960s efforts to cut industrial pollution have resulted in less heavy industry in the area and the establishment of a pastoral fringe around the area with lakes and wooded valleys. This same desire to clean up the region has resulted in a considerable diversification of the state's economic structure and the coal and steel industries now only employ one in twenty-five whereas it used to employ one in eight. There are now 1,600 firms focusing on environmental technology in the area and half the land has been given over to agriculture and forestry. 60% of the state's work force are employed in the service sector (media and culture) and almost half of Germany's top 100 firms (such as Bayer Leverkusen, VEBA AG and Bertelsmann) have their headquarters in the region. Düsseldorf is an important banking and international finance centre.

Bonn was made the capital of Federal Republic of Germany in 1949 and although since reunification Berlin has been reinstated as the Federal capital, Bonn will remain an important administrative and scientific centre. It has been designated the federal city for Science and Communications, home to Deutsche Telekom and the Centre for Advanced European Studies and Research (CAESAR). Duisburg on the Rhine is the world's largest inland port and Dortmund is home to

Beck's beer and has overtaken Munich as the 'beer city' of Germany. Cologne (Köln) has been largely re-built after it was almost completely flattened by bombing in the latter days of World War II but the famous cathedral, a gigantic gothic masterpiece, survived and the city is still a favourite tourist spot. The region has 99 theatres, 15 opera houses and 390 museums.

TERRITORY AND POPULATION

The *Land* comprises 34,079 sq. km. It is divided into 5 administrative regions, 23 urban districts, 31 rural districts and 396 communes. Capital: Düsseldorf. Population, 31 Dec. 1997, 17,974,487 (8,729,381 males, 9,245,106 females).

SOCIAL STATISTICS

Calendar years	Live births	Marriages	Divorces	Deaths
1994	186,079	104,200	40,523	192,669
1995	182,393	100,793	41,476	193,076
1996	188,493	99,922	42,839	194,548
1997	190,386	99,779	44,580	189,946

CONSTITUTION AND GOVERNMENT

Since Oct. 1990 North Rhine-Westphalia has had 6 seats in the Bundesrat.

RECENT ELECTIONS

The Diet, elected on 14 May 1995, consists of 108 Social Democrats (46% of votes cast), 89 Christian Democrats (37·7%) and 24 Greens (10%).

CURRENT ADMINISTRATION

North Rhine-Westphalia is governed by Social Democrats (SPD) and the Greens. *Prime Minister:* Wolfgang Clement (SPD).

ECONOMY

Budget

The predicted total revenue for 1998 was 82,578m. DM. The predicted total expenditure was 88,596m. DM.

BANKING

Central Bank

Landeszentralbank in Nordrhein-Westfalen: 40212 Düsseldorf, Berliner Allee 14. Tel: (0)211 874-0.

Stock Exchange

Rheinisch-Westfäliche Börse zu Düsseldorf: 40212 Düsseldorf, Ernst-Schneider-Platz 1; 40033 Düsseldorf, Postfach 104262. Tel: (0)211 13890. Fax: (0)211 133287.

ENERGY AND NATURAL RESOURCES

Agriculture

Area and yield of the most important crops:

	Area (in 1,000 ha)			Yield (in 1,000 tonnes)		
	1995	*1996*	*1997*	*1995*	*1996*	*1997*
Wheat	250·9	255·5	263·9	2,035·2	2,185·9	2,268·3
Rye	41·0	37·7	37·7	260·2	263·8	256·5
Barley	192·8	195·8	200·0	1,220·9	1,259·9	1,303·6
Oats	30·7	28·2	30·3	134·0	151·4	170·0
Potatoes	29·9	33·4	28·0	1,047·8	1,467·3	1,204·1
Sugar-beet	77·0	78·0	76·8	4,018·0	4,295·7	4,204·5

Livestock, 3 Dec. 1997: Cattle, 1,634,104 (including 451,151 milch cows); pigs, 5,800,743; sheep, 223,560; horses, 116,709 (1996); poultry, 10,859,348 (1996).

INDUSTRY

In Sept. 1997, 10,028 establishments (with 20 and more employees) employed 1,579,842 persons; of these, 104,378 were employed in production of food and tobacco; 237,518 in machine construction; 320,351 in metal production and manufacture of metal goods; 151,588 in the chemical industry; 154,087 in manufacture of office machines, computers, electrical and precision engineering and optics; 104,115 in motor vehicle manufacture.

Output and/or production in 1,000 tonnes, 1997: Hard coal, 39,118; lignite, 99,179; pig-iron, 18,168; raw steel ingots, 23,192; rolled steel, 29,461; castings (iron and steel castings), 932; cement, 11,367; fireproof products, 633; sulphuric acid (including production of cokeries), 1,233; staple fibres and rayon, 260; machine tools, 289 (1,000 pieces); equipment for smelting works and rolling mills, 1,925 (pieces); machines for mining industry, building and building materi-al, 83 (1,000 pieces); cranes and hoisting machinery, 453 (1,000 pieces); electricity distribution and control equipment, 9,374,248 (1,000 pieces); cables and electric lines, 168; springs of all kinds, 174; chains of all kinds, 37; locks and fittings, 256,251 (1,000 pieces); spun yarns, 93. Of the total population, 8·5% were engaged in industry.

Labour

The economically active persons totalled 7,391,000 at the 1%-sample survey of the microcensus of April 1997. Of the total, 677,000 were self-employed, 56,000 unpaid family workers, 6,658,000 employees; 142,000 were engaged in agriculture, forestry and fishing, 2,607,000 in power supply, mining, manufacturing, water supply and building, 1,713,000 in commerce, hotel trade and transport, 2,925,000 in other industries and services.

Trade Fair Organizers

Düsseldorfer Messegesellschaft/mbH-NOWEA: 40474 Düsseldorf, Stockumer Kirchstr. 61. Tel: (0)211 456001. Fax: (0)211 4560668.

COMMUNICATIONS

Roads

There were (1 Jan. 1998) 29,686 km of 'classified' roads, including 2,168 km of Autobahn, 5,098 km of federal roads, 12,632 km of first-class and 9,798 km of second-class highways. Number of motor vehicles, 1 July 1998, 10,448,097, including 8,979,844 passenger cars, 450,525 motor trucks/trucks, 17,171 buses, 213,245 tractors and 662,842 motor cycles.

Civil Aviation

In 1997, 86,929 aircraft landed at Düsseldorf, bringing 7,667,735 incoming passengers.

SOCIAL INSTITUTIONS

Justice

There are a constitutional court *(Verfassungsgerichtshof)*, 3 courts of appeal, 19 regional courts, 130 local courts, 3 *Land* labour courts, 30 labour courts, 1 *Land* social court, 8 social courts, 3 finance courts, a higher administrative court and 7 administrative courts.

Religion

The census on 25 May 1987 showed 35·2% Protestants and 49·4% Roman Catholics.

Education

In 1997 there were 4,205 primary schools with 62,669 teachers and 1,120,532 pupils; 703 special schools with 14,835 teachers and 87,751 pupils; 517 intermediate schools with 15,954 teachers and 294,623 pupils; 252 *Gesamtschulen* (comprehensive schools) with 16,624 teachers and 216,163 pupils; 620 high schools with 34,207 teachers and 519,329 pupils; there were 265 part-time vocational schools with 289,616 pupils; vocational preparatory year 157 schools with 11,392 pupils; 241 full-time vocational schools with 72,310 pupils; 166 full-time vocational schools leading up to vocational colleges with 14,508 pupils; 241 advanced full-time vocational schools with 38,823 pupils; 643 schools for public health occupations with 16,222 teachers and 44,403 pupils; 42 schools within the scope of a pilot system of courses with 83,717 pupils and 3,656 teachers.

In the winter term 1997–98 there were 8 universities (Bielefeld, 20,030 students; Bochum, 35,547; Bonn, 36,598; Cologne (Köln), 57,007; Dortmund, 24,281; Düsseldorf, 22,263; Münster, 44,398; Witten, 763); the Technical University of Aachen (30,960); 3 Roman Catholic and 2 Protestant theological colleges with a total of 682 students. There were also 3 colleges of music, 4 colleges of fine arts and the college for physical education in Cologne with 10,877 students in total; 24 *Fachhochschulen* (vocational colleges) with 97,434 students, and 6 *Universitäten-Gesamthochschulen* with a total of 121,865 students.

Health

In 1996 there were 1,907 hospitals in North Rhine-Westphalia with over 300,000 beds, which had an average occupancy rate of 79·3%.

CULTURE

Cinema

In 1996 there were 881 screens with 168,690 seats.

Tourism

At Dec. 1997 there were 5,666 places of accommodation (9 beds or more) providing 270,797 beds altogether. In 1997, 13,105,046 visitors (2,319,796 foreigners) spent 34,284,304 nights.

Libraries

In 1996 there were 2,599 public libraries lending a total of 67,094,481 items.

Theatre and Opera

8,963 productions were put on in 91 theatres and concert halls for audiences totalling 3,617,000 in 1996.

Museums and Galleries

In 1996 there were 604 museums which had 11,884,582 visitors.

FURTHER READING

Statistical Information: The Landesamt für Datenverarbeitung und Statistik Nordrhein-Westfalen (Mauerstr. 51, D-40476 Düsseldorf) was founded in 1946, by amalgamating the provincial statistical offices of Rhineland and Westphalia. *President:* Jochen Kehlenbach. The Landesamt publishes: *Statistisches Jahrbuch Nordrhein-Westfalen.* From 1949. More than 550 other publications yearly.

Först, W., *Kleine Geschichte Nordrhein-Westfalens.* Münster, 1986.

Land Library: Universitätsbibliothek, Universitätsstr. 1, D-40225 Düsseldorf. *Director:* Dr Niggemann.

RHINELAND-PALATINATE

KEY HISTORICAL EVENTS

The *Land* was formed from the Rhenisch Palatinate and the Rhine valley areas of Prussia, Hesse-Darmstadt, Hesse-Kassel and Bavaria.

The Palatinate was ruled, from 1214, by the Bavarian house of Wittelsbach; its capital was Heidelberg. In 1797 its land west of the Rhine was taken into France, and Napoleon divided the eastern land between Baden and Hesse. In 1815 the land taken by France was

restored to Germany and allotted to Bavaria. The area and its neighbours formed the strategically-important Bavarian Circle of the Rhine.

The rule of the Wittelsbachs ended in 1918 but the Palatinate
remained part of Bavaria until the American occupying forces
detached it in 1946.

The new *Land*, incorporating the Palatinate and other territory,
received its constitution in April 1947.

Rhineland-Palatinate is located almost at the centre of Europe and
profits from its position at the junction of an extensive modernized
network of Autobahns, federal highways, convenient rail links and
waterways as well as the state's proximity to three economically
powerful centres – the Rhine-Main, the Rhine-Neckar and Rhine-Ruhr
regions. The state is also Germany's most famous wine producing
region as well as being a major employer. Tourists pour into the area
all along the 'Weinstrasse' (Wine Road) that runs from Schweigen on
the French border to Bockenheim. Rhineland-Palatinate also has
other heavier industries. The many factories in and around
Ludwigshafen (including the chemical giant BASF) form a belt of
factories linked up with Mannheim across the Rhine in Baden-
Württemberg. Small and medium-sized businesses such as the
gemstone industry of Idar-Oberstein, the ceramic and glass industries of the Westerwald and the leather industry of the Hunsrück form
the backbone of the regional economy. Mainz, capital of the state,
was home to Johannes Gutenberg who invented the world's first
movable type printing press and is now home to Germany's two main
rival television networks – ZDF and SAT1. The area has some of the
most beautiful landscapes in Germany. The Rhine valley between
Bingen and Bonn is dotted with castles and historic sites. The old
Roman city of Trier, where the first bishopric north of the Alps was
established in 314, is 2,000 years old and its buildings appear on the
UNESCO world heritage list.

TERRITORY AND POPULATION

Rhineland-Palatinate has an area of 19,853 sq. km. It comprises 3
administrative regions, 12 urban districts, 24 rural districts and 2,305
communes. The capital is Mainz. Population (at 30 June 1998),
4,018,228 (2,049,559 females).

SOCIAL STATISTICS

Calendar years	Live births	Marriages	Divorces	Deaths
1994	40,539	23,182	9,003	42,857
1995	39,684	22,922	9,040	42,993
1996	40,926	22,741	9,385	43,752
1997	41,677	22,509	10,015	43,211

CONSTITUTION AND GOVERNMENT

The constitution of the *Land* Rheinland-Pfalz was approved by the
Consultative Assembly on 25 April 1947 and by referendum on 18
May 1947, when 579,002 voted for and 514,338 against its accep-
tance. It has 4 seats in the Bundesrat.

RECENT ELECTIONS

At the elections of 24 March 1996 the Social Democratic Party won
43 seats of the 101 in the state parliament with 39·8% of votes cast;
the Christian Democrats 41 with 38·7%; the Free Democrats 10 with
8·9%; and the Greens, 7 with 6·9%.

CURRENT ADMINISTRATION

The coalition cabinet is headed by Kurt Beck (b. 1949; Social Democrat).

BANKING

Central Bank

Landeszentralbank in Rheinland-Pfalz und im Saarland: 52122 Mainz, Hegelstr. 65. Tel: (0)6131 377-0. Fax: (0)6131 381664.

ENERGY AND NATURAL RESOURCES

Agriculture

Area and yield of the most important crops:

	Area (in 1,000 ha)			Yield (in 1,000 tonnes)		
	1994	*1995*	*1996*	*1994*	*1995*	*1996*
Wheat	77·7	85·3	86·9	484·0	543·2	587·7
Rye	19·0	20·6	15·6	94·3	107·6	93·5
Barley	118·8	113·3	121·1	541·0	542·7	681·7
Oats	22·8	18·3	17·1	87·1	74·0	84·0
Potatoes	10·6	11·1	11·0	329·1	329·7	372·6
Sugar-beet	22·9	23·1	22·6	1,228·1	1,261·5	1,440·0
Wine (1,000 hectolitres)	66·2	65·8	65·3	6,902·2	5,910·9	5,869·8

Livestock (1997, in 1,000): Cattle, 470·3 (including milch cows, 142·0); sheep, 126·7; pigs, 399·7; horses, 29·9 (1996); poultry, 1,874·4 (1996).

Forestry

Total area covered by forests in 1997 was 8,061·8 sq. km or 40·6% of the total area.

INDUSTRY

In 1997, 2,154 establishments (with 20 or more employees) employed 309,286 persons; of these 68,180 were employed in the chemical industry; 19,220 in electrical equipment manufacture; 6,992 in leather goods and footwear; 34,636 in machine construction; 23,493 in processing stones and earthenware.

Labour

The economically active persons totalled 1,709,900 in 1997. Of the total, 166,000 were self-employed, 18,000 were unpaid family workers, 1,525,900 employees; 54,400 were engaged in agriculture and forestry, 625,400 in power supply, mining, manufacturing and building, 371,600 in commerce, transport, hotels and restaurants, 658,500 in other industries and services.

COMMUNICATIONS

Roads

In 1998 there were 18,547 km of 'classified' roads, including 829 km of Autobahn, 3,042 km of federal roads, 7,132 km of first-class and 7,543 km of second-class highways. Number of motor vehicles, 1 July 1998, was 2,630,638, including 2,174,590 passenger cars, 110,373 trucks, 5,423 buses, 137,622 tractors and 170,652 motor cycles.

SOCIAL INSTITUTIONS

Justice

There are a constitutional court *(Verfassungsgerichtshof)*, 2 courts
of appeal, 8 regional courts, 47 local courts, a *Land* labour court,
5 labour courts, a *Land* social court, 4 social courts, a finance court,
a higher administrative court and 4 administrative courts.

Religion

The census on 25 May 1987 showed 37·7% Protestants and 54·5%
Roman Catholics.

Education

In 1997 there were 988 primary schools with 9,246 teachers and
188,700 pupils; 601 secondary schools with 16,461 teachers and
271,349 pupils; 146 special schools with 2,236 teachers and 14,710
pupils; 113 vocational and advanced vocational schools with 4,913
teachers and 118,031 pupils.

In the winter term 1997–98 (provisional) there were the University
of Mainz (28,169 students), the University of Kaiserslautern (8,007
students), the University of Trier (10,582 students), the University of
Koblenz-Landau (8,565 students), the *Hochschule für Verwaltungs-
wissenschaften* in Speyer (565 students), the *Wissenschaftliche
Hochschule für Unternehmensführung* (Otto Beisheim Graduate
School) in Vallendar (370 students), the Roman Catholic
Theological College in Trier (289 students) and the Roman Catholic
Theological College in Vallendar (87 students). There were also 9
Fachhochschulen with 22,076 students and 4 *Verwaltungs-
fachhochschulen* with 1,873 students.

CULTURE

Cinema

There were 178 screens in 1996 with 32,855 seats.

Tourism

3,776 places of accommodation provided 150,906 beds for 5,396,000 visitors in 1997.

Libraries

In 1996 there were 5,052 volumes held in 909 libraries.

Theatre and Opera

There were 20 theatres and concert halls in 1996. 619,000 people attended 1,629 productions.

Museums

339 exhibitions took place in 221 museums, visited by 3,779,000 people, in 1996.

FURTHER READING

Statistical Information: The Statistisches Landesamt Rheinland-Pfalz (Mainzer Str., 14–16, D-56130 Bad Ems) was established in 1948. *President:* Klaus Maxeiner. Its publications include: *Statistisches Jahrbuch für Rheinland-Pfalz* (from 1948); *Statistische Monatshefte Rheinland-Pfalz* (from 1958); *Statistik von Rheinland-Pfalz* (from 1949) 367 vols. to date; *Rheinland-Pfalz im Spiegel der Statistik* (from 1968); *Rheinland-Pfalz – seine kreisfreien Städte und Landkreise* (1992); *Rheinland-Pfalz heute* (from 1973); *Benutzerhandbuch des Landesinformationssystems* (1995); *Raumordnungsbericht 1993 der Landesregierung Rheinland-Pfalz* (Mainz, 1993).

SAARLAND

KEY HISTORICAL EVENTS

Long disputed between Germany and France, the area was occupied by France in 1792. The larger part was allotted to Prussia at the close of the Napoleonic wars in 1815. In 1870 Prussia defeated France and when, in 1871, the German Empire was founded under Prussian leadership, it was able to incorporate Lorraine. This part of France was the Saar territory's western neighbour so the Saar was no longer a vulnerable boundary state. It began to develop industrially, exploiting Lorraine coal and iron. In 1919 the League of Nations took control of the Saar until a plebiscite of 1935 favoured return to Germany. In 1945 there was a French occupation, and in 1947 the Saar was made an international area but in economic union with France. In 1954 France and Germany agreed that the Saar should be a separate and autonomous state, under an independent commissioner. This was rejected by referendum and France agreed to return Saarland to Germany. It became a *Land* of the Federal Republic on 1 Jan. 1957.

Saarland is Germany's smallest state, apart from the three city-states. The economy depends largely on wine making and its attendant tourist industries, although Saarlouis is an important industrial city producing cars, steel, food and electronics. Saarland has formed strong links with two neighbours, Lorraine in France and Luxembourg, known collectively as 'SAAR-LOR-LUX', largely because of new transportation projects. The Saarland is also a centre for sophisticated research in such fields as information and communications technologies, medical technology, production technologies and materials research. Institutes include the Max Planck Institute for Computers, the German Research Centre for Artificial Intelligence, the Frauhofer Institute for Non-Destructive Testing, the Frauhofer Institute for Medical Technology and the Institute for New Materials.

TERRITORY AND POPULATION

Saarland has an area of 2,570 sq. km. Population, 31 Dec. 1997, 1,080,790 (524,034 males, 555,756 females). It comprises 6 rural districts and 52 communes. The capital is Saarbrücken.

SOCIAL STATISTICS

Calendar years	Live births	Marriages	Divorces	Deaths
1994	10,028	6,427	3,035	12,711
1995	9,727	6,095	2,785	12,647
1996	9,976	6,181	2,938	12,529
1997	9,987	5,829	3,123	12,455

CONSTITUTION AND GOVERNMENT

Saarland has 3 seats in the Bundesrat.

RECENT ELECTIONS

The Saar Diet, elected on 5 Sept. 1999, is composed as follows: 26 Christian Democrats, 25 Social Democrats.

CURRENT ADMINISTRATION

Saarland is governed by Christian Democrats in Parliament. *Prime Minister:* Peter Müller (CDU).

ENERGY AND NATURAL RESOURCES

Electricity

In 1997, electricity production was 10,100m kWh. Supply from the electricity grid totalled 7,500m kWh.

Oil and Gas

8,700m. kWh of gas was used in 1997.

Agriculture

The cultivated area (1997) occupied 115,827 ha or 45·1% of the total area.

Area and yield of the most important crops:

	Area (in 1,000 ha)			Yield (in 1,000 tonnes)		
	1995	*1996*	*1997*	*1995*	*1996*	*1997*
Wheat	7·0	7·8	7·6	40·6	46·5	50·8
Rye	5·4	4·9	5·2	29·5	27·5	30·2
Barley	7·6	7·6	8·0	36·6	38·5	42·4
Oats	4·1	3·8	3·9	18·1	16·1	18·6
Potatoes	0·3	0·3	0·3	8·1	8·9	10·1

Livestock, Dec. 1997: Cattle, 62,223 (including 16,522 milch cows); pigs, 24,641; sheep, 15,476; horses, 6,115 (1996); poultry, 193,787 (1996).

Forestry

The forest area comprises nearly 33·4% of the total (257,045 ha).

INDUSTRY

In June 1998, 529 establishments (with 20 or more employees) employed 106,858 persons; of these 12,587 were engaged in coalmining, 18,524 in manufacturing motor vehicles, parts, accessories, 10,721 in iron and steel production, 15,460 in machine construction, 4,788 in electrical engineering, 4,778 in steel construction. In 1997 the coalmines produced 7·4m. tonnes of coal. 4 blast furnaces and 10 steel furnaces produced 3·6m. tonnes of pig-iron and 4·5m. tonnes of crude steel.

Labour

The economically active persons totalled 413,700 at the 1%-sample survey of the microcensus of April 1997. Of the total, 38,500 were self-employed, 373,700 employees; 5,100 were engaged in agriculture and forestry, 128,300 in power supply, mining, manufacturing and building, 101,300 in commerce and transport, 179,000 in other industries and services.

Trade Fair Organizers

Surmise GmbH: 66117, Saarbrücken, Messegelände. Tel: (0)681 954020. Fax: (0)681 954032.

COMMUNICATIONS

Roads

At 1 Jan. 1998 there were 2,031 km of classified roads, including 236 km of Autobahn, 352 km of federal roads, 820 km of first-class and 623 km of second-class highways. Number of motor vehicles, 31 Dec. 1997, 680,975, including 587,283 passenger cars, 28,128 trucks, 1,374 buses, 14,063 tractors and 42,773 motor cycles.

Shipping

During 1997, 1,753 ships docked in Saarland ports, bringing 2·7m. tonnes of freight. In the same period 561 ships left the ports, carrying 768,000 tonnes of freight.

SOCIAL INSTITUTIONS

Justice

There is a constitutional court *(Verfassungsgerichtshof)*, a court of appeal, a regional court, 11 local courts, a *Land* labour court, 3 labour courts, a *Land* social court, a social court, a finance court, a higher administrative court and an administrative court.

Religion

In 1995, 70·5% of the population were Roman Catholics and 20·3% were Protestants.

Education

In 1998–99 there were 293 primary schools with 49,595 pupils; 40 special schools with 3,331 pupils; 100 *Realschulen, Erweiterte Realschulen* and *Sekundarschulen* with 27,632 pupils; 37 high schools with 28,286 pupils; 15 comprehensive high schools with 10,748 pupils; 4 *Freie Waldorfschulen* with 1,072 pupils; 2 evening intermediate schools with 228 pupils; 2 evening high schools and 1 Saarland College with 198 pupils; 39 part-time vocational schools with 21,855 pupils; year of commercial basic training: 52 institutions with 2,274 pupils; 21 advanced full-time vocational schools and schools for technicians with 1,926 pupils; 50 full-time vocational schools with 4,929 pupils; 1 *Berufsaufbauschule* (vocational exten-sion school) with 12 pupils; 29 *Fachoberschulen* (full-time vocational schools leading up to vocational colleges) with 3,873 pupils; 43 schools for public health occupations with 2,268 pupils. The number of pupils visiting the vocational schools amounts to 37,137.

In the winter term 1998–99 (preliminary data) there was the University of the Saarland with 17,444 students; 1 academy of fine art with 328 students; 1 academy of music and theatre with 239 students; 1 vocational college (economics and technics) with 2,576 students; 1 vocational college for social affairs with 262 students; and 1 vocational college for public administration with 219 students.

Health

In 1997 the 28 hospitals in the Saarland contained 8,265 beds and treated 244,652 patients. The average occupancy rate was 83·3%. There were also 22 out-patient and rehabilitation centres which treated 27,376 patients in 1997. On average they were using 69·3% of their capacity.

CULTURE

Cinema

Saarland had 87 cinema screens with 14,987 seats in 1996.

Tourism

In 1997, 13,966 beds were available in 300 places of accommodation (of 9 or more beds). 568,677 guests spent 1,947,847 nights in the Saarland, staying an average of 3·4 days each.

Libraries

In 1996, 179 libraries held 1,372,000 volumes.

Theatre and Opera

In 1996 there were 5 theatres and concert halls. 231,000 people attended a total of 589 productions.

Museums

44 museums hosted 88 exhibitions in 1996. Attendances were 378,000 for the year.

FURTHER READING

Statistical Information: The Statistisches Landesamt Saarland (Virchowstrasse 7, D-66119 Saarbrücken) was established on 1 April 1938. As from 1 June 1935, it was an independent agency; its predecessor, 1920–35, was the Statistical Office of the Government Commission of the Saar. *Chief:* Direktor Josef Mailänder. The most important publications are: *Statistisches Handbuch für das Saarland,* from 1950. – *Statistisches Taschenbuch für das Saarland,* from 1959. – *Saarland in Zahlen* (special issues). – *Einzelschriften zur Statistik des Saarlandes,* from 1950. – *Statistik-Journal* (monthly), from 1996.

SAXONY

KEY HISTORICAL EVENTS

Saxony was ruled by a dynasty of Saxon Kings from the 15th century until 1918 and has been home to much of Germany's cultural history. In the 18th century, the capital of Saxony, Dresden, became the cultural capital of northern Europe earning the title 'Florence of the North, and the other great eastern German city, Leipzig, was a lively commercial city with strong artistic trends. The three cities of Dresden, Chemnitz and Leipzig formed the industrial heartland of

Germany which after World War II was the manufacturing centre of the GDR. After reunification, many of Saxony's factories were shut down – the Trabant automobile factory has been taken over by private enterprise and now makes parts for Mercedes Benz amongst others. Dresden has a long history of pottery production and the famous names of Meissen and Dresden still live on. The factories of Meissen (with their famous crossed-swords' trademark) have been producing pottery and porcelain continuously since 1710. Many innovations have been developed here – among them the first reflex cameras and the first CFC-free fridges. Numerous banks have opened branches in Leipzig and the city is starting to compete with Frankfurt and Düsseldorf to become one of Germany's main financial centres. Leipzig has always had a thriving book trade and now has the world's largest mail order house. The former airport has been converted into a conference and trade fair centre. Post reunification Saxony has attracted a considerable amount of inward investment from global corporations – BP, Shell and Phillips have all begun to operate here and the electronics giant Siemens is investing in a microelectronics centre in Dresden. Saxony is rich with tourist attractions – visitors can enjoy a wealth of palaces, landscaped parks and gardens, the 'silver route' in the Ore Mountains and the 'Saxon Wine Route' as well as many cultural and folk festivals.

TERRITORY AND POPULATION

The area is 18,412 sq. km. It is divided into 3 administrative regions, 7 urban districts, 22 rural districts and 787 communes. Population on 1 Jan. 1998 was 4,522,412 (2,338,244 females, 2,184,168 males); density, 246 per sq. km. The capital is Dresden.

SOCIAL STATISTICS

Calendar years	Live births	Marriages	Divorces	Deaths
1994	22,734	14,795	6,519	58,234
1995	24,004	15,474	7,043	57,550
1996	27,006	15,402	7,754	55,756
1997	29,008	15,287	8,470	53,483

CONSTITUTION AND GOVERNMENT

The *Land* was reconstituted as the Free State of Saxony on former GDR territory in 1990. It has 4 seats in the Bundesrat.

RECENT ELECTIONS

At the Diet elections on 19 Sept. 1999 the Christian Democrats won 76 seats, with 56·9% of the vote; the Party of Democratic Socialism (former Communists), 30, with 22·2%; the Social Democrats, 14, with 10·7%.

CURRENT ADMINISTRATION

The *Prime Minister* is Kurt Biedenkopf (b. 1930; Christian Democrat).

BANKING

Central Bank

Landeszentralbank in den Freistaaten Sachsen und Thüringen, 04253
Leipzig, Postfach 301316. Tel: (0)341 8600. Fax: (0)341 8602389.

ENERGY AND NATURAL RESOURCES

Agriculture

Area and yield of the most important crops:

	Area (in 1,000 ha)			Yield (in 1,000 tonnes)		
	1996	*1997*	*1998*	*1996*	*1997*	*1998*
Wheat	143·1	146·2	151·7	965·0	964·6	1,003·7
Rye	50·2	47·8	50·0	249·1	200·8	269·9
Barley	150·2	156·8	150·3	750·8	928·9	852·2
Maize	86·9	80·7	74·5	3,106·7	3,215·0	3,224·9
Potatoes	9·9	7·9	8·0	375·9	276·4	308·4
Fodder	196·3	195·3	196·6	1,682·1	1,682·7	1,682·0

Livestock in 1997 (in 1,000): Cattle, 618 (including milch cows, 250);
pigs, 582; sheep, 116.

INDUSTRY

In Nov. 1998, 2,650 establishments (with 20 or more employees)
employed 214,116 persons.

COMMUNICATIONS

Roads

On 1 Jan. 1998 there were 572 km of motorways and 2,474 km of main roads. There were, 1 July 1998, 2,490,049 registered motor vehicles, including 2,160,172 motor cars, 223,629 trucks and tractors, 4,285 buses and 81,476 motor cycles.

SOCIAL INSTITUTIONS

Religion

In 1997, 24·7 of the population belonged to the Evangelical Church and 4·2% were Roman Catholic.

Education

In 1997–98 there were 1,193 primary schools with 200,487 pupils and 11,748 teachers; 651 secondary schools with 221,100 pupils and 14,347 teachers; 190 grammar schools with 145,981 pupils and 9,496 teachers and 205 high schools (*Förderschulen*) with 27,752 pupils and 3,887 teachers. There were 798 professional training schools with 165,945 students and 6,075 teachers. There were 6 universities with 51,266 students, 10 polytechnics with 18,645 students, 6 art schools with 2,292 students and 1 management college with 1,341 students.

CULTURE

Cinema

In 1997 there were 99 cinemas with seating for 41,047 persons. 7m. tickets were sold.

Tourism

In 1997 there were 2,097 places of accommodation with 109,145 beds. There were 4,362,000 visitors that year.

Libraries

In 1996, 869 public libraries with 522,010 active users lent out 20,760,058 items.

Theatre and Opera

During the 1996–97 season there were 72 productions and seating for 24,431 persons. Audiences totalled 1,900,778.

Museums

270 museums hosted 853 exhibitions in 1996. There were 7,747,000 visitors.

FURTHER READING

Statistical office: Statistisches Landesamt des Freistaates Sachsen, Postfach 105, D-01911 Kamenz. It publishes *Statistisches Jahrbuch des Freistaates Sachsen* (since 1990).

SAXONY-ANHALT

KEY HISTORICAL EVENTS

Saxony-Anhalt has a short history as a state in its own right. Made up of a patchwork of older regions ruled by other states, Saxony-Anhalt existed between 1947 and 1952 and then, after reunification in 1990, it was re-established. Geographically, it lies at the very heart of

Germany and despite the brevity of its federal status, the region has some of the oldest heartlands of German culture. The south of the region was the industrial centre with Dessau producing the first ever all metal commercial airliner (the Junkers Ju52). Heavy machinery and vehicle construction still dominates the economies of Dessau and Magdeburg. Chemical production has featured in the Halle-Mersburg-Bitterfeld triangle since the 19th century and continues today with large chemical corporations like Bitterfeld using much cleaner technology. Considerable investment has been made into cleaning up industrial pollution in the region. Agriculture is also important to the region's economy and the forelands of Magdeburger Börde and Harz have rich fertile soil that produce an abundance of crops including grains, sugar beet, potatoes and vegetables. The region also produces wine from the Germany's northernmost vineyards. Dessau was the birthplace of the architect Walter Gropius who in the 1920s went on to found the Bauhaus movement in Weimar. The region also has many historic and picturesque towns. The half-timbered houses have made the old town of Quedlinburg a UNESCO World Heritage Site. Magdeburg boasts the first gothic cathedral to be built on German soil (it contains the tomb of the Emperor Otto I) and the Abbey of Our Lady, which has remained virtually unchanged since its completion in 1160. Martin Luther set the reformation in motion by nailing his 95 Theses to the door of Wittenberg church in 1517.

TERRITORY AND POPULATION

The area is 20,446 sq. km. It is divided into 3 administrative regions, 3 urban districts, 21 rural districts and 1,297 communes. Population in 1997 was 2,701,690 (1,390,490 females). The capital is Magdeburg.

SOCIAL STATISTICS

Calendar years	Live births	Marriages	Divorces	Deaths
1994	14,280	9,415	4,287	33,816
1995	14,568	9,667	3,867	33,519
1996	16,152	9,534	3,432	32,639
1997	17,194	9,285	4,494	30,892

CONSTITUTION AND GOVERNMENT

The *Land* was reconstituted on former GDR territory in 1990. It has 4 seats in the Bundesrat.

RECENT ELECTIONS

At the Diet election on 26 April 1998 the SPD received 35·9% of votes cast giving them 47 seats, the CDU 22·0% (28 seats), the PDS (former Communists) 19·6% (25 seats) and the DVU (extreme right) 12·9% (16 seats). The Free Democratic Party received 4·2% and the Greens 3·2%. Turn-out was 71·7%.

CURRENT ADMINISTRATION

The *Prime Minister* is Dr Manfred Höppner (SPD).

ENERGY AND NATURAL RESOURCES

Agriculture

Area and yield of the most important crops:

	Area (in 1,000 ha)			Yield (in 1,000 tonnes)		
	1995	*1996*	*1997*	*1995*	*1996*	*1997*
Cereals	539·7	563·8	602·8	3,607·5	3,473·1	3,860·3
Potatoes	17·5	18·2	15·7	521·8	710·1	561·5
Sugar-beet	61·5	61·4	60·3	2,716·8	2,869·5	2,798·5
Maize	66·3	78·8	70·4	2,299·1	3,420·3	2,459·5

Livestock in 1997 (in 1,000): Cattle, 420·6 (including milch cows, 189·1); pigs, 745·9; sheep, 120·2.

INDUSTRY

In 1997, 1,257 establishments (with 20 or more employees) employed 104,066 persons; of these, 48,420 were employed in basic industry, 30,565 in capital goods industry and 18,292 in food industry. Major sectors are machine and transport equipment, electrical engineering, chemicals and energy and fuel.

Labour

In 1996 there were 1,085,959 economically-active persons. Of these, 469,327 worked in local authorities, social security and services, 187,894 in mining and manufacturing, 198,646 in building, 125,616 in trade, 68,637 in transport and communications and 35,839 in agriculture, forestry and fisheries. Unemployment rate (1996), 18·8%.

COMMUNICATIONS

Roads

In 1997 there were 232 km of motorways, 2,329 km of main and 3,839 km of local roads. In 1997 there were 1,439,439 registered motor vehicles, including 1,247,995 passenger cars, 99,144 trucks, 2,669 buses and 41,927 motor cycles.

SOCIAL INSTITUTIONS

Religion

There are Saxon and Anhalt branches of the Evangelical Church. There were some 0·2m. Roman Catholics in 1990.

Education

In 1997–98 there were 1,521 schools with 374,351 pupils. In 1997 there were 11 universities and institutes of equivalent status with 30,707 students.

CULTURE

Cinema

There were 78 screens with 19,675 seats in 1996.

Tourism

1,013 places of accommodation provided 50,376 beds in 1997. There were 1,976,000 visitors during the year.

Libraries

In 1996 there were 540 libraries holding 5,925,000 books.

Theatre and Opera

There were 56 theatres and concert halls in 1996. 779,000 people attended 4,972 productions during the year.

Museums

In 1996 there were 169 museums which put on 479 exhibitions for 2,675,000 visitors.

FURTHER READING

Statistical office: Statistisches Landesamt Sachsen-Anhalt, Postfach 20 11 56, D-06012 Halle. It publishes *Statistisches Jahrbuch des Landes Sachsen-Anhalt* (since 1991).

SCHLESWIG-HOLSTEIN

KEY HISTORICAL EVENTS

The *Land* is formed from two states formerly contested between Germany and Denmark.

Schleswig was a Danish dependency ruled since 1474 by the King of Denmark as Duke of Schleswig. He also ruled Holstein, its southern neighbour, as Duke of Holstein, but he did so recognizing that it was a fief of the Holy Roman Empire. As such, Holstein joined the German Confederation which replaced the Empire in 1815.

Disputes between Denmark and the powerful German states were accompanied by rising national feeling in the duchies, where the population was part-Danish and part-German. There was war in 1848–50 and in 1864, when Denmark surrendered its claims to Prussia and Austria. Following her defeat of Austria in 1866 Prussia annexed both duchies.

North Schleswig (predominately Danish) was awarded to Denmark in 1920. Prussian Holstein and south Schleswig became the present *Land* in 1946.

Schelswig-Holstein is the only German state that is bordered by two seas, the North Sea and the Baltic, and is home to mixed ethnic groups. Everyday communication is a mixture of German, Low German, Danish and Friesian (the Friesian islands to the north are home to 50,000 Danes). The region is a holiday maker's and nature lover's paradise with the coastal islands, the red cliffs of Helgoland, the mud flats of the Wattenmeer National Park and the inland lakes of 'Holstein Switzerland' all attracting large numbers of annual visitors. The Kiel Canal, which links the Baltic and the North Sea, was the pre-war home of the German navy and was heavily bombed. Although the region depended on agriculture and fishing, Kiel's economy depended on shipbuilding and has only survived by specializing. The rest of the state has invested in new technologies. Schleswig-Holstein has more than 1,000 wind turbines, making it Germany's largest supplier of 'green' electricity and there are more than 4,000 firms involved with the communications and information technologies. Three universities and four polytechnics provide this sparsely populated state with a skilled workforce.

TERRITORY AND POPULATION

The area of Schleswig-Holstein in 1996 was 15,771 sq. km. It is divided into 4 urban and 11 rural districts and 1,131 communes. The capital is Kiel. The population (estimate, 31 Dec. 1996) numbered 2,742,293 (1,339,326 males, 1,402,967 females).

SOCIAL STATISTICS

Calendar years	Live births	Marriages	Divorces	Deaths
1993	28,632	18,451	6,250	31,223
1994	27,542	18,295	6,196	30,766
1995	27,430	17,671	6,679	31,288
1996	28,766	17,832	6,822	31,314

CONSTITUTION AND GOVERNMENT

The *Land* has 4 seats in the Bundesrat.

RECENT ELECTIONS

At the elections of 24 March 1996 the Social Democrats won 33 seats with 39·8% of votes cast, the Christian Democrats 30 with 37·2%, the Greens 6 with 8·1%, the Free Democrats 4 with 5·7% and the (Danish) South Schleswig Association 2 with 2·5%.

CURRENT ADMINISTRATION

Prime Minister: Heide Simonis (b. 1943; SPD).

ENERGY AND NATURAL RESOURCES

Agriculture
Area and yield of the most important crops:

	Area (in 1,000 ha)			Yield (in 1,000 tonnes)		
	1994	*1995*	*1996*	*1994*	*1995*	*1996*
Wheat	157·2	155·8	166·4	1,223·3	1,333·5	1,433·4
Rye	32·6	35·1	30·5	188·0	207·6	190·9
Barley	67·5	74·8	84·8	430·3	541·4	554·0
Oats	16·9	9·6	8·6	76·4	50·6	50·2
Potatoes	4·8	5·2	5·8	146·3	154·1	192·9
Sugar-beet	15·0	15·3	15·4	699·5	715·3	716·6

Livestock, 3 Dec. 1996: 1,396,970 cattle (including 422,213 milch cows); 1,293,356 pigs; 222,495 sheep; 54,707 horses; 2,885,175 poultry.

Fisheries
In 1996 the yield of small-scale deep-sea and inshore fisheries was 59,306 tonnes valued at 92·6m. DM.

INDUSTRY

In 1996 (average), 1,455 establishments (with 20 and more employees) employed 146,742 persons; of these, 6,976 were employed in shipbuilding (except naval engineering); 25,903 in machine construction; 20,187 in food and kindred industry; 10,368 in electrical engineering.

COMMUNICATIONS

Roads

There were (1 Jan. 1997) 9,886·1 km of 'classified' roads, including 447·9 km of Autobahn, 1,760·2 km of federal roads, 3,600·8 km of first-class and 4,077·2 km of second-class highways. Number of motor vehicles, 1 July 1997, was 1,706,336, including 1,432,722 passenger cars, 78,012 trucks, 2,940 buses, 69,981 tractors, 94,359 motor cycles.

Shipping

The Kiel Canal (*Nord-Ostsee-Kanal*) is 98·7 km (51 miles) long; in 1996, 37,055 vessels of 32·8m. NRT passed through it.

SOCIAL INSTITUTIONS

Justice

There are a court of appeal, 4 regional courts, 28 local courts, a *Land* labour court, 5 labour courts, a *Land* social court, 4 social courts, a finance court, an upper administrative court and an administrative court.

Religion

The census on 25 May 1987 showed 73·3% Protestants and 6·2% Roman Catholics.

Education

In 1996–97 there were 624 primary schools with 7,263 teachers and 119,937 pupils; 266 elementary schools with 2,772 teachers and 39,178 pupils; 171 intermediate schools with 2,863 teachers and

52,678 pupils; 102 grammar schools with 5,234 teachers and 63,234 pupils; 23 comprehensive schools with 1,236 teachers and 13,585 pupils; 162 other schools (including special schools) with 2,222 teachers and 16,254 pupils; 353 vocational schools with 4,170 teachers and 86,312 pupils.

In the winter term of the academic year 1997–98 there were 26,059 students at the three universities (Kiel, Flensburg and Lübeck) and 18,419 students at 11 further education colleges.

CULTURE

Cinema

In 1996 there were 173 cinema screens with 29,392 seats.

Tourism

5,016 places of accommodation provided 177,579 beds in 1997 for 4,057,000 visitors.

Libraries

In 1996 there were 188 libraries holding 4,857,000 volumes.

Theatre and Opera

23 theatres and concert halls put on 1,639 productions for 494,000 visitors in 1996.

Museums

In 1996 there were 145 museums that put on 313 exhibitions for 3,032,000 visitors.

FURTHER READING

Statistical Information: Statistisches Landesamt Schleswig-Holstein (Fröbel Str. 15–17, D-24113 Kiel). *Director:* Dr Kirschner. Publications: *Statistisches Taschenbuch Schleswig-Holstein,* since 1954. *– Statistisches Jahrbuch Schleswig-Holstein,* since 1951. *– Statistische Monatshefte Schleswig-Holstein,* since 1949. *– Statistische Berichte,* since 1947. *– Beitrage zur historischen Statistik Schleswig-Holstein,* from 1967. *– Lange Reihen,* from 1977.

Baxter, R. R., *The Law of International Waterways.* Harvard Univ. Press, 1964

Brandt, O., *Grundriss der Geschichte Schleswig-Holsteins.* 5th ed. Kiel, 1957

Handbuch für Schleswig-Holstein. 28th ed. Kiel, 1996

State Library: Schleswig-Holsteinische Landesbibliothek, Kiel, Schloss. *Director:* Prof. Dr Dieter Lohmeier.

THURINGIA

KEY HISTORICAL EVENTS

Erfurt is the capital of Thuringia, a fairytale land of mountains and forests criss-crossed by rivers. Perched on the Harz mountains, the rivers Saale, Werra and Weisse Elster run through a region covered by the Thuringian Forest. Martin Luther spent his exile in Eisenach where he translated the New Testament into German during his incarceration in the castle. Weimar became the centre of German intellectual life in the 18th century and by the 19th century the city had a reputation for its keen appreciation of the arts. In the early 1920s Walter Gropius founded the Bauhaus Movement. (He moved it to Dessau in 1925 and from there to Berlin). In 1919, Weimar was the seat of a briefly liberal Republic. Only ten miles from Weimar lies Buchenwald, the site of a war time Nazi concentration camp, which is now a national monument to the victims of fascism.

Germany's industrialization began in Thuringia with the mining of
potash, followed by gunsmithing, glass making and the manufacture
of machine tools. Germany is famous for its optical industry. Zeiss and
Schott both have works in Jena. Eisenach has replaced the manufacture of the East German Trabant's sister car, the Wartburg, with the
manufacture of Opels. As part of a post reunification adjustment,
Thuringia now has a strong academic and scientific base with three
universities, a number of Fachhochschulen (technical colleges),
roughly 50 research institutes and 20 technology centres. Jena is still
the centre of the optical industry in Germany and machinery is still
manufactured in Gera and Erfurt. More than half of Thuringia is agricultural land producing grains, rape, potatoes and sugar beet.
Visitors to the region can walk through the Thüringen Wald, along
some of the oldest and most beautiful hiking paths in Germany. The
region also boasts a wealth of mineral springs and spas. The
'Thüringen Classical Route' is a 300-kilometre long tour of the state's
beauty spots, palaces and the region's rich cultural history.

TERRITORY AND POPULATION

The area is 16,172 sq. km. Population on 31 Dec. 1997 was 2,478,148
(1,271,481 females); density, 153 per sq. km. It is divided into 6 urban
districts, 17 rural districts and 1,053 communes. The capital is Erfurt.

SOCIAL STATISTICS

Calendar years	Live births	Marriages	Divorces	Deaths
1994	12,721	8,581	3,795	28,877
1995	13,788	8,781	3,493	29,027
1996	15,265	8,646	3,955	28,468
1997	16,475	8,619	4,527	27,694

CONSTITUTION AND GOVERNMENT

The *Land* was reconstituted on former GDR territory in 1990. It has 4 seats in the Bundesrat.

RECENT ELECTIONS

At the Diet elections on 12 Sept. 1999 the Christian Democrats (CDU) won 49 seats, with 51% of the vote; the Party of Democratic Socialism (PDS), 21, with 21·4%; the Social Democrats (SPD), 18 with 18·5%.

CURRENT ADMINISTRATION

The *Prime Minister* is Dr Bernhard Vogel (CDU).

BANKING

Central Bank

Landeszentralbank in den Freistaaten Sachsen und Thüringen, 04253
Leipzig, Postfach 301316.Tel: (0)341 8600. Fax: (0)341 8602389.

ENERGY AND NATURAL RESOURCES

Agriculture

Area and yield of the most important crops:

	Area (in 1,000 ha)			Yield (in 1,000 tonnes)		
	1995	*1996*	*1997*	*1995*	*1996*	*1997*
Wheat	187·6	185·8	183·3	1,240·5	1,290·9	1,229·2
Rye	27·6	20·9	17·2	170·1	130·5	117·9
Barley	122·7	138·7	146·0	678·9	775·5	814·2
Oats	6·3	6·7	8·2	31·8	33·7	41·6
Potatoes	5·4	5·7	4·3	178·2	235·2	161·6
Sugar-beet	13·5	13·1	13·2	618·9	589·5	619·0

Livestock, 3 Dec. 1997: 445,125 cattle (including 161,658 milch
cows); 660,074 pigs; 226,099 sheep; 14,048 horses (1996);
4,065,825 poultry (1996).

INDUSTRY

In 1997, 1,448 establishments (with 20 or more employees) employed
110,091 persons; of these, 48,507 were employed by producers of
materials and supplies, 28,360 by producers of investment goods,

9,236 by producers of durables and 23,988 by producers of non-durables.

Labour

The economically active persons totalled 1,082,300 in April 1997, including 494,800 professional workers, 465,900 manual workers and 82,700 self-employed. 39,000 persons were engaged in agriculture and forestry, 373,400 in production industries, 229,800 in commerce, transport and communications and 440,000 in other sectors. There were 232,004 persons registered unemployed in Dec. 1997 (130,478 females) and 5,889 on short time; unemployment rate was 20·4%.

COMMUNICATIONS

Roads

In 1996 there were 7,905·6 km of 'classified' roads (310 km of Autobahn, 1,952·9 km of federal roads, 5,642·7 km of first- and second-class highways). Number of motor vehicles, Jan. 1998, 1,401,902, including 1,204,304 private cars, 97,904 trucks, 2,843 buses, 34,968 tractors and 41,368 motor cycles.

SOCIAL INSTITUTIONS

Religion

In 1997, 216,850 persons were Roman Catholic and 299 were Jewish. In 1996, 740,635 persons were Protestant.

Education

In 1997–98 there were 628 primary schools with 113,935 pupils, 365 core curriculum schools with 121,630 pupils, 113 grammar schools with 86,107 pupils and 101 special schools with 19,102 pupils; there were 86,731 pupils in technical and professional education, and 4,118 in professional training for the disabled.

In the winter term 1997–98 there were 11 universities and colleges with 31,215 students enrolled.

Health

In 1997 there were 57 hospitals with 18,803 beds. There was 1 doctor per 366 population.

Welfare

1996 expenditure on social welfare was 883·7m. DM.

CULTURE

Cinema

In 1996 there were 126 cinema screens with 21,487 seats.

Tourism

In 1997, 1,435 places of accommodation (with 9 or more beds) received 2,549,800 visitors who stayed 7,327,700 nights.

Libraries

There were 514 public libraries in 1996 with 315,000 active users who borrowed 6,052,000 items.

Theatre and Opera

In 1996 there were 41 theatres and concert halls. 851,000 people attended 3,947 different productions.

Museums

There were 165 museums in 1996 putting on 453 exhibitions for 4,686,000 visitors.

FURTHER READING

Statistical information: Thüringer Landesamt für Statistik (Postfach 900163, D-99104 Erfurt; Leipziger Str. 71, D-99085 Erfurt). *President:* Gerhard Scheuerer. Publications: *Statistisches Jahrbuch Thüringen,* since 1993. *Kreiszahlen für Thüringen,* since 1995. *Statistische Monatshefte Thüringen,* since 1994. *Statistische Berichte,* since 1991. *Faltblätter,* since 1991. *State library:* Thüringer Universitäts- und Landesbibliothek, Jena.